WILD swimming
Walks

YORKSHIRE
28 waterfall, river and coastal days out

Sarah Banks

WILD THINGS PUBLISHING

River Wharfe, Burnsall p105

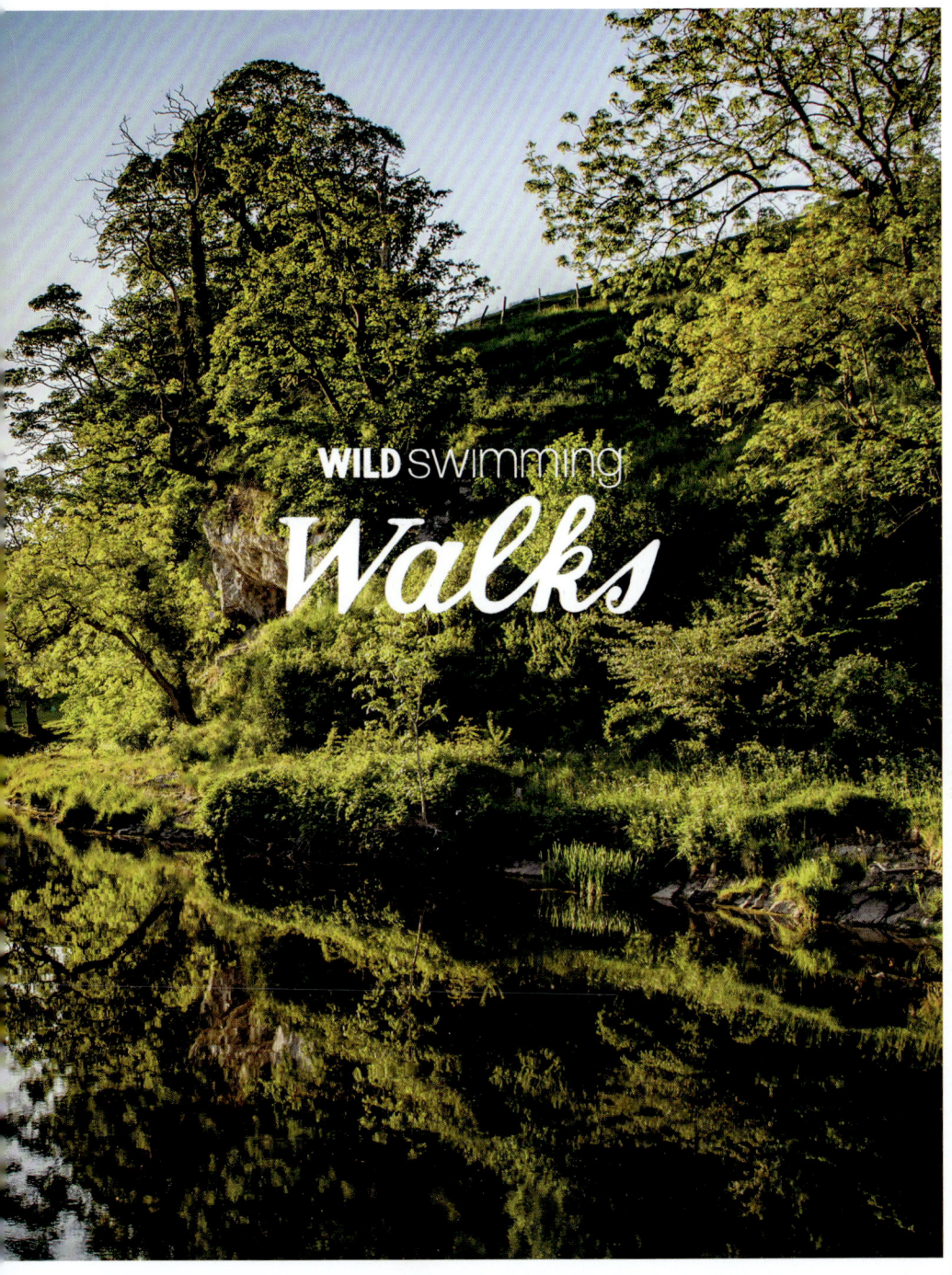

WILD swimming
Walks

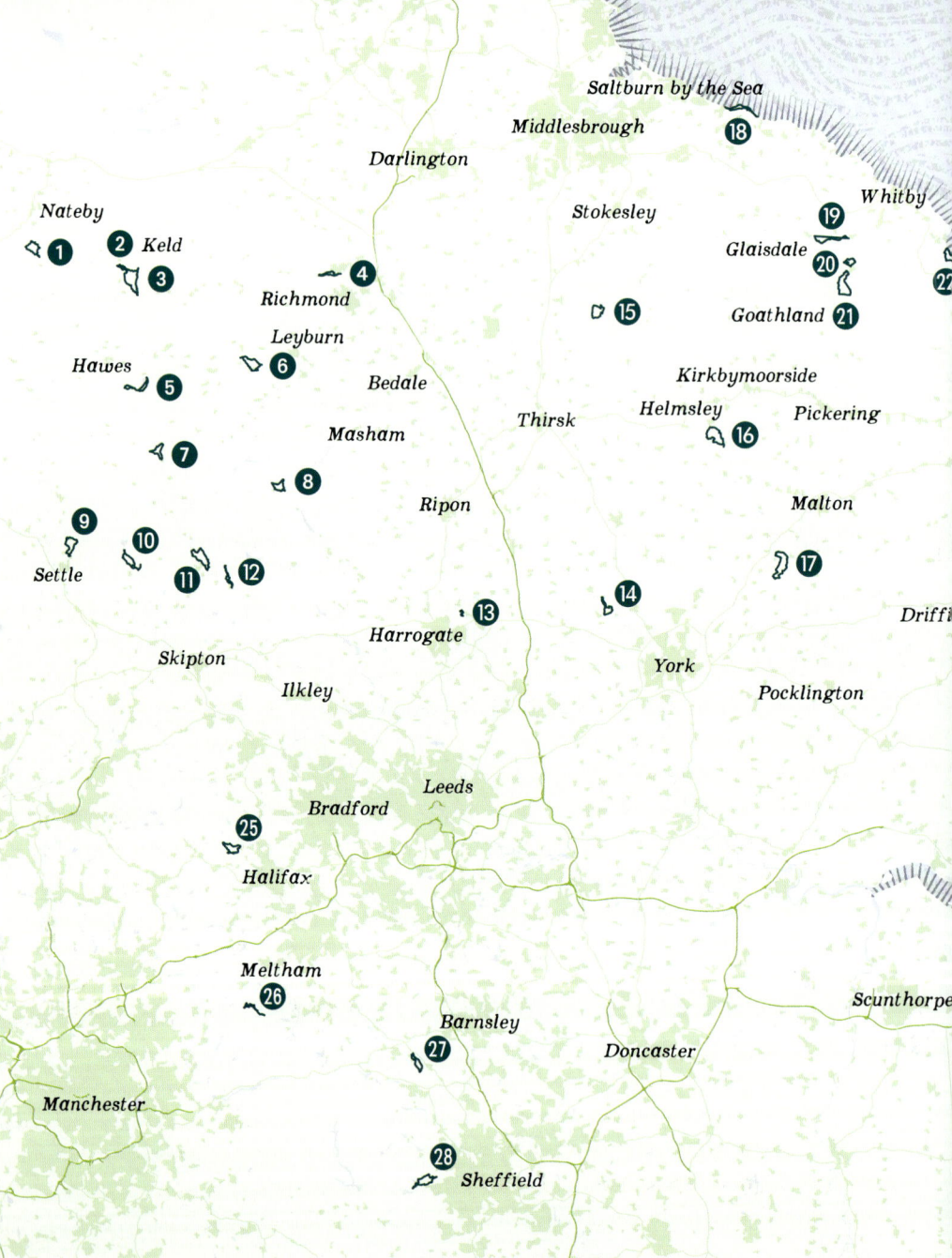

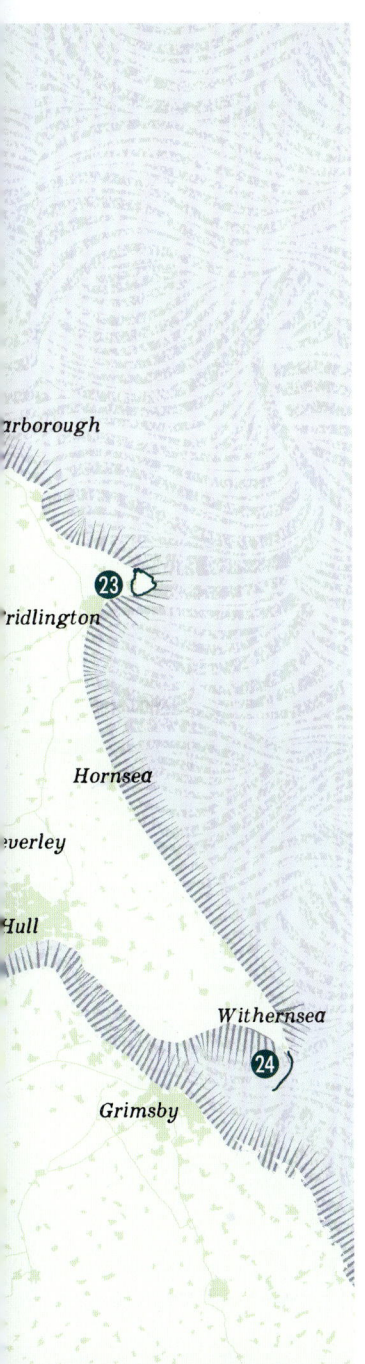

THE WALKS

TABLE OF WALKS

No.	NAME	SWIMMING
1	Pendragon Castle and Catagill Scar	Waterfall and pools at Catagill Scar and river pools along the River Eden
2	Keld Waterfalls	Waterfall pools at East Gill Force, Currack Force, Wain Wath Force and Hoggarth's Leap
3	Muker, Swinner Gill and Kisdon Force	Waterfall pools along Swinner Gill Beck, East Gill Force and Kisdon Force
4	Richmond Foss, River Swale and Round Howe	Waterfall at Richmond Foss and several spots along the River Swale
5	Semer Water and Bardale Beck	Lake swimming at Semer Water and waterfall pools along Bardale Beck
6	Redmire Force and River Ure	Waterfall at Redmire Force and several spots along the River Ure
7	Cray Gill Waterfalls and River Wharfe	Waterfall pools along Cray Gill and Crook Gill and river swimming along the River Wharfe
8	Upper Nidd Falls and How Stean Gorge	Waterfall and pools along the River Nidd and Howe Stean Beck
9	Catrigg Force, Stainforth Force and the Eel Pool	Waterfall pools at Catrigg Force and Stainforth Force, Eel Pool and river swimming along the Rive
10	Janet's Foss and Gordale Scar	Waterfall pool at Janet's Foss and small waterfall at Gordale Scar
11	Grassington and River Wharfe	Several spots along the River Wharfe
12	Hebden, Loup Scar and Burnsall	Two spots along the River Wharfe, waterfall pool at Scale Haw Force
13	Nidd Gorge	River swimming along the River Nidd
14	River Ouse at Beningbrough	River swimming along the River Ouse
15	Douglas Ridge and Upper Rye Falls	Waterfall pools along the River Rye
16	Nunnington and River Rye	Several spots along the River Rye
17	Kirkham Abbey and Howsham Mill	Two spots along the River Derwent
18	Saltburn and Cattersty Sands	Sea swims at Saltburn and Cattersty Sands
19	Esk Valley Rail Trail	Several spots along the River Esk
20	Water Arc and Thomason Foss	Waterfalls at Water Arc Foss and Thomason Foss
21	Goathland Tarn, Simon Howe and Nelly Ayre Foss	Moorland Tarn at Goathland and waterfall pool at Nelly Ayre Foss
22	Ravenscar, Stoupe Beck Sands and Boggle Hole	Sea swims at Stoupe Beck Sands and Boggle Hole
23	Flamborough Coves and Caves (options)	Sea swims at Thornwick Bay, North Landing, Selwicks Bay and South Landing
24	Spurn Point Out-and-Back	Sea swims along Spurn Point
25	Luddenden Dean and Midgely Moor	Small waterfall pool at Luddenden Brook and reservoir on Midgely Moor
26	Wessenden Falls and Blake Clough	Waterfalls at Wessenden Falls and Blake Clough
27	Oxspring and River Don	River swimming along the River Don
28	Wyming Brook and Rivelin Plunge Pool	Waterfall pool at Rivelin Plunge Pool and very small pools along Wyming Brook

RRAIN	REFRESHMENTS EN ROUTE	MILES	DIFFICULTY
paths, bridleways, country lanes and rland road	None - cafés and pubs in Kirkby Stephen	4.5 miles	Easy
paths, bridleways and country lanes	Two cafés in Keld (start and finish)	2.5 miles	Easy
paths and bridleways. Steep, rocky nd	Pub and tearoom in Muker (start and finish)	7 miles	Moderate
odland and riverside paths, footpaths bridleways	Pub just off route and cafés and pubs in Richmond	4.5 miles	Moderate
paths, bridleways and country lanes.	None - cafés in Bainbridge/Hawes	6 miles	Easy
paths and bridleways	Two pubs in West Witton (start and finish)	5 miles	Easy
paths and bridleways and quiet ntry lanes	Pub at Buckden (start and finish) and Hubberholme (halfway round)	4 miles	Easy
rside paths, woodland paths, footpaths bridleways	Café (almost at finish)	4 miles	Moderate
paths, bridleways and quiet country s	Pub (halfway round)	5 miles	Moderate
paths and bridleways, rocky, uneven nd and tussocky moorland	Kiosk/van at Gordale Bridge	6.5 miles	Moderate
an, footpaths, bridleways and riverside s	Cafés and pubs in Grassington	5.5 miles	Easy
ntry lanes, footpaths and bridleways	Tearoom in Hebden (start and half way round), pub at Burnsall (halfway round)	4.5 miles	Easy
odland tracks and some uneven rside paths	Cafés and pubs in Knaresborough	1.75 miles	Easy
mac driveway, riverside paths, footpaths bridleways	Pub in Newton-on-Ouse (start and finish)	4 miles	Easy
rland tracks, footpaths and indistinct s across open access land	Pub and tearooms in Hawnby (off route)	4 miles	Moderate
rside paths, tracks and fields	Café at Nunnington (start and finish) and pub in Harome (just off route, half way round)	5.5 miles	Easy
odland paths and tracks, riverside paths country roads	Pub at Kirkham Abbey (start and finish)	7 miles	Easy
top paths, footpaths, steep steps	Cafés, pubs, restaurants and fish and chips in Saltburn (start and finish)	6 miles	Moderate
odland footpaths, tracks, country roads	Cafés and pubs in Grosmont and Egton Bridge (start, finish and halfway round)	3.5 miles	Easy
rland footpaths, riverside paths, steep, ciptitous paths near the falls, country lane	Cafés and pubs in Goathland (start, finish and halfway round)	3 miles	Moderate
paths and bridleways, indistince paths ss heather moorland, scramble to falls	Cafés and pubs in Goathland (start and finish)	5.5 miles	Moderate
top paths, footpaths, steep steps, ed walking and cycle track	Cafés at Ravenscar and Boggle Hole (start, finish and halfway round)	6 miles	Moderate
top paths, steep climbs, road walking shorter routes	Cafés and fish and chips at North Landing, Thornwick Bay, Flamborough Head and Flamborough village (start, finish and halfway round)	7.5 miles (or 3 and 5.5 mile options)	Moderate
mac and sandy tracks	Café at Spurn Discovery Centre (start and finish) and pub at Kilnsea (just off route)	7 miles	Easy
odland paths, country lanes, fields, ep climbs	Café near Jerusalem Farm (start, finish, halfway round)	5 miles	Easy
cks, footpaths, steep climbs	None - cafés and restaurants in Meltham, Slaithwaite, Marsden and Holmfirth	5 miles	Moderate
paths, bridleways, fields, woodland ns	Pub at Oxspring (start and finish)	4 miles	Easy
paths and bridleways, steep climbs, ven ground	Seasonal café (halfway round)	6 miles	Moderate

7

Goathland Tarn p159

INTRODUCTION

*T*rying to encapsulate the vast and varied county of Yorkshire in a single sentence or two feels somewhat daunting. Affectionately called 'God's Own Country' by those of us who live here, Yorkshire is the biggest county in Britain, and home to an astonishing variety of landscapes. From glacier-carved pastoral valleys to soaring peaks and crags, undulating chalk wolds to purple-tinged heather moorlands - not to mention magnificent waterfalls, meandering rivers and a dramatic coastline - it's all here, woven together by a rich cultural heritage that stretches to sacred Neolithic sites, romantic ruined abbeys, post-industrial architecture and wartime relics.

Yorkshire is also a swim-walker's delight, the landscapes outlined above peppered with some of the best wild swimming spots in the country, and a network of wonderful walks running between them. Several cherished national trails run through the county as well as thousands of miles of footpaths, bridleways, woodland tracks and ancient packhorse routes. A number of walks in this book also take in swathes of open-access land where hikers are free to roam, unrestricted by fences or footpaths.

With so many waterfalls, rivers and tarns, and a coastline dotted with secret coves and dune-fringed beaches, Yorkshire really does promise a swim spot to suit everyone's tastes. All abilities are catered for, too, from seasoned year-round swimmers to occasional summer dippers.

Picture yourself exploring a secret canyon and discovering a run of cascades and waterfalls to plunge into on a hot summer's day, meandering through wildflower meadows to reach a wide, glassy river pool where you can float beneath a canopy of oaks, or scrambling down to a secret cove beneath towering sea cliffs then swimming through smugglers' caves as puffins wheel above. It is magical swims such as these that you will discover on each of the walks in this book.

River Wharfe, Grassington p99

Wain Wath Force p45

TAKING THE PLUNGE

Being near water is good for us. Whether that involves picnicking beside a tinkling brook, the thrill of watching a waterfall in full spate, wandering along a riverside path as dappled light dances on the water beside you or marvelling as mighty waves crash onto a sandy shore, the sense of wellbeing such experiences bring us is irrefutable. Negative ions – electrically charged particles created around moving water such as waves or the rush of a waterfall - leave us feeling refreshed and rejuvenated. The same forces are in action when we venture outside after a rainstorm and feel a renewed sense of energy. Take this one step further by entering the water and wild swimming offers us the opportunity to form an intimate connection with nature. Watching a fallen leaf float by in a gently flowing river, being mesmerised by the ripples created by tiny water boatmen as they skate across a moorland tarn or gazing out at the endless horizon of the sea all give us a different perspective on the world. In Roger Deakin's seminal book, Waterlog, charting his swimming journey around Britain, he calls this "the frog's eye view." When we

allow ourselves to become immersed in the rich aquatic life of fish, amphibians, birds and mammals we gain an enormous sense of wellbeing.

The fantastic health benefits of cold-water swimming are also now common knowledge. The surge in popularity of outdoor bathing in recent years is testament to this. Not only is wild swimming great for our immune systems, blood pressure and circulation, it also boosts our mental health, helping to reduce anxiety and stress - a sensory experience that anchors us in the moment, enabling us to shrug off everyday cares and worries. Wild swimming is also jolly good fun! Just observe a group of wild swimmers as they edge deeper into the water. Their shrieks of laughter are contagious as they slowly surrender their bodies to an enticing river pool, or plunge beneath the cascades of a waterfall or dash into frothing waves. In our modern, digital age, when we spend so much of our time tethered to electronic devices - always connected, always available - this element of adventure, and the unleashing of freedom it brings, is a valuable way to restore human happiness.

A SENSE OF COMMUNITY

The sense of community among wild swimmers is well-known; stripping down to just a swimsuit and entering the water together is a great leveller, helping conversation and laughter flow easily. Wild swimmers will also tell you about rewarding post-dip chats, sips from steaming mugs of tea and bites of scrumptious cakes (there's always lots of cake!) as they warm up. It is all part of the adventure. This book was created with the help of a wonderful wild swimming community and I am extremely grateful to the many like-minded people from the Facebook group, Wild Swimming Walks Yorkshire, who joined me during a year of research to 'test-swim' some of the walks. In checking out the most scenic routes and the best swim spots there was much scrambling over rocks or slith-

Richmond Foss p57

Saltburn-by-the-Sea p141

Swinner Gill p51

River Ouse, Beningbrough p117

Bardale Beck p63

Upper Nidderdale p81

Swaledale p51

ering down muddy banks (places can be quite different in real life from how they appear on a map)! These same people also shared their local knowledge, enthusiasm and photography skills as we trekked over moor and dale to find magical waterfalls, idyllic river pools or hidden coves. Many were keen to share their own expertise and generously helped us to forage for hedgerow snacks, or connect to the earth's natural energy by grounding (barefoot walking), as we strolled through ancient broadleaved woodlands. Barriers came down as we walked, talked and swam. I recall grabbing my camera at one secluded riverside location and turning round to see my companions had decided on a spontaneous skinny-dip! Others set their own challenges; one wild swimmer was notching up an impressive 70 swims before her 70th birthday.

These shared adventures played a huge part in the enjoyment of creating this book. The idea behind it was to showcase the best of the region's diverse landscapes, and the most beautiful places to walk and swim within them. Over a year of walks with my wonderful wild swimming community I think that goal was definitely achieved. If you're

strapping on your boots and packing your swimming gear in your backpack as you read this, I wish you happy swim-walking. I hope you enjoy these adventures as much as we have. If you'd like to join us, you can find regular updates on swim walk meet-ups by joining the Wild Swimming Walks Yorkshire group on Facebook, or by following me on Instagram @sarahbanksphoto.

THE LANDSCAPES OF YORKSHIRE

Yorkshire is huge. Encompassing 2.9 million acres - an area bigger than Greater London - and 5.5 million people - roughly double that of Wales, it stretches from the Yorkshire Dales in the west to the North York Moors in the east, taking in miles of spectacular coastline as it continues through East Yorkshire to the Humber and South Yorkshire. Down its north-south length, rippling through the old industrial heartlands of West Yorkshire, the Pennine Hills form a wild, rugged counterpoint to the busy conurbations in their valleys.

Flanking the central Pennines is the Yorkshire Dales National Park while, further south, parts of

Burnsall p105

Scale Haw Force p105

West and South Yorkshire lie within the northern and eastern fringes of the Peak District National Park; the North York Moors National Park lies off to the east. The county also contains two National Landscapes, Nidderdale and the Howardian Hills; a third, the Yorkshire Wolds, is currently under consultation. Each of these regions and landscapes has its own cultural identity, heritage and geography.

THE YORKSHIRE DALES

The Yorkshire Dales are what many people have in mind when they think of Yorkshire. The region is synonymous with natural beauty and bucolic scenery, their sheltered, glacial valleys (the "dales") ribboned by pastures criss-crossed by dry stone walls and divided by wild, heather-clad moorlands.

From Wensleydale to Wharfedale, Swaledale to Ribblesdale, each of the dales has its own character but most lie on limestone. This geology gives rise to some spectacular natural features, including the dramatic natural amphitheatre of Malham Cove, the magnificent gorge of Gordale Scar and the enchanting waterfall of Janet's Foss, whose iridescent plunge pool is lined with limestone tufa. Swathes of rare limestone pavement can also be found in several dales, a vital habitat for a large number of ferns and plants. The soluble nature of the limestone has also created a labyrinth of tunnels, caverns, potholes, rivers and waterfalls below ground; there are more than 2,500 known caves in the Yorkshire Dales, including one of the longest chambers in Britain at Gaping Gill. Thanks to the lime-rich soil, the UK's last remaining traditional upland hay meadows are also found in the Dales, where a huge range of native wildflowers and plants thrive. Wandering through the flower-filled meadows at Muker in high summer is a truly unforgettable experience.

Gazing across the pastoral landscapes of the Dales today it is hard to imagine there was a prolific lead-mining industry in operation here between the mid-17th and the early 20th centuries. The scattered remains of old mine workings and other industrial infrastructure are legacies of this heritage, still visible on the higher fells in dales such as Swaledale.

For wild swimmers, however, the key thing is that water is everywhere. It cascades off the moors, creating tumbling waterfalls with exquisite tree-fringed plunge pools like those at Catrigg Force or Cray Gill, winding rivers, such as the Wharfe, the Swale and the Ure, and shimmering moorland tarns such as Semer Water.

Keld p45

Goathland p153

THE NORTH YORK MOORS

Purple-hued uplands, speckled with stone crosses and Bronze Age standing stones, characterise the North York Moors. Home to one of the largest unbroken expanses of heather moorland in England and Wales, stretching across an impressive 44,000 hectares, these rugged slopes were cut through by glacial meltwater to form dales. In the crinkled folds of these dips a mosaic of meadows, farmsteads and hamlets nestle. Each valley, from Farndale to Fryup Dale, Bransdale to Bilsdale, has its own features but much of the land within them is designated as open-access, offering swim-walkers the freedom to explore beyond marked footpaths.

Many of those footpaths, like the stone trods through Arncliffe Woods at Glaisdale, follow in the footsteps of pilgrims and monks. Others trace routes along the remains of ironstone mining;

these include a scenic cycling and walking trail through Rosedale, where remnants of the old ore-roasting kilns remain, and of the valley's former goods railway. Elsewhere, walks pass the signs of old Roman camps and roads, and boundary stones and crosses erected by our Christian forebears.

This region promises rich pickings for wild swimmers, too. Eskdale, at the eastern edge of the national park, is dissected by the River Esk as it meanders towards the coast at Whitby. As well as enjoyable walks and swims along wooded riverside paths, it is in these far reaches of the North York Moors that waterfall seekers will delight; an array of cascades and falls around Goathland have been formed by the tumbling streams of the Eller Beck and West Beck. Adventurous swim-walkers can clamber down to the secluded falls of Nelly Ayre Foss, Thomason Foss and Water Arc Foss, and marvel at Mallyan Spout, the tallest waterfall in the North York Moors.

EAST YORKSHIRE AND THE WOLDS

Bordering North Yorkshire is the East Riding of Yorkshire, sometimes abbreviated to East Yorkshire, where the undulating chalk hills of the Yorkshire Wolds flatten towards the Holderness plain and the coast. The Yorkshire Wolds form one of the county's least-trammelled corners. Though 'wolds' are areas of high, open moorland, the charm of the Yorkshire Wolds lies in the deeply-incised valleys that interlace its rolling arable uplands. Formed by glaciers rather than rivers, these billowing, wide-skied hills famously captured the imagination of artist David Hockney over many years.

The northerly ledge of chalk on which the Wolds sit drains water so effectively that the valleys are dry; with no springs or streams the only water to be found is in the region's dew ponds. This may not sound like good news for a wild swimmer but the answer is to divide your swim-walk in two; first make your way to Thixendale, Fridaythorpe or Huggate, or the lesser-visited southern corner of the Wolds - Welton, North Newbald and Londesborough – for a hike along the Wolds Way national trail, then head to the coast for an end-of-walk dip. Choose Flamborough for dramatic sea cliffs and secluded coves, or the sand and pebble beaches at Filey, Fraisthorpe, Hornsea and Withernsea. Or, for a river swim, look to the River Hull at Baswick Landing and Tickton where there are plenty of tranquil stretches for a swim in this picturesque chalk-fed waterway.

THE YORKSHIRE COAST

The Yorkshire coast is magnificent. From surfing beaches, sandy shores and smugglers' coves to towering chalk sea cliffs, caves and stacks, all manner of fantastic aquatic adventures can be had here. Stretching for 100 miles, from Redcar in the north to the tip of Spurn Head in the Holderness, the Yorkshire coastline is fringed with picturesque

Flamborough Head p171

Spurn Point p177

Saltburn-by-the-Sea p141

Blake Clough p189

fishing villages such as Staithes, Runswick Bay and Robin Hood's Bay, and popular resorts like Whitby, Scarborough and Filey, the existence of which helps make day trips a doddle.

One highlight is the coastal town of Saltburn, once a notorious smuggling haunt, then a Victorian seaside resort and today a hotspot for surfing. It also has a buzzing sea swimming community whose members meet every morning for a dip in the bracing North Sea. From Saltburn the coastal path ribbons round to the dune-backed beach at Cattersty Sands along the Cleveland Way. Further south, wildly beautiful Ravenscar perches on a magnificent stretch of coast overlooking miles of secluded coves and caves; this area was also once popular with smugglers, who hid their contraband in the hollows of Boggle Hole. Along with the wooded cove of Stoupe Beck Sands, this span of coastline forms part of Robin Hood's Bay; both are wonderful beaches for a scenic swim.

Further south still, some of the most magnificent chalk cliffs in England can be found at Flamborough Head, plus the UK's largest mainland seabird colony at neighbouring Bempton. Just outside Flamborough, the tiny coves of Thornwick Bay, North Landing and South Landing feature fascinating caves that you can spend hours exploring. Beyond Flamborough, however, the area's most spectacular wild scenery is right at the tip of the Yorkshire coastline - the unique and constantly shifting peninsula of Spurn Point. A walk along its wildflower-festooned paths in summer, dropping down to pristine sandy beaches, makes for an outstanding swim-walk.

SOUTH AND WEST YORKSHIRE

It is easy to look at a map of South and West Yorkshire and see only cities and industrial heritage, but great efforts have been made to preserve the regions' wild and unspoilt areas. Coal-mining may have left an enduring mark on the countryside but much of this landscape has been restored, and nature reserves created where wildlife now thrives.

Wessenden Valley p189

Midgely Moor p183

Nelly Ayre Foss p159

Thornwick Bay p171

Upper Rye Falls p123

The string of green valleys that stretch over South Yorkshire's north-eastern moors towards Sheffield include the Rivelin Valley, for example, where a nature and heritage trail takes in river pools, a fabulous waterfall and relics of the mills that once operated here. And, in the lush valleys, hills and moorland of the South Pennines, between the Yorkshire Dales and the Peak District national parks, a ramble beside the youthful River Don at Oxpring will lead you through peaceful and picturesque countryside well away from the urban bustle.

By the same token, while West Yorkshire may be synonymous with 19th-century industrialisation, conjuring images of smoke billowing from the chimneys of textile mills, many of those mills have been transformed into boho art galleries and trendy offices. The surrounding Pennine countryside, particularly in its western reaches, now offers up truly wild landscapes, including the rugged, unpopulated moors that proved so inspiring for the literary Brontë sisters.

If it's a slice of that kind of wilderness you're after, the dramatic moorland of Marsden Moor, around the Wessenden Valley, hides an array of scenic cloughs (clefts in the hillside) washed through by tumbling streams and waterfalls that are ideal for intrepid swim-walkers. Or, head to Calderdale, in West Yorkshire, to walk amid lush, steep-sided valleys like Luddenden Dean, cloaked in ancient woodland. The tumbling brook that once powered water mills here is now a delightful spot for a dip.

The myriad streams and rivers rising on these moors have long been dammed to create huge reservoirs, supplying the inhabitants of Manchester, Leeds, Bradford and Sheffield with water. These glistening 'lakes', such as Redmires, Broomhead, Agden and Wessenden, may appear to be ideal swim spots but the catch is that swimming is not permitted in them (see 'Rights and Responsibilities'). Clearly, many people do swim in these under-appreciated oases, and the tide may slowly be turning to allow this. In the meantime, I've sought out those Yorkshire reservoirs where you are allowed to swim – including Gadding's Dam, near Todmorden - often dubbed England's highest beach - and Sparth Reservoir, near Marsden, which sits beside the picturesque Huddersfield Narrow Canal.

21

RIGHTS AND RESPONSIBILITIES

Goathland p159

The act of swimming in natural bodies of water such as lakes, ponds, rivers and seas goes back centuries. The Greeks and Romans embraced the therapeutic benefits of water by building bath-houses and plunge pools near natural springs. Romantic poets such as Byron, Coleridge and Wordsworth swam in open water to connect with nature and nurture their creativity. During the Victorian era a surge of interest in the healing powers of bathing led to the development of spa-focused seaside resorts such as Scarborough. And, by the late 19th and early 20th centuries, amateur swimming clubs had sprung up, many of them creating 'natural' swimming pools in rivers. After the Second World War, however, the popularity of 'wild' swimming declined as concerns grew over water pollution and both indoor and outdoor swimming pools became the norm.

Over the past few years, the tide has turned once more, though. Swimming in natural bodies of water has seen a huge resurgence as increasing numbers of people are discovering the wellbeing benefits of swimming outdoors, and connecting with others who share their passion through social media networks. While this is undoubtedly a welcome shift, there is some (justified) concern that the upsurge in interest is putting too much pressure on fragile environments that were previously off the radar. Certain swimming spots have become honeypot sites where footfall is so high that it is having an adverse impact on these precious places. With this in mind, the Wild Swimming Code (below) offers some guidance to help care for and preserve these natural beauty spots.

THE WILD SWIMMING CODE

Respect others

- Be considerate to those living in, working in and enjoying the countryside
- Car-share where possible and park sensibly to avoid blocking gates, narrow roads or passing places
- Respect other water users, including anglers, kayakers and paddle boarders
- Keep to marked paths unless wider access is permitted
- Get changed discreetly and keep noise to sociable levels

Protect the environment

- Take your litter home and take a bag to pick up any litter left by others
- Do not light fires, or disposable BBQs
- Avoid damaging riverbanks when entering or exiting the water

- Be bio-secure. 'Check, clean, dry' your swimwear and kit between visiting different bodies of water to avoid the spread of invasive species
- Avoid disturbing livestock or wildlife, including animals, birds, fish and invertebrates. Keep your distance from nesting birds in spring and summer
- Keep clear of areas important for fish breeding and spawning, such as gravel shoals and riffles, especially between autumn and spring

Enjoy the Outdoors

- Check your route and local weather conditions
- Keep yourself and others safe and know how to get help
- Enjoy your visit, have fun and take away memories

RIGHT TO ROAM

All of the walks in this book are in areas where there is designated public access, including rights of way, access land and some waters with navigation rights. In Yorkshire, many of the upland areas, including the Yorkshire Dales, North York Moors and the moorland around West Yorkshire, lie on open-access land. Some of the walks involve making your own way across access land, which is denoted on OS maps by a thick orange border. It is legal to roam anywhere on this land and you are not restricted to footpaths or bridleways. However, there are some exceptions. You can find more information on access land on the Ramblers website - **ramblers.org.uk**

RIGHT TO SWIM

Reservoirs: Yorkshire, particularly in the south and west, is dotted with reservoirs that look like fantastic swim spots. However, current bylaws prohibit swimming in almost all active reservoirs. So, although you may pass reservoirs on some of these walks, at the present time we cannot encourage you to enter the water. An increase in campaigning for access to these blue spaces means swimming may be allowed in them in the not-too-distant future.

The Sea, Rivers and Lakes: The right to swim in the sea and tidal waters is clear and undisputed. Access rights to rivers and lakes is more complicated and restrictive. There are many places with a legal right of access to swim, many more where there are good arguments that this right exists, and several places where swimming is tolerated.

River Swale, Richmond p57

Keld p45

FURTHER READING

You may like to read '16 Reasons for Swimming Access in Reservoirs', written by Owen Hayman and Imogen Radford from SOUP (Sheffield OUtdoor Plungers): **outdoorswimmingsociety. com/sixteen-reasons-reservoirs/**

For more information on where people can legally swim, visit the Outdoor Swimming Society website: **outdoorswimmingsociety.com/is-it-legal**

CLEANER WATERS

Yorkshire's rivers, streams and coastal waters are beautiful places to swim. However, we cannot ignore the fact that our waterways and seas are under huge pressure from pollution, caused by intensive agricultural practices and sewerage releases from water companies. This means that each time we enter the water we have to make a compromise between the joy of swimming in these blissful outdoor pools and acknowledging the risks this might bring.

At the time of writing, three Yorkshire swim spots have been issued Bathing Water Status - stretches of the River Wharfe at Ilkley and Wetherby and the River Nidd at Knaresborough. Bathing water designation means the Environment Agency has to conduct weekly testing at the designated sites between May and September, putting pressure on water companies, farmers and local communities to cut pollution levels. It doesn't mean these places will necessarily be clean to swim in but it is a good starting point.

It says much that so many people continue to swim in our rivers, lakes and seas even in this time of public concern over water pollution. For many the benefits of outdoor swimming clearly outweigh the risks. As swimmers we can also be advocates; there are numerous campaigns and citizen science projects we can get involved in, as well as lobbying our local MPs. By continuing to swim we are demanding change, telling water companies and the government that everyone has the right to access clean water, and giving them an incentive to clean things up.

Thornwick Bay p171

Cray Gill p75

WALKING AND OPEN WATER SWIMMING SAFETY

*A*lthough Yorkshire is not as rugged as some other mountainous areas of the UK, it is still home to some remote and wild uplands that can present challenges for walkers. The key to a successful walk is in the planning. Familiarising yourself with the route and terrain before you set out will make for a more enjoyable excursion. I have endeavoured to offer tips and advice where I feel it is helpful in the description and information panel for each walk. Almost all the photographs for the walks in this book were taken in the less inclement months of April to October, although with climate change extreme weather can occur at any time. Because the landscape is constantly changing, there may be new or recent hazards that have not been identified - trees fall, paths can erode, particularly along coastal routes, and some trails may become overgrown, so you should make your own assessment on the day.

Check the weather forecast for the day of your walk as this can be variable and you need to be prepared for changing conditions. Mist and fog can appear all year round, particularly on higher ground or by the coast, and terrain can become water-logged after heavy rain, or paths slippery. Becks, streams and rivers can all swell and flood and, as this is a book of swim-walks, it is important to be well-informed before you set out. You will find some recommended apps for weather, surf and beach forecasts, river flow and pollution etc. under Practical Information.

Most of the walks in this book are easy to follow, with identifiable footpaths and signposts along the route. However, some more remote routes require navigation skills. The illustrated maps in this guide

Swinner Gill p51

give you an indication of the route and assist with directions, but they should be used alongside a map, ideally an OS Explorer 1:25,000 scale map. You can find out which map to use by referring to the information panel next to each walk. Armed with your map, make sure you know how to locate yourself using a grid reference in case you need to share this in an emergency. You can also download each map from the Wild Things Publishing website. Digital mapping apps are useful but remember to download the map before you set off; mobile phone reception can by patchy, or non-existent, on some of the more remote walks.

Crook Gill p75

River Don, Oxspring p195

Upper Nidd Falls p81

Thornwick Bay p171

OPEN WATER SWIMMING SAFETY ADVICE AND TIPS

When you add swimming in cold water into your walk, you will need to factor in a few more pre-cautions. The majority of wild swimming walks detailed in this book are not extreme in any way but several are far away from any direct help, sometimes with poor mobile phone signal. It is, therefore, advisable to take a few more safety measures prior to and during your walk:

- Always be prepared not to swim. You may arrive at a swim spot and find it isn't safe to swim - the water may be too fast-flowing or full, a tree may have fallen or the water may not look or smell good. Or you might just not feel in the mood. If it doesn't feel right, leave it for another day.
- Swim with others. If this is not possible, let people at home know your plans and whereabouts.

- Don't swim in a river that is in spate. Always make an assessment on the current and flow of the water before getting in. Even seemingly sedate rivers can have a fast flow. Throw a leaf or stick into the water to see how fast it moves with the current.
- Before entering the water check your exit point. Make sure you know where you can get out safely and easily. Remember that your hands will be cold and less dexterous if your swim involves clambering out.
- Take care on rocks near water. Wet rocks can be slippery and sharp so tread carefully.
- Enter the water gradually. Allow your body to acclimatise to the change in temperature by getting in slowly and calm your breathing before you start swimming.
- Don't jump in at the beginning. Always check the depth and look out for hidden objects, even if it is somewhere you have jumped in before.
- Do not swim beneath weirs or large waterfalls. The water is powerful here and can drag you under.
- Avoid swimming after heavy rain. Water levels can rise quickly and debris and pollution may increase, including run-off from surrounding farmland.
- Get out of the water before you start to feel too cold. It is easy to stay in the water too long but your core temperature continues to drop even after you have got out. Get out while you feel good and get dressed quickly to warm up.

SEA SWIMMING

With sea temperatures averaging between 4 to 7 degrees in winter and 14 to 17 degrees in summer, the Yorkshire Coast certainly offers an exhilarating dip. Currents, tides and weather, including on-shore and off-shore winds, all play a part in the ever-fluctuating nature of the coast and it is important not to underestimate the power of the sea. Having a good understanding of the water is crucial, as is knowing what to do if you, or anyone with you, gets into difficulty. It is advisable to take a few more safety precautions to ensure everyone stays safe:

- Always check the tide times before you set out. You can check the Met Office for beach forecasts and tide times. Surfline also offers a surf report listing details of swells and wind conditions (see Further Information).
- Beware of tidal currents, especially around headlands, and estuary mouths, particularly around mid-tide, and on fortnightly spring tides when flows are strongest.
- Be aware of rip currents - strong currents running out to sea that can quickly take you out of your depth. If you do find yourself caught in a rip, follow this advice from the RNLI:
  - Don't try to swim against it or you'll get exhausted
  - If you can stand, wade don't swim
  - If you can, swim parallel to the shore until free of the rip and then head for shore
  - Always raise your hand and shout for help

IN EMERGENCY

If something does go wrong know who to ring. If you are at the coast, dial 999 and ask for the Coastguard. If you are on remote moorland or hills, dial 999 and ask for the police, then Mountain Rescue. Have as much information as you can about your location and the nature of the emergency.

WILD SWIMMING WALKS KIT

Whilst you could argue that you need very little for a wild swimming walk apart from a comfortable pair of shoes, a swimming costume and small towel, for more isolated hikes, or hikes in the shoulder months either side of high summer, appropriate clothing

and some further equipment is essential. Here are some suggestions on what to pack for a swim walk:

- A 25 – 30l rucksack
- A sturdy pair of walking boots or shoes, preferably waterproof
- A waterproof jacket, both to keep you dry and to give some protection from wind-chill
- Layers of clothing that you can add or remove
- A swimming costume for each swim spot (see Rights and Responsibilities)
- Aqua shoes
- A waterproof bag, or zip-lock bag, for stowing wet swim clothes
- A small, hammam-style, microfibre or poncho-type towel
- A basic first aid kit - waterproof plasters, blister plasters (sheep's wool also does the trick in an emergency), antiseptic cream, tick remover
- A paper OS map
- A mobile phone and fully-charged power bank
- Food, snacks, water and a flask of something hot - tea/ coffee/ hot chocolate
- Optional extras - a brightly-coloured tow float and hat for visibility

Cray Gill p75

Upper Wharfedale p75

Thornwick Bay p171

HOW TO USE THIS BOOK

*E*ach of the 28 wild swimming walks in this book feature a walk description and photographs, detailed walk directions, a route map with key waypoints plus swimming and dipping spots. The information panel includes both essential and useful information including:

- A short description of the terrain you can expect on the walk
- The distance of the walk measured in miles with an estimated walking time (the time will vary depending on the pace of your walk; note that swimming time is not included)
- The starting point for each walk - usually a car park, or a lay-by large enough to offer parking space
- Public transport options
- At least two swim spots per walk
- Places or points of interest along the way, or in the vicinity
- Refreshments en route - cafés, pubs or kiosks plus other facilities such as toilets
- Other local swim spots
- Option for easier access to the swim spots in each walk, or a more accessible local swim spot

GETTING THERE AND PUBLIC TRANSPORT

Many of the walks in this book have been designed to start near bus stops or train stations, the details of which are listed in the information panel next to the walk description. Be aware that the frequency of these services can vary; more regular rural bus services include the DalesBus, Moors Bus (summer only) and coastal bus services while some community transport services operate a more limited schedule. Be mindful that these rural bus routes can change, or be axed altogether. The suggested services should be taken as a guide only so always check if the service is still operating. If travelling by car, every effort has been made to use village car parks or spacious parking lay-bys.

DOWNLOADABLE ROUTE INFORMATION

PDF and GPX route information to print out or transfer to your smartphone can be found at **wildthingspublishing.com/yorkshire** - Insert the last two words of each chapter introduction, with no spaces or capitals. For example, for Walk 1 go to **wildthingspublishing.com/yorkshire/ pendragoncastle**

A GLOSSARY OF YORKSHIRE TERMS

Some terms you might come across in this book and on your Yorkshire swim-walks:

Beck – a small stream or brook
Clough - frequently used in the South Pennines to describe a steep-sided ravine
Foss or Force - the name force comes from the time of the Vikings; their word for waterfall was foss (ie Janet's Foss) which, over time, sometimes became force
Gill - frequently used in the North Pennines and Yorkshire Dales to describe a small narrow valley or ravine
Snicket or ginnel - an alleyway between a fence or wall
Squeeze/ Squeeze stile (in a stone wall) - a break in a stone wall, created by vertical stones, which you can just about 'squeeze' through!
Tarn - a lake or a pond

Nelly Ayre Foss p159

COLLECTIONS

WALKS TO DO WITH KIDS

2. Keld Waterfalls
4. Richmond Foss, River Swale and Round Howe
5. Semer Water and Bardale Beck
7. Cray Gill Waterfalls and River Wharfe
8. Upper Nidd Falls and How Stean Gorge
10. Janet's Foss and Gordale Scar
11. Grassington and River Wharfe
12. Hebden, Loup Scar and Burnsall
13. Nidd Gorge
14. River Ouse at Beningbrough
15. Douglas Ridge and Upper Rye Falls
16. Nunnington and River Rye
18. Saltburn and Cattersty Sands
19. Esk Valley Rail Trail
22. Ravenscar, Stoupe Beck Sands and Boggle Hole
23. Flamborough Coves and Caves
27. Oxspring and River Don

LONGER SWIMS

4. Richmond Foss, River Swale and Round Howe
5. Semer Water and Bardale Beck
6. Redmire Force and River Ure
9. Catrigg Force, Stainforth Force and the Eel Pool
11. Grassington and River Wharfe
12. Hebden, Loup Scar and Burnsall
14. River Ouse at Beningbrough
17. Kirkham Abbey and Howsham Mill
18. Saltburn and Cattersty Sands
21. Goathland Tarn, Simon Howe and Nelly Ayre Foss
22. Ravenscar, Stoupe Beck Sands and Boggle Hole
23. Flamborough Coves and Caves
24. Spurn Point Out-and-Back
25. Luddenden Dean and Midgley Moor

SPECTACULAR SCENERY

1. Pendragon Castle and Catagill Scar
2. Keld Waterfalls
3. Muker, Swinner Gill and Kisdon Force
5. Semer Water and Bardale Beck
7. Cray Gill Waterfalls and River Wharfe
8. Upper Nidd Falls and How Stean Gorge
9. Catrigg Force, Stainforth Force and the Eel Pool
10. Janet's Foss and Gordale Scar
11. Grassington and River Wharfe
12. Hebden, Loup Scar and Burnsall
18. Saltburn and Cattersty Sands
21. Goathland Tarn, Simon Howe and Nelly Ayre Foss
22. Ravenscar, Stoupe Beck Sands and Boggle Hole
23. Flamborough Coves and Caves
24. Spurn Point Out-and-Back
26. Wessenden Falls and Blake Clough
25. Luddenden Dean and Midgley Moor

HISTORICAL JOURNEYS

3. Muker, Swinner Gill and Kisdon Force
4. Richmond Foss, River Swale and Round Howe
17. Kirkham Abbey and Howsham Mill
18. Saltburn and Cattersty Sands
19. Esk Valley Rail Trail
22. Ravenscar, Stoupe Beck Sands and Boggle Hole
24. Spurn Point Out-and-Back
25. Luddenden Dean and Midgley Moor
27. Oxspring and River Don
28. Wyming Brook and Rivelin Plunge Pool

FURTHER INFORMATION

The following websites and apps offer useful information to help plan a safe, enjoyable and responsible swim walk:

The Met Office
Provides localised weather forecasts
metoffice.gov.uk

Surfers Against Sewage
Marine conservation charity's real-time map, tracking sewage discharge and pollution risks around the UK's coastline
sas.org.uk

Surfline
Provides tide tables and surf forecasts
surfline.com

Yorkshire Water Storm Overflow Map
Search for Storm Overflow Map to find a live storm overflow map, including date, time and duration
yorkshirewater.com

The Rivers Trust
Umbrella organisation for local river conservation trusts
riverstrust.org

Shoothill GaugeMap
Interactive map with latest river level, flow and groundwater data from Environment Agency stations in UK and Ireland
gaugemap.co.uk

National Trust
Further information on National Trust properties included in some of the walks
nationaltrust.org/visit/yorkshire

Midgely Moor p183

Outdoor Swimming Society
Inspiration, connection and advice for the outdoor swimming community
outdoorswimmingsociety.com

Welcome to Yorkshire
Official tourist information website for Yorkshire
yorkshire.com

FINDING FELLOW SWIMMERS

Facebook groups for swimmers in Yorkshire are plentiful. Some popular ones include:

The Dales Dippers - the Yorkshire Dales
FLOWS (Fabulous Leeds Outdoor Wild Swimmers) - Leeds area
Hebden Bridge and Calderdale wild swimbling - Hebden Bridge and Calderdale
Knaresborough Swimmers Group - Knaresborough area
KAPOWS - Kirklees and Penistone Outdoor Wild Swimmers - South and West Yorkshire
Saltburn Sea Swimmers and Saltburn Mermates - Saltburn-by-the-Sea
SOUP Swims (Sheffield OUtdoor Plungers) - Sheffield/South Yorkshire area
The Hub Sea Swimmers - Scarborough North Bay
Whitby Wild Swimmers - Whitby/Sandsend area
Wild Swimming Walks Yorkshire – swim-walk meet-ups across Yorkshire
Yorkshire Dippers - swim meet-ups across Yorkshire
York Swimmers - river swimming around York

Wild Swimming
Wild swimming tips and advice from Wild Things Publishing, including a wild swimming community map
wildswimming.co.uk

SEMI-WILD SWIMMING

For a wild swimming experience in a more managed environment you might like to visit these two swimming lakes near York (paid entry):

Pool Bridge Farm
poolbridgefarm.co.uk

Chaloner Pond
chalonerpond.co.uk

SAUNA AND SWIM

The Finnish cultural tradition of steam and a cold-water plunge is growing in the UK with saunas popping up beside the country's beaches, riversides, waterfalls and even city docklands. Some popular wild saunas in Yorkshire include:

Whitby Well-Being
Pop-up Finnish tent sauna at locations across Yorkshire
whitbywellbeing.com

Iglu Sauna
Nordic-style wood-fired sauna and plunge pools outside Hebden Bridge
iglusauna.co.uk

Pool Bridge Farm
Wood-fired saunas overlooking private swimming ponds outside York
poolbridgefarm.co.uk

Richmond Castle, River Swale p57

Walk 1

PENDRAGON CASTLE AND CATAGILL SCAR

A dramatic and captivating adventure in the remote Mallerstang Valley, with breathtaking views and delightful swims in idyllic river pools and cascades.

A walk that's also something of a geographical brainteaser, although this picturesque upland loop is technically in Cumbria, it happens to sit within the Yorkshire Dales National Park – a throwback to the fact that, when the Park was created, in 1954, its peaceful north-western fringes were still part of the West Riding. Further expansion of the Park in 2016 took in even more of Cumbria, scooping up burly fells peppered with castles and cascades, including the wild and exceptionally beautiful Mallerstang Valley.

This narrow dale is bounded on one side by the distinctive peak of Wild Boar Fell and by Mallerstang Edge and High Seat on the other. At times the road through it runs parallel with the Settle to Carlisle railway line, en route from Garsdale Head to Kirkby Stephen. Most excitingly for swim-walkers, the gorgeous River Eden flows through the dale, creating a series of 'secret' pools and falls on the bend of an idyllic, wooded river glade downstream of Pendragon Castle. As the river winds further along its journey there are more opportunities for swimming and dipping in meadow-fringed pools on the lower slopes of Birkett Common, in the shadow of Lammerside Castle ruins.

Undoubtedly, these western reaches of the Yorkshire Dales National Park have a different feel and appearance to the dales on the eastern side of the watershed. The landscape is rugged and more remote here, and less populated. Those already familiar with the Dales will find this captivating western corner of them surprisingly distinct – and, if you're like me, yearning to explore more of it.

INFORMATION

Tracks, footpaths, bridleways, country lanes and remote moorland roads with passing traffic. Basic navigation skills required on open-access land. You may encounter livestock.

DISTANCE: 4.5 miles
TIME: 2.5 hours
MAP: OS Explorer OL19 Howgill Fells and Upper Eden Valley
START & END POINT: Parking lay-by opposite Pendragon Castle (NY 782 026, 54.41865, -2.3367)
PUBLIC TRANSPORT: Train station at Kirkby Stephen then taxi to start
SWIMMING: River Eden at Catagill Scar and other pools up and downstream
PLACES OF INTEREST: Pendragon Castle, Lammerside Castle, Mallerstang Pillow Mounds
REFRESHMENTS: None on route but The Black Bull, Nateby (CA17 4JP, 01768 371588), and Owen's Farm Shop, nr Kirkby Stephen (CA17 4HE, 07972 485794), are nearby
NEARBY SWIM SPOTS: River Eden, Stenkrith Bridge
EASIER ACCESS: It is less than half a mile's walk along a country lane from the parking lay-by to the first swim spot but it is possible for anyone with limited mobility to be dropped off even closer, by the cattle grid before the track.

The walk begins next to the romantic ruins of Pendragon Castle ❶, where there is parking for a few cars in a small lay-by opposite. Legend has it that the original castle was built in the 5th century by Uther Pendragon, father of King Arthur, and may have been the site of his death (by poisoned well). Although an intriguing tale, this is stretching the truth since there appears to be no evidence of a castle here before the 12th century. Another claim to fame is that it was once home to Sir Hugh de Morville, one of the knights who murdered the Archbishop of Canterbury, Sir Thomas Becket, in 1170. Having fallen into disrepair by the 16th century, the castle then passed into the hands of landowner Lady Anne Clifford, when it was restored and improved. However, after Lady Clifford's death the castle fell into disrepair again, leaving the ruined shell we see today.

After exploring the ruins, the walk continues along a quiet country lane, crossing a bridge over the River Eden before deviating onto a track skirting the base of Birkett Common, with grand vistas ahead ❷. Keep an eye out for red squirrels in the trees, and for your first proper glimpse of the bronze-hued river shimmering below. A short tramp down tussocky hillside leads to a sun-dappled river pool, with falls and cascades tumbling over jagged rocks at either end. It is a gorgeous spot in summer with foxgloves, cushions of bilberries and emerald ferns cloaking the hillside. Although the peaty pool is more suitable for a dip than a longer swim, a wade downstream brings you to more cascades and deeper pools.

Back on the track the route continues past the industrial remains of an old lime kiln - once used to burn locally quarried limestone to produce quicklime and slaked lime. Just after a fenced area, the river meanders beneath Catagill Scar, one of

the steep limestone rockfaces synonymous with the Yorkshire Dales ❸. Here it is squeezed through a narrow channel, creating some tumultuous cascades and frothing pools. Reaching this secluded ravine requires navigating your own path across grassy open-access land. This can be bracken-smothered in parts during high summer so always remember to check your legs for ticks after bashing through the ferns and, if possible, follow sheep tracks. As you near the water, a rocky path ribbons over a hillock and down to the river's edge.

There are interesting rock formations on the riverbed here and impressive waterfalls that cleave down large boulders into seething, swirling pools. Clamber over large pot-holed rocks and you reach a captivating pool and shingle beach a little further downstream. A little more exploring up and downstream rewards you with more gems but, as the rocks are slippery, it is a good idea to don a pair of aqua shoes for scrambling over them. Afterwards dry off on the rocks, or grassy riverbank, and enjoy a summer picnic, far from civilisation.

Post-swim, there is a short climb out of the ravine to rejoin the main track, picking out your own preferred route to ascend soft slopes that are seamed with tiny rills. Snowy tufts of common cotton-grass stipple the boggy moorland like cotton wool flags swaying in the breeze. The route continues, following the river downstream and shrouded by the wild beauty of the fells, dotted with occasional farmsteads and cottages.

Marked on the OS map as the track veers off to the left are 'pillow mounds' which lie to the north of Birkett Common, near the summit of Round Hill ❹. These four intriguing rectangular banks cut into the hillside are also known in Mallerstang as Giants' Graves, and are most conspicuous when travelling along the main road to Kirkby Stephen. Artificial

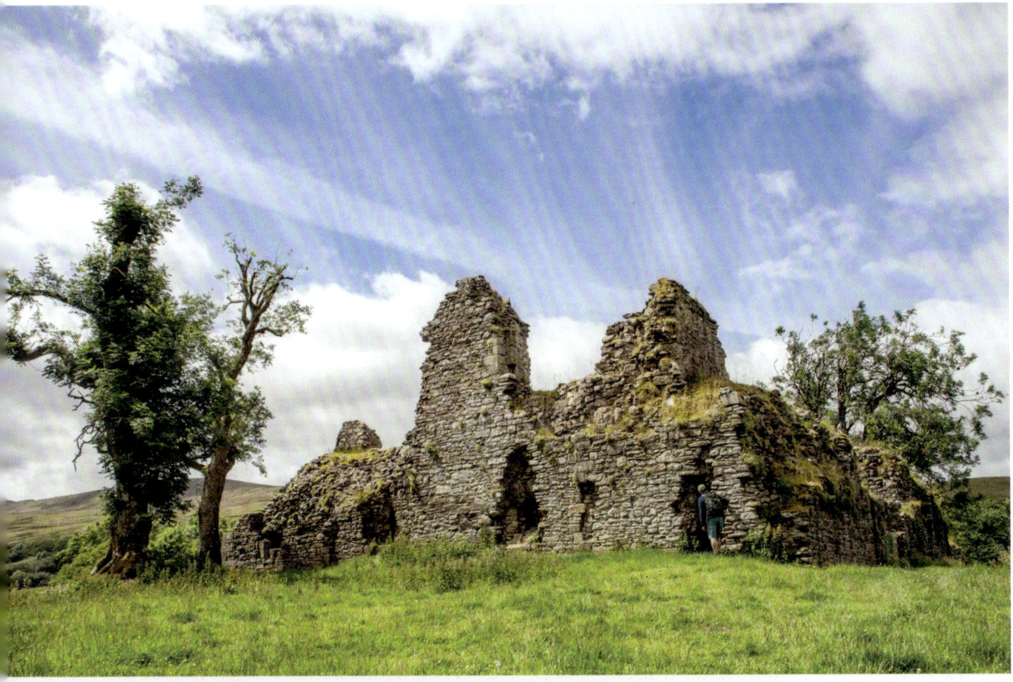

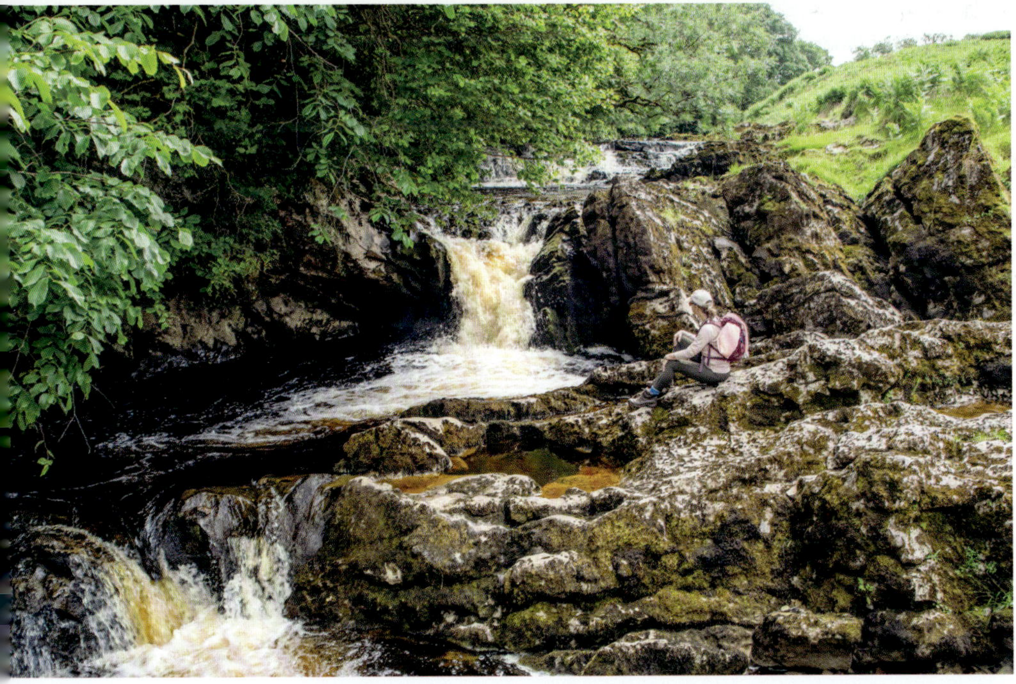

rabbit warrens, created in the 12th century by the Normans, who introduced rabbits to England for their meat and fur, each mound consists of a low, flat-topped bank of earth surrounded by a ditch.

The River Eden forms a broad, graceful bend here, the water sliding smoothly then creating riffles over the stony river bed. Its journey is unusual in that, unlike most of England's rivers, it flows northwards from its source in the fells above Hell Gill Force out to sea via the Solway Firth. Although it is quite shallow here, there are a couple of deeper pools suitable for a swim, tucked in beneath the fells with ample sheep-nibbled grassy banks to sprawl out on and dry off afterwards ④. Another good reason to pause here is the opportunity for a brief detour to Lammerside Castle, a ruined 14th-century peel tower and small castle, built to keep Scots raiders at bay.

Turning sharply left here and passing a row of cottages and farm buildings, the route joins an attractive green lane, bounded by mossy stone walls ⑤. With height gained, it is worth pausing to look back at the splendid view behind; on a bright day, the sun's rays flood the fells with brilliant gold

light. The railway bridge that you pass beneath soon afterwards carries the Settle to Carlisle railway on one of the most scenic lines in the UK, travelling over countless bridges and viaducts and through numerous tunnels along its 72-mile track. After being run down in the 1970s, it was thankfully saved from closure in 1989 after a long and determined campaign and is now a major tourist attraction in its own right.

With one final uphill push you arrive at the Tommy Road ⑥, a classic moorland thoroughfare over Wharton Fell. The panoramic views from this lofty vantage point are glorious: Ash Fell and Ravenstonedale to the west, Mallerstang to the east, Kirkby Stephen to the north and tent-shaped Wild Boar Fell to the south. As along much of this walk, you are likely to be in your own company save for the aerial acrobatics of skylarks, soaring in song-flight before parachuting back down to earth, or the distant rumbling wheels of a passing train as it burrows through Birkett Tunnel. The last mile or so is a gentle stroll along this road, which eventually rejoins a verdant lane back to Pendragon Castle.

1 You may wish to start with a visit to 12th-century Pendragon Castle. Afterwards, turn immediately left out of the gate onto a narrow lane, marked not suitable for HGVs and with a notice about Red Squirrels. After crossing a bridge, the route rises sharply to the right, passing a house on the left. Look for a cattle grid ahead and a fingerpost to Wharton on the right.

2 Leave the road to follow the Wharton track as views open up ahead of you. Just beyond the wall the River Eden is visible below. Make your way down the grassy bank to the water, which tumbles over jagged rocks with deeper pools for bathing. Explore downstream to find more small cascades and pools. Afterwards rejoin the track and continue with occasional glimpses of the river below, passing an old lime kiln on the left and Catagill Scar to the right, where the river narrows through a wooded gorge.

3 There is a fence between the path and the scar which then turns right down towards the river. Here you need to follow faint tracks across open-access land to reach the water. A stony path leads down to the riverside with numerous cascades, waterfalls and pools. After your swim, it is a case of finding the best route back up to re-join the track - with the river to your back, head straight uphill and the track will become visible once you crest the slope out of the gorge. The ground can be boggy in

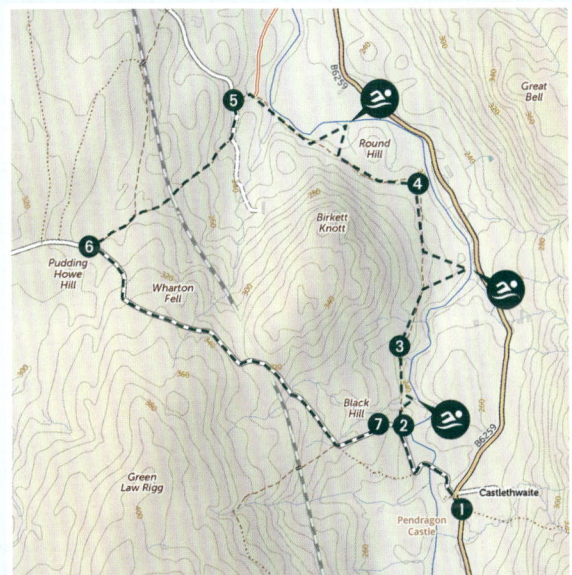

parts. Re-join the track and continue, following the river downstream as it meanders left.

4 The river here runs shallower but there are a couple of deeper meadow-fringed pools for swimming. The track drops down almost to river level, crossing a flat bridge over a stream before rising again to a metal gate. To the right is Lammerside Castle, which is worth a short detour to visit; follow a bridleway across the field to reach it.

5 Back on the track the route then ascends, swinging sharp left to a tarmac lane. Turn left, past houses and farm buildings. Do not cross the cattle grid. Instead, go through a less obvious metal gate

on the right and ascend along a grassy, walled track to a gate. Continue through a field, with a stone wall to your right and the railway bridge ahead. Pass beneath the railway bridge and continue across open moorland until you reach the moorland road. There are superb views of the surrounding fells from this vantage point, including the peaked Wild Boar Fell.

6 At the road turn left and continue along this scenic road for 1.5 miles, passing over a railway tunnel.

7 You eventually reach the cattle grid you crossed at the start of the walk. From here retrace your steps back to Pendragon Castle and the parking lay-by.

Walk 2

KELD WATERFALLS

A fabulous short ramble stringing together some of the most enchanting waterfalls in the Yorkshire Dales, along with spectacular scenery and a lovely tea garden.

With what's claimed to be the highest concentration of waterfalls in England (there are at least nine of them within a mile of this secluded, Upper Swaledale hamlet) it is little wonder that the tiny village of Keld has inspired writers like Alfred Wainwright and WH Auden, who immortalised Swaledale in his poem, *'Streams'*:

Lately, in that dale of all Yorkshire's the loveliest,
Where off its fellside helter-skelter Kisdon Beck
Jumps into Swale with a Boyish shouting,
Sprawled out on grass, I dozed for a second

This short walk takes in five of these gorgeous cascades, four of them with plunge pools. If waterfall-bagging is your aim, you could pinch another of the falls, Kisdon Force, from the Muker, Swinner Gill and Kisdon Force walk, without adding too strenuous a detour. Or you could combine both walks for an epic waterfall-chasing yomp.

With its plethora of cascades, it is little surprise that the name Keld stems from the Norse word *'Kelda,'* meaning spring or well. The village's stone-built cottages and rustic farmsteads give the place a timeless character. In his 1973 Coast to Coast Walk, Wainwright mused that *"a sundial records the hours but time is measured in centuries in Keld"*. The sundial in question sits above the doorway of the United Reformed Church in the village centre. Despite being one of the most remote villages in the Yorkshire Dales, Keld is popular as a starting point for walkers; it sits where Wainwright's Coast to Coast and the Pennine Way meet. It is also very well

INFORMATION

Well-trodden footpaths, bridleways and country lanes. You may encounter livestock.

DISTANCE: 2.5 miles
TIME: 1.5 hours
MAP: OS Explorer OL30 Yorkshire Dales, Northern and Central
START & END POINT: Park Lodge Car Park (Rukin's Park Lodge Campsite - honesty box £3 per day) (NY 892 011, 54.4067, -2.1695)
PUBLIC TRANSPORT: DalesBus, Service 30 - The Swaledale Shuttle (may require booking in advance, 01969 667400)
SWIMMING: Waterfalls at East Gill, Currack Force and Wain Wath Force plus Hoggarth's Leap
PLACES OF INTEREST: Keld Resource Centre
REFRESHMENTS: Rukin's Park Lodge Campsite café (summer-only), Keld Green Café
NEARBY SWIM SPOTS: Kisdon Force
EASIER ACCESS: East Gill is a short walk from Keld. Hoggarth's Leap is easily accessed from Rukin's Park Lodge Campsite.

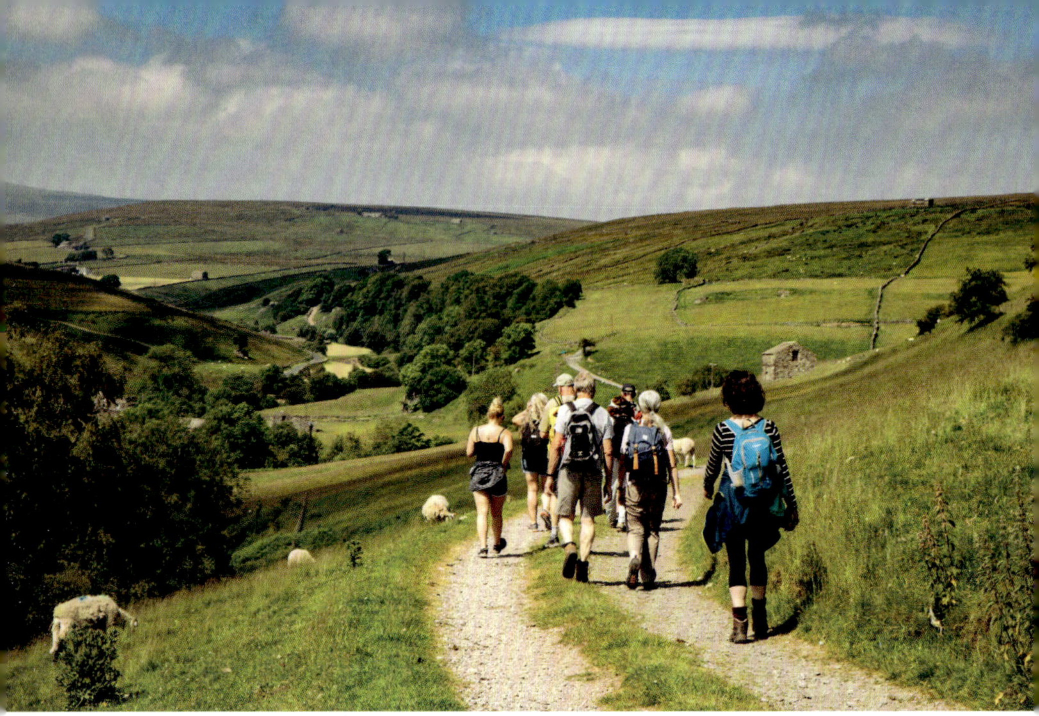

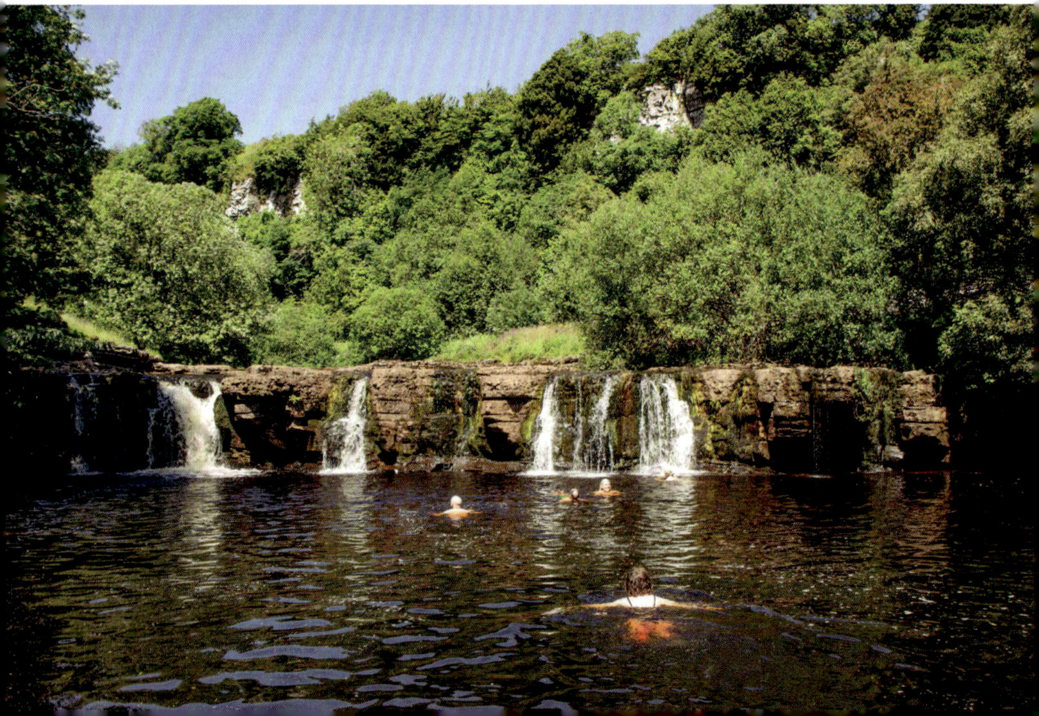

served with amenities, including two charming tea rooms, an idyllic riverside campsite, various other accommodation options and the must-visit Keld Resource Centre ❼. The latter is a village-based charity preserving and sharing the heritage of Swaledale in general, and this former lead-mining village in particular, by restoring several historic buildings in the village and opening them to the public as holiday cottages, museums and community gardens.

The walk starts at the large Park Lodge Car Park, winding along a bridleway towards the River Swale, with soaring views of Kisdon Hill ahead. Picking up an attractive path through a tunnel of trees, fringed with garlicky-scented ransoms in spring, this leads to the tumultuous river ❶.

After crossing the footbridge, the sound of the frothing white water of East Gill Force grows louder as it cascades in tiers to join the river. The lower falls are just visible through the leaves. The higher falls, with a plunge pool, can be reached by following the gill a few metres upstream ❷. You may find yourself in the company of long-distance walkers hiking the Pennine Way or The Swale Trail; both pass through here and two well-sited benches above the falls provide a scenic spot to pause. The falls are a lovely place to take a quick dip, setting you up for the rest of this delightful ramble.

From here you are likely to leave other walkers behind as the route rises along a stony track towards an isolated farmhouse. Spectacular views abound, though some of the best scenery is behind you, looking back towards the crags of Kisdon Gorge and the commanding grassy mound of Kisdon Hill. Keld's cluster of solid stone-built houses sit at the summit of the river valley, encircled by a patchwork of rolling green hills, criss-crossed with dry stone walls and speckled with cow barns. These

little stone cow houses, or cow'usses as they are known locally, have been a feature of the Swaledale landscape for centuries. The traditional cow house comprised of bosses, or stalls, where cattle were tied; a mew, where dried hay was stored and the faux, above the cattle, where green hay or bedding was placed to dry out. Today many of the barns are empty, used only for storage or as shelter for ewes and lambs in poor weather.

Although farming has been the lifeblood of people living in these remote uplands for centuries, the hills have also been exploited for lead. So rich with lead veins and ore shoots was the northern side of Swaledale that, in the 18th and 19th centuries, the valley became the largest and most productive lead-mining area in Britain. Looking across this

peaceful rural landscape today it is hard to imagine the network of tunnels and mine workings that still lie beneath the undulating hills and remote moors. However, some of the old mine ruins, including the smelt mill, can be seen around Swinner Gill (see Muker, Swinner Gill and Kisdon Force walk).

At a fork in the track the route passes behind a farmhouse with ever-widening views across the dale. Hillside streams sluice over mossy stones, creating miniature waterfalls, and hardy Swaledale sheep nibble the grassy slopes, errant strands of their wool flapping on stretches of wire fencing. This wool is the perfect remedy if you happen to get a blister. Place a piece of it on the blister, or the area most likely to cause irritation, and put your sock back on over it. It really works!

As the track descends, the falls of secluded Currack Force are audible before you glimpse them through the trees. These are the top falls,

however; the larger falls are the lower ones, reached by crossing the bridge over Stonesdale Beck ❸ and following the stone wall down to a grassy bank, shrouded by trees. Few realise this enchanting cascade is here since it is so well hidden. The water tumbles over the rock face here, the beck having scoured out a wide plunge pool before hurrying off to its confluence with the Swale. It is a magical setting.

Continue along the path to a country road and then zig zag down this to Park Bridge, catching a glimpse upstream of Wain Wath Force ❹. With grassy banks and several rocky ledges for changing and summertime picnics, Wain Wath's falls are broad and graceful, cascading into a magnificent plunge pool while the limestone cliff of Cotterby Scar rises behind ❻. Unsurprisingly, these roadside falls are popular, although outside school holidays and weekends you may have them to yourself.

After frolicking beneath the spray of the falls, the route winds back to Keld through gorgeous scenery. The Keld Green Café ❼ is on the main road before the turn for Keld, a tempting summer pitstop before the last two waterfalls. Catrake Force and Hoggarth's Leap are accessed from Rukin's Campsite by kind permission of its owners. Flowing through a steep gorge, impressive Catrake Force is best admired from above ❽. There isn't really a safe way down. For one last dip, however, Hoggarth's Leap is much more accessible. A multi-tiered wedding cake of a waterfall, at the far end of the campsite, it has a string of smaller cascades and a small pool ❾. Afterwards, the farm teashop at Rukin's Campsite serves up an array of treats from ice creams to bacon butties, all of which can be enjoyed in the garden - the perfect place to end a day spent chasing waterfalls in this beautiful, remote valley.

1 Leave the car park (honesty box by the gate) in the direction of the village. Cross the road to the track opposite (signed Swale Trail, Coast to Coast, Public Bridleway). Continue to a decorative stone-flagged track on the left (signed Pennine Way and The Swale Trail), to descend steeply through woodland to the footbridge. (To detour to Kisdon Force, continue straight ahead and look for a path on the left leading down to the falls). Cross the footbridge. The lower falls of East Gill are to the right, where the Gill flows into the River Swale.

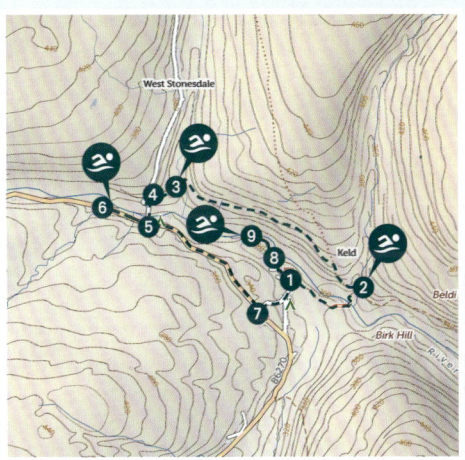

2 Follow the water upstream to the main East Gill Falls for your first dip. Afterwards, return to the footbridge, and follow the track leading up and round to the right. At the T-Junction turn left, onto a bridleway (signed Pennine Way). Follow this stony track to a farmhouse. Go through the gate and, at a fork, take the lower path that runs behind the house. Continue, passing through two gates. After passing a small barn on the left, the track gradually veers right before crossing Stonesdale Beck.

3 You catch a glimpse of the top falls of Currack Force just before a stone bridge over Stonesdale Beck. To reach these, you need to beat your own path across the grass to the water's edge; there may be nettles here in summer. To reach the lower, more spectacular, falls cross the bridge and follow the edge of the wall to the falls

and plunge pool. After your dip, return to the track and continue to a country road.

4 Turn left down the steep zig-zag road and cross over the bridge just before Park House. Wain Wath Force is just visible upstream.

5 At a T-junction, turn right. After a few metres you will see a gate on the right leading to a grassy bank by the falls.

6 Go through the gate to Wain Wath Force, a fantastic swim spot. Afterwards, return to the road and turn left. The route back to Keld is along this road. It is not terribly busy, but be mindful of passing traffic.

7 Turn left just before Keld Green Café and follow the country lane back to Keld. The route passes the Keld Resource Centre, which is well worth a visit. From

here, continue along the lane to return to your starting point at Rukin's Campsite and the final two final waterfalls.

8 To reach these, follow the stony track by the farm buildings down to the riverside campsite. At the river, turn right between two wooden gate posts onto a path above Catrake Force to admire the falls, particularly dramatic in spate. There is no safe way to access the pool below. However, for Hoggarth's Leap, return to the track and follow the river upstream beside the camping pitches.

9 A narrow path leads to the pools of Hoggarth's Leap and your last dip. Return to the car park.

Walk 3

MUKER, SWINNER GILL AND KISDON FORCE

From the hay meadows of Muker delve into the hidden canyon of Swinner Gill then swim at Kisdon Force, before treading an old corpse road to journey's end.

INFORMATION

Mostly well-trodden footpaths and bridleways. Some unmarked footpaths and scrambling over steep, rocky ground at Swinner Gill. Steep, sometimes muddy, descent to Kisdon Force. You may encounter livestock.

DISTANCE: 7 miles
TIME: 4 hours
MAP: OS Explorer OL30 Yorkshire Dales, Northern and Central
START & END POINT: Muker village car park (SD 910 978, 54.3760, -2.1388)
PUBLIC TRANSPORT: DalesBus, Service 30 - Swaledale Shuttle (Keld, Reeth, Richmond route). May need booking in advance (01969 667400)
SWIMMING: Pools at Swinner Gill, East Gill and Kisdon Force waterfalls
PLACES OF INTEREST: Muker hay meadows, Swinner Gill mines, Crackpot Hall, Corpse Road
REFRESHMENTS: Muker Village Store and Teashop offers a warm welcome along with homemade cakes, cream teas and light lunches (DL11 6QH, 01748 886409) The Farmer's Arms, also in Muker, is a community-owned Dales pub serving homemade pub classics and local ales (DL11 6QG, 01748 343130)
NEARBY SWIM SPOTS: Wain Wath Force, Keld
EASIER ACCESS: East Gill waterfall is easily reached by following the start of the directions for the Keld Waterfalls walk

This swim-walk adventure begins with an amble through some of the most beautiful wildflower meadows in the country. The tiny village of Muker sits on the banks of the River Swale, huddled between Thwaite and Gunnerside, at the western end of Swaledale. Its name, pronounced Mewker, comes from the Old Norse mjór akr, meaning the 'new, narrow cultivated field' and its fields, or meadows, are what attract most visitors to this corner of the Yorkshire Dales between late May and early July when its species-rich hay meadows are a blaze of colour. For its diminutive size, Muker boasts a rich array of services - the Village Store and Teashop, the Farmer's Arms pub, a public hall and even a Literary Institute. The latter is home to the Muker Silver Band, formed to celebrate Queen Victoria's Diamond Jubilee in 1897; every village in Swaledale had a band of 'ten and a drummer' back in those lead-mining days but today only Muker and Reeth still have them.

Leave the wildflower meadows behind, though, and the delights of this glorious swim-walk will more than compensate, taking in a hidden canyon, old mining ruins, several gorgeous waterfalls, a romantic ruined house, an ancient corpse road and superb views.

From the small car park next to Straw Beck (WiFi is patchy if using a parking app so arrive with a pocketful of coins for the meter just in case), the route crosses a bridge, leaving the village on an uphill lane towards sublime hay meadows. A stone-flagged footpath weaves through pastures, with narrow squeezes - gaps in the dry-stone walls - and rustic cow houses creating a quintessential Dales scene. These are some of the best upland hay meadows in the Yorkshire Dales, traditionally managed to maintain their unique plant diversity; some are protected as sites of special scientific interest or conservation.

If you are lucky, you might bump into a visiting botanist to help you identify the flowers. Look out for meadow buttercup, pignut, red clover, yellow rattle, betony, meadow grasses and species that are particularly associated with this habitat such as globeflower, lady's mantle, wood cranesbill and melancholy thistle. When they're in bloom the tableau is reminiscent of a time gone by with huge enjoyment to be had roaming through this picturesque landscape. The hay is harvested around mid-July so time your visit accordingly if you want to see the meadows at their best.

Beyond the meadows the River Swale comes into sight, tumbling over stones and rocks along the valley bottom. The walk then joins a well-laid bridleway, running alongside and above the river as Kisdon Hill rises on the other side of the water, tumble-down barns and hawthorn trees clinging to its lower slopes. This stretch of the route is very popular so expect to meet other walkers before detouring off into the deep-cut tributary valley of Swinner Gill, soon visible ahead.

A map would be helpful in locating the correct footpath into the gill ❸. As the river bends to the left, before its confluence with Swinner Gill, a steep, narrow (unmarked) path on the right leads into the gorge. The narrow dirt path becomes more obvious the further you go, enticing you into the gill as the glistening water of Swinner beck cascades over a series of pretty falls beneath a footbridge. Keep an eye on younger explorers here; a very short section of the track is eroded and will be slippery after rain, though the path soon resumes with a hop and a skip over the beck to the other side.

After the uphill climb, your reward is solitude, and a refreshing dip in the falls and plunge pools

down the grassy slope ❸. The main waterfall, and slightly larger pools, are further up the path but these smaller infinity pools are tucked away in the heart of the gill and are easy to reach. There are lovely views along the gorge with only the melancholy calls of curlews above, and maybe a curious ewe and her lamb nibbling patches of grass. The higher falls and remains of Swinner Gill Lead Mine are reached by re-joining the path and cresting a short, craggy section of the canyon. East Grain is a small gill running into the head of Swinner Gill Valley from Ivelet Moor, creating the main waterfall. You may wish to dip here too, via a scramble down, or mooch around exploring the old mine workings, tunnels and the crumbling buildings.

It is hard to imagine that this peaceful location was at one time a thriving hub of industry; in the 18th and 19th centuries Swaledale was one of the largest lead mining areas in Britain. A rich system of lead veins ran along the north side of Swaledale, with several good ore shoots, and the valley was worked extensively. The landscape may look remote and rural today but beneath the surface of the undulating hills and wild moors is a labyrinth of interconnecting tunnels and mine workings. As you stand and admire the views from this spot, you might ponder the precarious lives of the men (and sometimes children) who once toiled beneath this soil, and the women who dressed the stone above, laboriously hammering the rock to separate out the ore.

Taking a higher path, beneath Buzzard Scar, the route then leaves the gill with dramatic views of the River Swale as it flows between Kisdon Hill and Ivelet Moor against the backdrop of Muker Common. Continuing along the contours of the hill, the path passes a small stone barn and the ruins of Crackpot Hall, its name a blend of the Old Norse 'kràka,' for crow, and Old English 'pot,'

for cave ❹. This atmospheric building was once a hunting lodge, then a mine office and latterly a farmhouse, abandoned in the 1950s due to subsidence. In the 1930s Yorkshire authors Marie Hartley and Joan Ingleby wrote about a girl called Alice who ran with her dogs in the countryside around Crackpot. More recently children's writer David Almond made a radio programme about these stories after tracking down the real Alice and discovering that she had lived as a child at Crackpot Hall, with her farming family, enjoying a free-range Dales childhood.

Rejoining the bridleway towards Keld, the path crosses a bridge over East Gill ❺ and another beautiful waterfall with plunge pools, a grassy bank and benches. Beyond a wooden footbridge, a footpath leads towards Kisdon Force, whose tumble of water you will soon hear. A narrow trail descends to the river, bordering the spectacular crags of Kisdon Gorge where huge mossy boulders are strewn across the slopes ❻.

Kisdon Force itself is a spectacular double waterfall, hidden deep in a wooded gorge ❼. The top falls pour into a wide plunge pool, with views down the valley, while a deeper pool swirls beneath the lower falls. Swathes of moss drape over the rim of the cascades like a luxurious green pelt and makeshift rope swings have been strung up above the water; make sure to test the depth and check for any hidden underwater objects before leaping into the ebony pool. The falls are surrounded by ash, wych elm and rowan trees, and a carpet of primroses in spring. The noisy 'peep-ing' call of oystercatchers can often be heard overhead; these coastal waders have relocated inland to nest here.

After your swim, the next section is a little tricky to navigate as it ascends Kisdon Hill; a map would be handy to make sure you pick up the right paths.

After following the contours of the hillside, the route joins the medieval Swaledale Corpse Way ❾. This timeworn track was used by mourners to carry their dead to the nearest sanctified ground - St Andrew's Church in Grinton - before St Mary the Virgin Church in Muker was built, in 1580. It is steeped in folklore and it is said that rituals were often performed at river crossings and crossroads to help prevent the spirits of the dead from returning. There have been reports of ghostly sightings along it but the only creatures you are likely to encounter on a bright, summer's day are hardy Swaledale sheep roaming the exposed hillsides.

Superb views of the Dales landscape abound along the length of the track, a mosaic of fields crossed by dry stone walls and dotted with traditional cow houses. Lapwings wheel and tumble through the air while curlews call above the moorland and, eventually, Muker comes into sight as the path winds back down to the village.

1 From the car park cross the bridge to Muker Village Store. Follow the lane to the right of the shop to an information board and fingerpost, pointing to the hay meadows. Go through the gate and follow the flagged path to the end of the meadows.

2 Turn right, signposted FP Gunnerside, crossing a bridge over the river. Continue uphill on rocky stone steps, bearing left onto a well-laid bridleway beside the river.

3 As the bridleway and river veer left, just before the mouth of Swinner Gill, follow a steep unmarked footpath up the grass slope, with a fence and plantation on the right, to join a more obvious path. Cross the beck and follow the path on the other side of the gorge. Look to your right for a series of falls and plunge pools below. Afterwards, climb back to the path and continue over a craggy section to the head of the gill, and a larger waterfall, pools and mine workings. You can scramble down to the plunge pool.

4 Afterwards relocate the original footpath but take the higher path (a right fork) leading out of the gorge, passing Crackpot Hall, to a junction of paths. Turn right to rejoin the original bridleway, in the direction of Keld.

5 Cross a footbridge and go through the gate on the left to the falls of East Gill for another dip. Afterwards continue, crossing another bridge onto a decorative path through woodland, to a footpath on the left.

6 Follow the footpath and take note of a green metal gate on the right

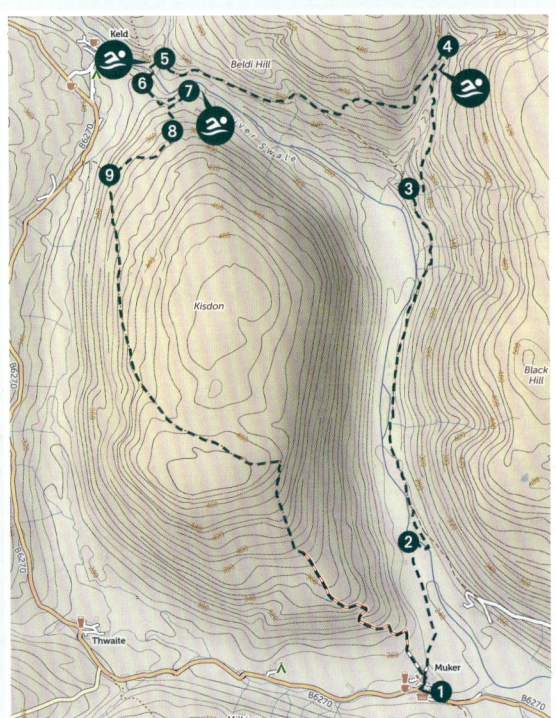

that you will return to. Look for a path that diverges left down to Kisdon Force, following a narrow trail bounded by rocky crags.

7 There are two ways down to the falls: a quick route, with a rope, which can be muddy or continuing along the narrow path to a switchback leading down to the falls. Afterwards retrace your steps to the footpath and return to the green metal gate. Pass through the gate onto an unmarked footpath, keeping the stone wall on your left, and go through a gap in the wall. Cross the field heading diagonally right, towards two gates.

8 Go through the left-hand gate, higher up the slope (not the right-hand gate next to a sheep fold). Continue along this footpath, with a stone wall on your right, through several gates to a junction of paths.

9 Follow the bridleway on the immediate left, not the gated footpath. This is the medieval Swaledale Corpse Way. The track passes through several wooden gates around the contours of Kisdon Hill. Eventually Muker comes into sight and the path veers right down the hill, past a farmhouse and onto a lane that winds down to Mucker.

Walk 4

RICHMOND FOSS, RIVER SWALE AND ROUND HOWE

Wander through riverside meadows and ancient woodland paths to pools along the River Swale, before returning to the tumbling cascades of Richmond Foss.

INFORMATION

Woodland and riverside paths, some uneven terrain and steps. Several stiles. You may encounter livestock.

DISTANCE: 4.5 miles
TIME: 2 hours
MAP: OS Explorer 304 Darlington and Richmond
START & END POINT: The Fosse car park, Richmond, NZ 173 006, 54.4007, -1.7345 (4 hours max.) or Yorke Square car park (long stay)
PUBLIC TRANSPORT: Services 29 (Richmond, Darlington), 30 (Keld, Reeth, Richmond), 34 (Darlington, Catterick, Richmond), 55 (Northallerton), 79, X79 (Barnard Castle), 159 (Ripon), 825 (York, Fountain's Abbey), 830 (Ribblehead), 831 and 832 (Darlington, Hawes, Kirby Lonsdale route), 858 (Ribblehead, Darlington), 859 (Leyburn), Richmond Rover (Catterick, Northallerton), X26 and X27 (Catterick, Darlington)
SWIMMING: Richmond Foss and River Swale river pools
PLACES OF INTEREST: Richmond Castle, Easby Abbey
REFRESHMENTS: Barries Ices kiosk (DL10 4JR, 01748 811861) serves drinks and ice creams in The Fosse car park. Soak up Swaledale views from The George and Dragon, Hudswell (DL11 6BL, 01748 518373), just off-route.
OTHER AMENITIES: Toilets in The Fosse car park
NEARBY SWIM SPOTS: River Swale, Easby Abbey
EASIER ACCESS: Richmond Foss is by the car park

elve into the name of the River Swale – it comes from the Anglo-Saxon word *sualuae*, meaning 'rapid and liable to deluge' - and you get a hint at its fast-flowing nature. Said to be the fastest rising river in England, in the late 16th century, the antiquary William Camden wrote that the Swale *"rusheth rather than runneth"*. Be warned that it still swells swiftly and treacherously if there is heavy rain further up the valley.

As it curves beneath the castle at Richmond, the Swale plunges over a series of slabs on the riverbed, leaping from one waterfall to the next to create Richmond Falls, or Richmond Foss, as it is known locally. The power of these falls has been harnessed by humans for at least a thousand years; in 1865, paper maker James Cooke built Castle Paper Mills on the site of an ancient corn mill here, adding brick to the natural waterfall. Ever true to its name, however, the Swale swept the mill away in a mighty flood, in 1883.

That being said, don't let the Swale's reckless character put you off. This walk takes in some serene stretches of the river, including riverside meadows and beaches that slope gently into tranquil pools and, further along, secluded, wooded shores. The falls at Richmond offer a dramatic - and accessible - swimming hole with myriad pools to splash in. Although the walk begins next to the falls, leaving these until the end means you can enjoy a refreshing finale to your day in the natural jacuzzi of the foss.

Starting out from Richmond Foss, the route follows the river upstream, beneath Richmond Castle. One of the finest fortresses in England, with a commanding view over the town from its lofty position ❶, the castle was originally built in the 1070s by

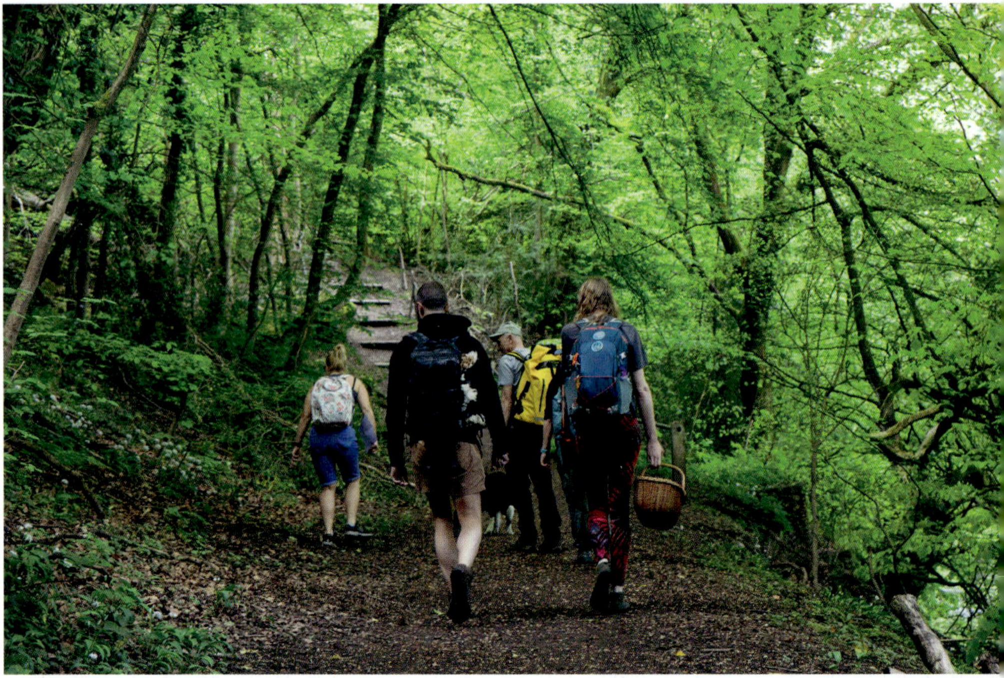
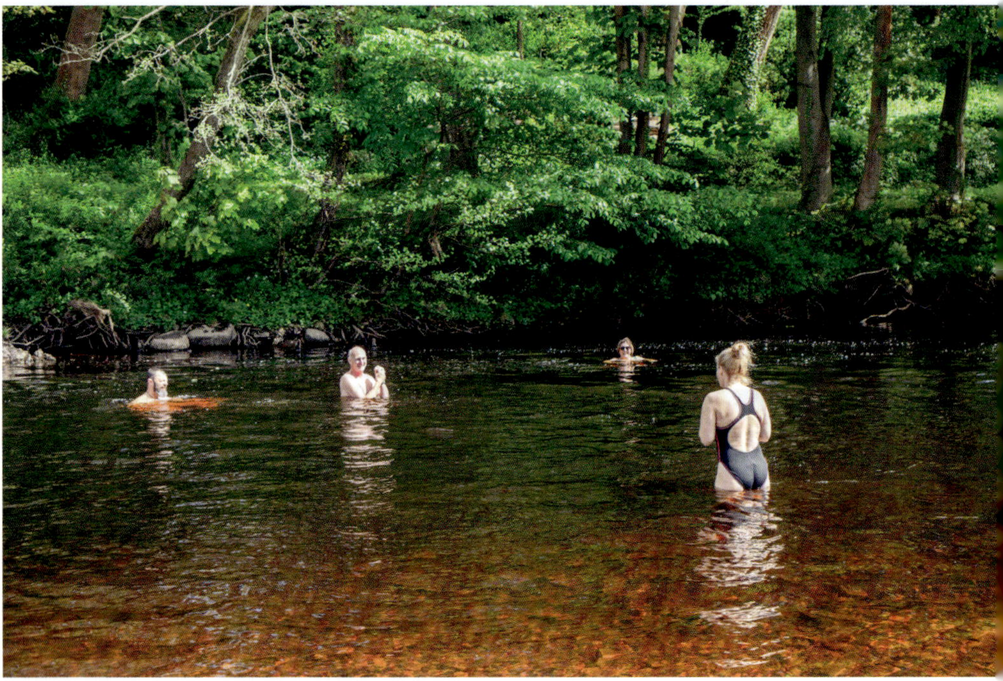

Alan Rufus who fought alongside William the Conqueror at the Battle of Hastings. Designed to subdue rebellious Anglo-Saxon nobles in the north of England, by the 16th century it was mostly derelict. Still a powerful feature of the landscape, however, its romantic ruins have inspired many artists, including JMW Turner, whose dreamy watercolours of the castle, and nearby Green Bridge, hang in London's Tate Britain.

Starting below the castle, after crossing the 18th-century bridge, the walk follows the river upstream, rising high above the Swale as it winds through woodland dominated by ash, oak, lime and beech trees. In spring the slopes of this ancient woodland are carpeted with ransoms and bluebells, exuding their heady scents ❷. Enjoying this walk with a group, in springtime, one of our band of swim-walkers turned it into a foraging expedition, nourishing us with snacks plucked from the woodland floor; not only wild garlic but also sweet cicely, gorse flowers, speedwell and great burnet.

The bluffs along this stretch are remnants of the copper quarrying that took place here from the 15th century - with little commercial success. The flagged walkway hugging the river is another industrial throwback – the remains of a causeway, with rails for a tramway, that edged the riverside and shuttled tubs of copper ore from a mine to Green Bridge; ponies then transported the ore to Richmond train station.

Gaining height, the walk reveals superb views back across the town. Through the trees you might catch a glimpse of Culloden Tower, a Gothic folly built in 1746 on the estate of local artistocrat and sometime-MP, John Yorke. Named after the Battle of Culloden, the final Jacobite rising, it is now a Landmark Trust holiday let, with exquisite period interiors. Along the walk's tree-lined path tendrils

of ivy, mosses and lichen cling to the craggy cliffs of Billy Bank Wood and glossy, green fronds of hart's-tongue fern sprout from crevices as the path descends towards riverside meadows ❸.

Highland cattle graze these pastures. Using their long tongues to rip vegetation from the ground means the grass is left at varying heights while the animals' movement around the fields breaks up the ground, creating bare patches of earth that allow wildflowers to seed and germinate. These photo-genic cattle tend to be docile. Nonetheless, always give them a wide berth, particularly if they have young calves and/ or you have a dog in tow.

The grassy meadows drop gently down to a pebble beach at a sharp bend of the river ❸. With both shallow and deeper pools, this is the first of several lovely swim spots along this stretch. In summer the sweet fragrance of the flower-filled meadows makes it an idyllic location for a riverside picnic. Even if the water appears calm, there is sometimes a discernible flow - try swimming upstream then gently swooshing down the river.

After a refreshing swim, the walk continues towards the conical mound of Round Howe (between ❸ & ❹). Detached from the surround-ing woodland, this small hill may have been the site of ancient druidic rituals, though others believe it is simply a geological quirk. Either way, this is not entirely untamed countryside. Both Round Howe and Billy Bank Wood were modified during the 18th century to suit the contemporary fashion for arcadian landscapes. Laying out a romantic walk by the Swale, local merchant, Cuthbert Readshaw, also landscaped Round Howe, building a temple at its summit. This offered a viewpoint to the town, castle and river and also served as an eye-catcher from the town. The temple's lifespan was short, however; by 1791 the hilltop was bare once again.

At Hudswell Woods, a network of trails fans out through the ancient woodland. A tree-fringed permissive path edges the river, offering further opportunities for a secluded swim **4** in calm, deeper pools with sandy beaches. These are perfect for a longer swim – and, perhaps, some discreet skinny-dipping. You may have the company of grey wagtails and dippers, brave little birds that wade in and under the water, hunting for insect larvae and crustaceans on the riverbed. Keep an eye out, too, for the blue flash of a kingfisher.

After drying off, the woodland path winds uphill, passing an old quarry that has gradually been subsumed by nature, and a recumbent tree trunk indented with coins; you might wish to add some of your own for good luck. A heart-pumping climb up a steep set of steps leads to a higher path and the return leg of the walk **5**. A chalked blackboard a little way along the path points to the George and Dragon pub in Hudswell, which might lure you off route. This friendly inn was the first community pub in Yorkshire and has splendid views over the dale from its beer garden.

Following the upper reaches of the wooded escarpment for most of the way back to Richmond,

the River Swale glints through the trees below. The path is narrow and rocky in places, with knotted tree roots bulging from the ground. After passing through a series of narrow field strips and several stiles, the walk re-enters Billy Bank Wood, joining a tree-top path above the Swale with an excellent view of Culloden Tower **8**. The trail emerges from the woodland next to a house, formerly The Good Intent pub. Once a popular pitstop for thirsty copper miners, it closed in 1914, shortly after local copper mining ended, in 1912. Many of the young men who drank here would have been called up to fight on the battlefields of Europe during World War One.

After crossing Green Bridge, the route returns to The Fosse car park, with time for one last dip in Richmond Foss **1**. The falls are only accessible when the river is not in spate; if the red flag is flying do not enter the water. If it is safe to do so, the easiest way to enter the water is from the rocky steps beside the cascades, just beyond the car park wall. This is a popular town centre spot so expect an audience; nonetheless, splashing about in the myriad of pools and waterfalls is tremendous fun and a thrilling finale to the day.

1 Leave The Fosse car park and walk up the road, with the river to your left (if you park at Yorke Square car park, pick up directions from the bridge). At the junction, turn left across the bridge then take the footpath opposite, following the river upstream.

2 The path rises above and away from the river, with a rocky escarpment to the left and some stone steps. Cross a wooden bridge over a small ravine to Billy Bank Wood. Keep to the high path and continue to a wooden gate, leading to a riverside meadow.

3 Bear right along a permissive path towards the bend in the river and a small pebble beach. You can swim here or continue beside the river to another swim spot with a sandy beach. Afterwards, continue towards the tree-covered mound of Round Howe, between a tunnel of trees, to a gate into Hudswell Woods.

4 Instead of taking the rising footpath, follow the narrow permissive path that edges the river, to discover more swim spots. Descend some stone steps to a wide sandy beach and a shallow, but faster-flowing, stretch of water. Further upstream you will find more pools for a secluded swim. The path then winds up Hudswell Bank, passing an old quarry, to some steep steps.

5 Go up three flights of steps and turn left onto a path at the bottom of the fourth set of steps.

A short way along is a sign for the George and Dragon; follow this if you want a short detour to the pub. Otherwise, continue on the path and go through an open metal gate, partially obscured by foliage, onto another narrow path.

6 At a fork, take the left-hand path, descending to cross a stream (dry in summer). Go through a narrow gap in the fence into Calfhall Wood. Follow the narrow trail along the woodland boundary. Climb some wooden steps on the right and continue along the path, with a wooden fence to the right. Pass through a gate into a meadow to another gate, leading back into the woodland. Continue to a gate and fingerpost, on the right, leading into a narrow field. Cross the field diagonally, to a gate in the hedge and another field with open views. The route then follows a succession of stiles and gates through narrow field strips, occasionally returning to

woodland paths, but remaining at the top of the escarpment. It is well signposted but the following directions offer more detail.

7 After crossing a field diagonally towards a white house, climb a stile into a field behind the house, and another stile onto a footpath running between two fenced plantations. After another stile, the route passes through two narrow fields to a large field with horses and jumps. Head across the field towards a clump of trees in a dip, climb a stile over a wire fence then follow the edge of the field with woodland to the left.

8 Go through a gate into the woods and continue along the path, with the river far below. The path descends and emerges to the right of a house. Turn left, cross the bridge, then turn right. Walk back to the car park and Richmond Foss, for a final dip.

Walk 5

SEMER WATER AND BARDALE BECK

A walk in two parts - a scenic ramble along the shoreline of legend-sprinkled Semer Water then a wild dip in the captivating waterfalls of remote Bardale.

Semer Water is one of only three natural lakes in the Yorkshire Dales National Park, the other two being Malham Tarn and Sunbiggin Tarn. It was formed by glacial action and, as a rare feature of the Dales landscape, it is not surprising that legends have proliferated around it. The most common is that the lake conceals a drowned town beneath its silvery surface, the folk tale bolstered somewhat by archaeological evidence of an Iron Age settlement. The story tells of a wandering hermit who visited Semer Town disguised as a pauper, begging for food and shelter. He was refused hospitality by all in the prosperous valley apart from a poor, elderly couple. The following day he cursed the town with the words:

Semer Water rise! Semer Town sink!
And bury the place all save the house
Where they gave me meat and drink

The whole valley was said to be submerged, saving only the home of the husband and wife who had given him refuge.

This sublime hike takes in a swim in the fabled Semer Water, either at the beginning or end of your walk, or both. The route then wends its way along the eastern fringes of the lake to explore more of remote Raydale, and the tiny valley of Bardale with its delightful waterfalls and expansive fell views. Don't forget to pack your binoculars for this one, for spotting birds of prey. A map and compass would also be useful for navigating open-access land above Marsett, where there is no mobile phone signal.

The walk starts from the northern shoreline of Semer Water ❶, past Low Blean Farm, picking up a footpath that skirts the lakeside

INFORMATION

Footpaths, bridleways, tracks and country lanes. Basic navigation skills needed for part of the walk since mobile signal is patchy.

DISTANCE: 6 miles
TIME: 3 hours
MAP: OS Explorer OL30 Yorkshire Dales, Northern and Central
START & END POINT: Semer Water car park (modest charge, payable at Low Blean Farm) (SD 922 874, 54.2831, -2.1208)
PUBLIC TRANSPORT: Bus to Bainbridge - services 156 (Gayle, Leyburn), 856 (Gayle, Northallerton), 857 (Castle Bolton, Garsdale), 858 (Darlington, Ribblehead), 874, 875, 876 (Ilkley, Hawes) then walk up River Bain footpath to Semer Water.
SWIMMING: Semer Water, Bardale Beck
PLACES OF INTEREST: St Matthew's Old Church, Stalling Busk, Semer Water
REFRESHMENTS: No refreshments en route but A Taste of Wensleydale, a bakery and tearoom in Bainbridge serves brunch, light lunches and homemade bakes (DL8 3EH, 07790 665799) while the Green Dragon Inn at Hardraw (DL8 3LZ, 01969 667392) is an atmospheric Dales pub with excellent food. Behind the Green Dragon is Hardraw Force, the highest single-drop waterfall in England.
NEARBY SWIM SPOTS: Hardraw Force, Hardraw
EASIER ACCESS: There is parking right next to Semer Water

just above the water's edge. The lake and its surrounding wetlands are a haven for waders, geese, lapwings and winter wildfowl, their southern reaches protected as a nature reserve, which the route briefly passes through. Beyond a stone barn, the path drops closer to the lake, the sandy foreshore lapped gently by water and spangled with crimson common spotted-orchids.

As the path rises through Semer Water Nature Reserve it enters a gorgeous leg of the walk, awash with peace. Less frequented than the northern lakeshore, in early summer, the spongy ground here is graced with a wide variety of water-loving plants, including bog bean, marsh valerian, marsh cinque-foil and ragged robin. Turn your eyes skywards and you may spot oystercatchers, redshank, lapwings and possibly even an eagle or osprey.

At the end of the nature reserve it is worth pausing to look back; the views across the lake become increasingly beautiful with growing elevation, the sparkling sapphire lake cupped in the creases and folds of the surrounding hills as an ever-widening view of the fellside opens up ahead.

Just beyond the nature reserve are the ruins of Old St Matthew's Church ❷. The shell of the old building and an array of higgledy-piggledy tomb-stones are all that remain of the old parish church of Stalling Busk. The church dates to 1722 and was still in use in the early 20th century, albeit in a poor state of repair. When work on a new church was started, in 1908, Old St Matthew's was stripped of its roof and furnishings.

The route now ribbons through several flower-filled meadows dotted with barns; some inhaling is needed to wedge yourself through the squeeze stiles. The route is easy to follow, eventually reaching a stone barn and stile into a field, which can be boggy, leading to Semer Water Nature Reserve. Beyond the gate, the flagged path cuts a route through marsh grass and, in summer, the tattered pink flowers of ragged robin. After crossing a couple of footbridges over streams, the route joins a rocky track that weaves alongside Marsett Beck to the farming hamlet of Marsett ❹.

As you cross the village green, don't be surprised to see free-range cows grazing; as always, take care with dogs.

The next leg of the walk involves an expedition into Bardale, following the beck upstream into the higher reaches of the valley. Successive years of heavy rainfall have caused erosion so the beck's soft embankment has been built up and a wooden platform added. As the route dips into Ash Gill Woods, the beck is bounded by a stone wall and fence, though there are occasional glimpses of it through the trees; interesting rock formations have been carved out where the water is squeezed through rocky chutes, creating cascades and a waterfall.

You can only access this stretch of the beck further along, as you enter open-access land beyond the stone wall that rises up the hillside. Ahead you will see a higher waterfall - a good place to start exploring the watery delights of Bardale ❺. The upper falls comprise a rocky lip over which water cascades. The pool beneath the falls is not very deep in summer but there is great fun to be had showering beneath the spray of water. Look closely at the rocks here and you will spot some impressive fossils. You can also explore downstream to discover a delightful waterfall, well-hidden and requiring a scramble down onto rocks where a chute of water tumbles over limestone rocks into a delicious, dark, shady pool ❻. The inky water offers a blissful swim in a pool fringed with feathery strands of larch, rowan and ivy, and it is surprisingly warm, despite the shrouded, sequestered setting.

This entire valley is a wonderful place to while away an afternoon on a hot summer's day, cooling off in the pools along the beck then basking like lizards in the sunshine. The next leg of the walk is across open-access land where a map is helpful. The moorland is riven with streams and gills and, on winter walks here, it is quite a spectacle to see Low Ash Gill Scar waterfall **❽** and the tiered cascades of High Ashgill Scar waterfall **❾** in spate. In summer, however, they are no more than a trickle. With height gained, the feel is one of remoteness and solitude with magnificent views of the surrounding fells.

As the route rejoins a footpath, the walk descends through buttercup-studded meadows back to Marsett **⓫**, retracing the route to the footbridge and nature reserve with a steep climb to Stalling Busk **⓬**. As you pass through the hamlet, look out for a plaque on one of the cottages indicating *The Stalling Busk Conference*. This is where the Ramblers met to draft what became the

Countryside and Right of Way Act 2000 (CROW), the legislation that gave the public access to land mapped as 'open country'.

The last leg of the walk meanders along a quiet country lane, offering a chance to admire Semer Water, sparkling beneath moorland slopes, from a higher vantage point.

Arriving back on the shores of Semer Water, seek out the spot where artist JMW Turner sat to make his famous sketch of the lake for his painting *Simmer Lake*, in 1816. Gazing out across the lake, small waves of white water rippling across its pewter surface and occasionally catching the sun's rays, you can see why Turner, the master of light, found inspiration here.

For a swim at the end of the walk, enter the water beside two large, sculpted rocks. You will need to wade out, teetering across pebbles, to reach deeper water. It's worth the effort, though, the wonderful silvery-blue water rippling out ahead of you with every stroke.

1 Before parking your car, call at Low Blean Farm for a parking ticket (around £3 per day). Park up on the north shore of Semer Water, then turn right, back towards the farm, to a footpath on the right, signed Stalling Busk. Follow the footpath through several fields, navigating step stiles and stile squeezes as you keep Semer Water on your right. At a stone barn the path becomes wooded, dipping almost to the shoreline of the lake. Keep to this path to reach a gated stile into Semer Water Nature Reserve. The path rises slightly here, with beautiful views behind you of the lake and ever-widening views ahead. At the end of the reserve, pass through a stone stile and gate towards the stone wall ahead.

2 Keep this wall to your right and follow it round to the ruined church and graveyard of Old St Matthew's, on the right. After exploring the ruins, go through a gate to the left of a large tree. Follow the fingerpost pointing right towards Marsett, continuing along the footpath through several fields with squeeze stiles to a metal gate with a stile to the right. Go through either. The path passes a ruin on the right. Continue through two more fields to a gated squeeze stile right next to a stone building. The route beyond follows an unmarked footpath through a field, a little marshy in places, to a gate and Semer Water Nature Reserve.

3 Go through the gate and keep left along a flagged path, then cross a footbridge over Crook's Beck. Follow the track to another footbridge next to a ford. Beyond the bridge, follow the stony track, which eventually runs alongside Marsett Beck, to Marsett. Cross the stone bridge and look for a footpath sign on the left.

4 The footpath follows the beck upstream, firstly heading towards a cottage then running adjacent to the beck. The path has been built up due to erosion and crosses a basic bridge. Continue along the riverside path then go through a squeeze stile into a field and Low Ash Gill Woods beyond. The beck is now fenced and bounded by a stone wall. Further along you will see some unusual rock formations of the beck and catch a fleeting glimpse of a waterfall. Make a mental note of this for later.

5 As the woods open out onto moorland, cross the small stream of Ash Gill as a higher waterfall becomes visible ahead. Follow the stone wall to a footpath sign and cross a stile.

6 This is open-access land. If water levels are low, you can reach these falls without crossing the beck. Otherwise, a hop across the beck is necessary, to reach the falls from the opposite bank. To reach the lower waterfall and plunge pool you glimpsed earlier, follow the beck downstream. Parts of the route are fenced so you need to navigate the most sensible access, which may require some clambering. After your dip, return to the first waterfall and retrace your steps back to Ash Gill Beck.

7 The next section is over open-access land and doesn't initially follow footpaths so a paper map and compass are useful. There is no mobile signal here so you cannot rely on digital mapping.

8 Climb the hill towards a metal gate with Ash Gill (fenced off) to your right. Beyond the fence is another waterfall, Low Ash Gill Scar - spectacular after rain but just a trickle when dry.

9 Go through the gate then cross a small boardwalk over Ash Gill Beck (to the left is another waterfall, High Gill Scar, which you might like to seek out). Continue straight ahead, keeping the stone wall to your right. Skirt a stone wall housing a barn but keep going straight.

10 Eventually you reach a footpath sign and a squeeze stile on the right. Follow the footpath down through a meadow to another stile and cross a field

towards a farmyard. Go through the gate to pick up a track back to Marsett.

11 From here, retrace your footsteps to the second footbridge over Crook Gill and the flagged path you walked earlier. Pass through the gate and this time climb the field to the top to join the stony track of Busk Lane.

12 Turn left here and continue to the end of the track towards the hamlet of Stalling Busk. Turn right, following Butts Lane round to Stake Road. The country lane leads back to Semer Water.

Walk 6

REDMIRE FORCE AND RIVER URE

A scenic stroll through riverside meadows to the tumbling cascades of Redmire Force, and further pools along the River Ure, in a quiet corner of Wensleydale.

INFORMATION

A level walk on well-trodden footpaths and bridleways through fields and riverside meadows. You may encounter livestock.

DISTANCE: 5 miles
TIME: 2.5 hours
MAP: OS Explorer OL30 Yorkshire Dales, Northern and Central areas
START & END POINT: Holl Gate, West Witton (SE 066 844, 54.2919, -1.8990)
PUBLIC TRANSPORT: Services 156 (Gayle, Leyburn), 856 (Gayle, Leyburn, Northallerton)
SWIMMING: Redmire Force, pools along the River Ure
PLACES OF INTEREST: Bolton Castle, Aysgarth Falls
REFRESHMENTS: The Fox and Hounds Inn, in West Witton (DL8 4LP, 01969 623650), is a characterful old Dales pub with active darts, dominoes and quoits teams, well-kept ales and a menu of pub classics. Restaurant with rooms, the Wensleydale Heifer (DL8 4LS, 01969 622322, is also in West Witton, with an in-house smokery and an excellent reputation for seafood. Fairhurts at Berry's Farmshop and Café (DL8 4UH, 07727 231202), just down the road in Swinithwaite, serves breakfasts, lunches and cakes.
NEARBY SWIM SPOTS: Cauldron Falls, West Burton or Lower Aysgarth Falls
EASIER ACCESS: Redmire Force can be reached by a shorter walk from Redmire village

The village of West Witton stretches out beneath the slopes of Penhill, a distinctive ridge fell that presides over the southern side of Wensleydale. While foodies visit to eat at the award-winning Wensleydale Heifer, a family-owned restaurant with rooms where the food is so exceptional that it often makes the pages of discriminating food guides, those more interested in folklore come to witness the strange, and somewhat terrifying, ancient custom that takes place here every August.

On a given Saturday around St Bartholomew's Day, as the sun is setting, the villagers take part in the Burning of the Bartle, a pagan ritual re-enacting supposedly real historical events when a local criminal was chased, caught and burned at the stake in place of a sacrificial lamb. These days a straw effigy, similar to those made on Guy Fawkes night, is escorted down the road to his fiery demise. As the raucous gathering stops for a pint or two at selected houses in the village, a chanter reads out Bartle's rhyme, name-checking the crags of Penhill:

"On Penhill Crags he tore his rags,
At Hunters Thorn he blew his horn,
At Capplebank Stee he brock his knee,
At Grisgill Beck he brock his neck,
At Wadham's End he couldn't fend,
at Grisgill End we'll mek his end!
- Shout lads Shout"

The exact origins of the ceremony are not known, and it is not clear who Bartle was, but the huge hill that looms over the village is

snicket to a squeeze in a stone wall. This feels like entering someone's garden but, beyond the wall, the path widens out onto a rolling expanse of grassy meadows. Fine views ahead set the scene for the rest of the walk.

Continuing through fields onto a verdant bridleway, purple wood cranesbill sprawling onto the path, the route joins an attractive holloway. Bordered by a dry stone wall and veteran ashes, sycamores, maples, elders and oaks, this time-worn path has been gently carved by generations of feet and hooves. As the track opens out there are splendid views over Wensleydale ❸.

A little further along ❹ you can spy Bolton Castle, standing proud on the hillside opposite. This stocky 14th-century fortress has remained in the same family for its entire 600-year history; the current owner, Thomas Orde-Powlett, is a direct descendant of Sir Richard le Scrope, who built it in 1379. Bolton Castle's most famous inhabitant was Mary, Queen of Scots, who was imprisoned here in 1568 after her capture by Queen Elizabeth I's forces in Scotland. By general prison standards, Mary's stay here wasn't too harsh; Catholic sympathisers supplied her with Turkish carpets and luxurious clothes, and she was given permission to hunt in the surrounding area.

From this viewpoint, the path ribbons on, through pastures, towards the river. Longhorn cattle graze these meadows in summer. This ancient breed tends to be gentle and friendly, with a placid temperament, but always take care with dogs, particularly if the cows have calves.

As the route enters attractive semi-ancient woodland, the gush of Redmire Force can be heard as it tumbles over several stepped shelves ❺. It is a serene place for a swim, sheltered by ancient oaks, with deep pools beneath the lower falls. The Ure is

unmistakable. One of Wensleydale's most enduring tales is a fable about the Giant of Penhill, an evil landowner who terrorised the locals until he was ultimately chased off the cliffs at Penhill. Some people believe the Giant may be the Bartle in the story.

Leaving legends of old behind, West Witton is the starting point for a number of attractive trails, including this picturesque walk on ancient pathways through wildflower meadows to the River Ure, and one of the Dales' lesser-known waterfalls, Redmire Force. A short distance downstream from busier Aysgarth Falls, there's more chance you might have these tumbling cascades to yourself.

The River Ure is the principal river of Wensleydale - a rare example of a dale being named after a town rather than its river. This wasn't always the case; the valley was once known as Yoredale, the river that flows through it morphing from Yore to Ure over the centuries. Downstream of Redmire Force, the Ure features several meadow-fringed river pools – ideal spots for a longer swim as you meander back to the start.

The walk begins, however, on the eastern edge of West Witton. Initially it follows the main street, passing the Fox and Hounds Inn and the Wensleydale Heifer, before diverging along a narrow

known for its fast flow and the water tends to rush and roar after heavy rain so take care. However, the wide river pool above the falls is generally more sedate, and deep enough for an enjoyable swim. Access involves sitting and shuffling your way into the water from the large stone slabs edging the riverbank. Once in the water, you are rewarded with fine views down the valley as the river hurries downstream around you.

After the falls the route continues through a field of rippling hillocks. A faint footpath weaves between thyme-cloaked anthills, humming with bees and the chirrup of grasshoppers in summer. To the right, Penhill rears up beyond a patchwork of meadows, cropped by cattle. Milk from cows grazed on the limestone grassland here gives a unique flavour to creamy, crumbly Wensleydale cheese – its producer's fortunes revived in the 1990s by the cheese's starring role in the Wallace and Gromit animations.

For a short distance the river is obscured by a stone wall but, at a sharp meander, a deep, wide pool is revealed (between ❻ and ❼). As the footpath rises behind a copse, following the course of the river, another leisurely stretch of river reveals itself, with several pools for a longer swim. The best is beyond another gate - a pebble beach and a long, peaty pool ❼. It's fun to swim against the gentle current here, swooshing back downstream to shallow rapids. The canopy of trees provide welcome shade on a hot day and the only disturbance to the peace is the occasional call of oystercatchers hunting on the water.

The rest of the route passes through wildflower meadows, creating a tapestry of colour in summer when meadow buttercups, scabious, bird's-foot trefoil and knapweed are in bloom. A narrow footpath bound by dry stone walls weaves back to the main road, just a short distance from where you parked your car.

1 From the parking lay-by walk into West Witton, passing the Fox and Hounds Inn, on the left. Cross the road and walk past the Wensleydale Heifer to a footpath, signed Oak Tree Farm, on the right.

2 Follow the footpath through a snicket beside a garden fence to a squeeze in the wall and onto a narrow path to a gate on the left at the end. Follow the faint path beyond the gate through a field to a metal gate. Go through this and head towards another gate, next to a squeeze and a small wooden gate.

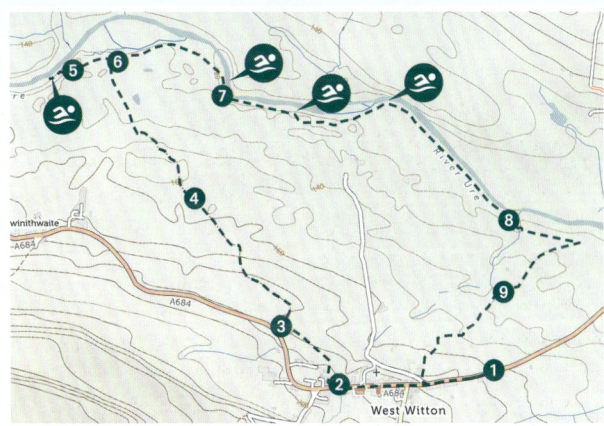

3 Pass through the squeeze and turn right, onto a bridleway, passing through a wooden gate. Continue along the tree-lined bridleway, bounded by a fence and stone wall. Continue to a wooden gate and public bridleway signpost. Go through the gate and follow the field headland with the dry stone wall on your right and open views ahead. Go through a small gate into another field with a bridleway signpost, then a stone wall and hawthorn trees to the right.

4 At a rustic bridleway signpost, cross the field diagonally with Bolton Castle on the opposite hill, in your sight line. Go through a metal gate with paving slabs strewn around it then follow a faint track (later becoming more obvious) to a metal gate straight ahead. Go through this gate and follow the path as it curves to the left, edging the field. Look for a small, wooden gate and public footpath signpost in front of some woods.

5 Go through the gate into the woodland and follow the path to Redmire Force for your first swim, if river levels allow. After your dip, retrace your steps to the wooden gate and return along the grassy footpath to a stone wall and a ladder stile.

6 Cross the stile into a field with undulating hillocks and follow a faint footpath through the field towards a wall opposite. Keeping the wall to your left, continue to a wide river pool on a bend of the river, another swim spot.

7 After your swim, the footpath continues above the river and behind some trees. At a footpath sign for Wensley Bridge, West Witton and Aysgarth, follow the direction for Wensley Bridge. Continue along the footpath, which runs parallel to the river below. Pass through a small wooden gate in a stone wall. There are river pools along here for a swim but the best is further on, through a wooden gate in a fence; look for a tree stump next to the rugged path down to it. After your swim re-join the footpath and go through a small gate to another field before crossing a rickety wooden fence and stile. A stile into another field leads to a metal gate into a field, with a small beck to cross.

8 Go through a metal gate into a field (cows, calves and bull in field sign on gate). The footpath continues straight ahead but you can take a shortcut by veering to the right. Climb uphill and double back to re-join the footpath beside a stone wall on the right. This leads to the corner of the field where it narrows to a gate/stile.

9 A narrow footpath, bound by stone walls, takes you back to the village. Turn left onto a metalled road and continue to the main road. Turn left again to Holl Gate, where you parked your car.

Walk 7

CRAY GILL WATERFALLS AND RIVER WHARFE

Hike past pretty waterfalls tumbling into cup-shaped pools, explore the haunt of one of England's greatest writers and swim in a serene stretch of the River Wharfe

INFORMATION

Well-trodden footpaths and bridleways, short hill ascent at the start, riverside paths, stepping stones, some rough terrain and quiet country lanes.

DISTANCE: 4 miles
TIME: 2 hours
MAP: OS Explorer OL30 Yorkshire Dales, Northern and Central
START & END POINT: Buckden car park (SD 941 772, 54.1920, -2.0897)
PUBLIC TRANSPORT: DalesBus services 874, 875/876 (Wetherby, Ilkley), 72, 72A and 72B (Skipton, Grassington, Buckden)
SWIMMING: Waterfalls on Cray and Crook Beck, river pools along the River Wharfe
PLACES OF INTEREST: Buckden Pike, St Michael and All Angels, The George Inn
REFRESHMENTS: Georgian coaching inn, the Buck Inn, at Buckden (BD23 5JA, 01756 761933), has outdoor seating with superb views of the village and valley. Along the route, the George Inn, at Hubberholme (BD23 5JE, 01756 760223), is a popular riverside pub steeped in history.
NEARBY SWIM SPOTS: Buckden Falls, just off the start of the route, and the River Wharfe at Starbottom and Kettlewell
EASIER ACCESS: The waterfalls can be reached via a footpath adjacent to Stubbing Lane, between Hubberholme and Cray

T his sublime ramble winds through Upper Wharfedale along the banks of Cray Beck as it carves a channel through the hidden valley of Cray Gill. Here, small streams from the limestone and peat uplands tumble over rocks and limestone ledges to create an abundance of sparkling cascades, waterfalls and cataracts laced with enticing plunge pools. These peaceful upper reaches of Wharfedale, curving west towards lovely Langstrothdale, reward hikers with breathtaking scenery and tranquility - not to mention a historic pub along the way and the sun-trap terrace of Georgian coaching inn at the finish.

Beginning at the visitor car park in Buckden, the walk initially follows Buckden Rake, the route of an old Roman road. Although there is archaeological evidence of people living in this valley for thousands of years, Buckden is a relative newcomer, dating back to the 12th century. Its old name Buck-dene, or the valley of the deer, refers to its location within the Norman hunting forest of Langstrothdale Chase; the village was created as the forest keeper's headquarters.

Today Buckden is a popular walking destination, particularly among ramblers hoping to scale 702m-high Buckden Pike, whose rugged slopes rise from the village. A memorial cross, south of the summit trig point, with fragments of aircraft parts embedded into its base, is dedicated to five Polish members of the Royal Air Force who died when their Wellington Bomber crashed into the hill during a snowstorm in 1942. The sole survivor, Josef Fusniak, only found his way to safety thanks to the unexpected assistance of a fox, whose tracks he followed in the snow - hence the addition of a fox's head to the memorial. For his bravery, Fusniak was awarded the British Empire Medal by King George V.

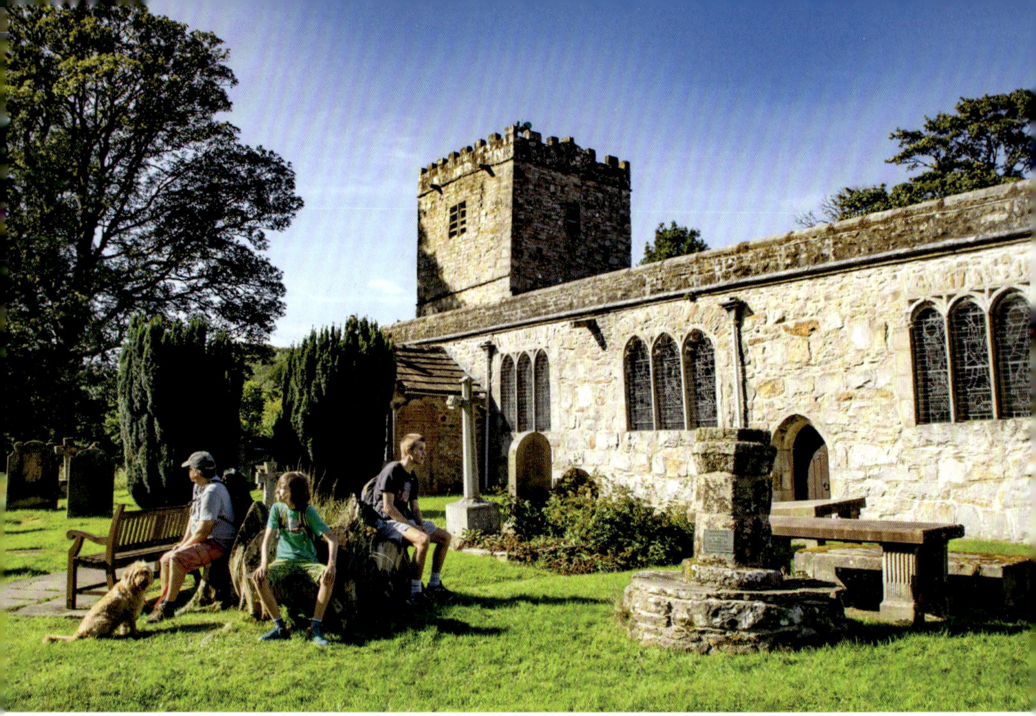

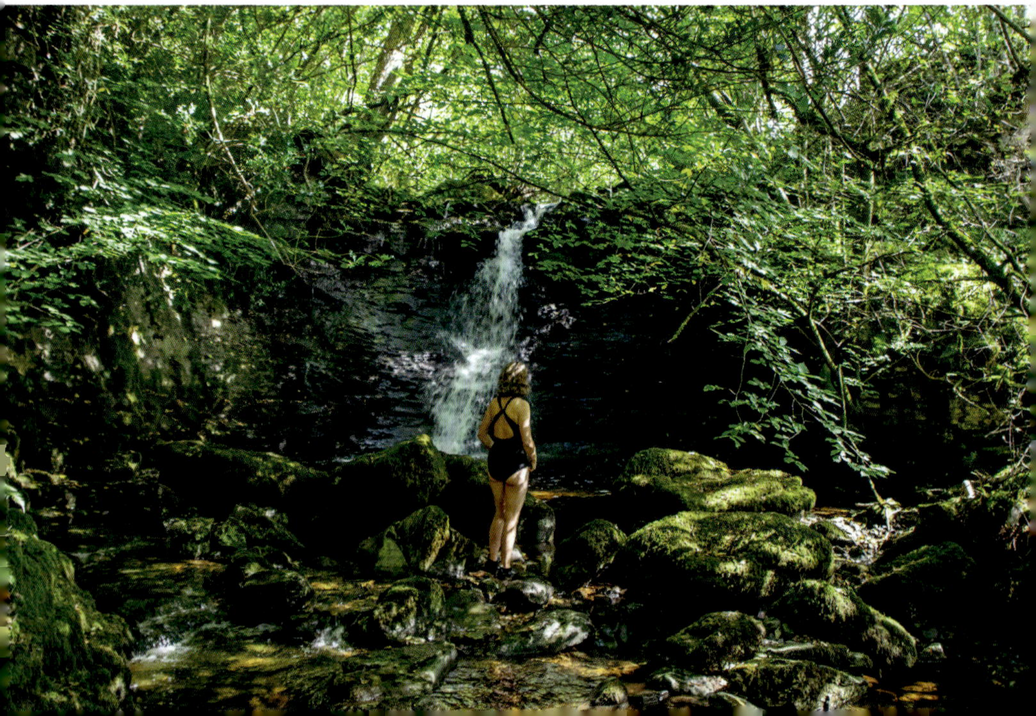

Buckden Rake, a track that was once part of a Roman road, rises among the wooded contours of Buckden Out Moor. This remote and wild expanse of land is managed by the National Trust's Upper Wharfedale Estate and is home to a scattering of cairns and an ancient settlement as well as disused shafts, quarries and shake holes that speak of the intense lead mining that took place here between the 17th and 19th centuries. As you gain height along the stony track, stop to admire the magnificent views of the natural amphitheatre that forms the head of the dale ❶.

The path veers right, passing through several spring-loaded gates before flattening out. Leaving this bridleway, the route descends via a footpath through a field to the hamlet of Cray. A hop across the beck over stepping stones leads to a footpath behind the White Lion pub opposite ❸.

A little further along, a footpath to the left leads into the secluded, steep-sided valley of Cray Gill. In summer, its fern-clad slopes are starred with hundreds of lilac-blue devil's-bit scabious. This tiny pincushion flower gets its Latin name scabere from 'to scratch,' a reference to the fact that it was once used as a treatment for scabies and the sores of bubonic plague - a rather unappealing backstory for such a dainty flower. The 'devil's bit' comes from its distorted black root, supposedly bitten off by the Devil after becoming enraged at its curative powers.

At the valley bottom, the waterfall-chasing begins ❹. The crashing cascades are audible before they are visible but, as you start to glimpse the first falls through the trees don't be tempted to clamber down to them from here. Instead, continue along the path to a switchback path a little further along. It's then a short scramble across rocks to reach the plunge pool. The slanted cascade pours over a curved rock into a pretty, bronze-hued basin, encircled by large mossy boulders. Dappled light filters through the canopies of trees clinging precariously to its rim, dancing across its surface to reveal a smooth, stony bottom beneath the translucent amber water. The surrounding rocks are perfect for changing, and for enjoying a flask of tea after your dip.

This delightful cascade is only a warm-up for the next waterfall, a 6m chute that spills into a perfect oval pool, deep in the limestone cleft of Crook Gill ❻. Sunshine seeps through the leaves of trees, bouncing light off the peat-stained water and giving it a dazzling copper glow. This pool is deeper and the water is icy but it's wonderfully refreshing. To warm up afterwards, return to the path and cross the single span packhorse bridge across the beck. Built from limestone slabs in the medieval era, the bridge ❼ lies on an old packhorse route from Bishopdale to Wharfedale and was designed to carry horses loaded with panniers across the stream. After following suit and crossing the bridge you will find a perfect picnic spot a few metres downstream, beside a series of tumbling cascades. The huge slabs of weathered limestone warm up beautifully on a sunny day, perfect for air-drying after a dip.

When you've soaked up enough of the sun's rays, continue along the footpath, passing several more

cascades along the beck before it dashes off to meet the River Wharfe. The path meanders through meadowland to reach a quiet country lane leading to the hamlet of Hubberholme. It's tempting to stop for refreshments at the historic George Inn but, before crossing the bridge to do so, pop into the picturesque 12th-century church of St Michael and All Angels ❾. Originally a Forest Chapel of the Norman hunting forest of Langstrothdale Chase, the church - and the village - were loved by the author JB Priestley, who described Hubberholme as *"one of the smallest and most pleasant places in the world"*. His ashes were scattered in the churchyard here, and there is a memorial and information panel about him inside the church. Fans of the TV reboot of *All Creatures Great and Small* will recognise the church's interior as the place where Yorkshire vet James Herriot, and his wife-to-be, Helen, made their wedding vows.

The 17th-century George Inn is reputed to have been one of Priestley's favourite watering holes and this quintessential Dales pub still observes several quaint traditions. A candle is kept burning when the pub is open, for instance: a throwback to when the inn was a vicarage and the parson lit the candle to let his parishioners know he was available. Candles also make an appearance on the first Monday after New Year's Day. This is when the annual meeting of the Hubberholme parliament takes place, and an auction is held for 16 acres of pasture land just up the road from the George. After a short service of prayer, the pub candle is lit to mark the start of the bidding and is extinguished when it finishes.

The return route to Buckden leaves Hubberholme along a country lane. Ahead is Buckden Pike and the route soon picks up the Dales Way, detouring onto a riverside path ❿. Soon afterwards, a track winds through the grass to a wide pebble beach and a lovely pool for one final swim. Following the river back to Buckden, the path rejoins a lane for the final stretch into Buckden.

1 From Buckden car park, go through the gate and follow the stony bridleway uphill towards Cray and Buckden Rake. As the path veers right there are fine views towards Hubberholme. Continue along the track, keeping left at a fork in the path and go through several spring-loaded gates until the path levels out.

2 At the footpath sign to Cray go through a gate on the left. Head downhill towards the pub and cross the stepping stones over the beck then cross the road and follow the uphill footpath to the right of the White Lion pub (currently closed).

3 Choose your path carefully here. A yellow way marker indicates the correct path. Continue until the path forks at a footpath sign. Follow the left fork, not the path to the house. A footpath sign directs you to a narrow path with a dry-stone wall on the left and the garden of the house on the right. Go through a wooden gate into a field, following the path through the valley, with Cray Beck down below to your left. The path descends towards the beck, and a wooden gate marked with a National Trust sign.

4 Pass through this gate into the woodland and continue along the footpath. Listen out for the first waterfall, which you can just about see through the trees. You cannot access it from here. Instead, continue along the path and look carefully for a track on the left that doubles back to the falls, just before two large stones. This path leads right up to the waterfall, your first swim spot.

5 After your dip, head back to the main footpath. Almost immediately you reach a stone packhorse bridge and, just before this, a path leading off to the right.

6 Take this path and, after 50m, you reach the second swim spot, a 6m-high waterfall that cascades down a limestone cleft into an oval plunge pool.

7 After your dip, head back to the main footpath and cross the arched bridge. Continue along the path for a few metres to a delightful picnic spot; a series of large, flat stones next to the beck, overlooking tumbling cascades. Afterwards, rejoin the footpath, passing several more cascades and pools. The path opens out onto meadowland leading to a gate.

8 Turn right along a country lane, towards the bridge across the River Wharfe at Hubberholme.

9 The historic church in Hubberholme is worth a visit. Afterwards cross the bridge. You might be tempted by the George Inn. Otherwise, turn left to follow the country lane out of the village with great views towards Buckden.

10 At the Dales Way sign turn left, through a field then onto a riverside path. There are several deep pools for a swim along this stretch. The best comes not long after you have joined the path. Look for a trodden grassy path to a wide beach and river pool. Afterwards, rejoin the riverside path as it eventually opens out into a field and head towards a gate, leading onto a lane.

11 Turn left along this lane, crossing the bridge back into Buckden and the car park - or into the pub!

Walk 8

UPPER NIDD FALLS AND HOW STEAN GORGE

Follow the river that 'vanishes' from Lofthouse and savour valley views from Middlesmoor before descending to How Stean Gorge and a string of enticing pools.

INFORMATION

Narrow riverside and woodland paths, moderate hill climb to Middlesmoor, country lanes. Stiles. May be muddy after rain. You may encounter livestock.

DISTANCE: 4 miles
TIME: 1.45 hours
MAP: OS Explorer 298 Nidderdale, Fountain's Abbey, Ripon & Pateley Bridge
START & END POINT: Lofthouse Village Car Park (SE 101 734, 54.1571, -1.8461)
PUBLIC TRANSPORT: Bus Services 820/821 (Keighley, Otley, Scar House Reservoir)
SWIMMING: Falls and pools along the River Nidd, pools and cascades along How Stean Beck
PLACES OF INTEREST: How Stean Gorge, St Chad's Church, Middlesmoor
REFRESHMENTS: How Stean Gorge Café (HG3 5SF, 01423 755666) serves bacon sandwiches, soups and homemade cakes and has excellent views of the gorge through its glass floor and windows. The family-run Crown Hotel, in Lofthouse (HG3 5RZ, 01423 755206), serves fish and chips, shepherd's pies, ham and chips and real ales.
NEARBY SWIM SPOTS: River Nidd, Pateley Bridge
EASIER ACCESS: Upper Nidd Falls are a short walk from Lofthouse

When the boundaries of the Yorkshire Dales National Park were drawn up 70 years ago, Nidderdale, on the eastern fringes of the Dales, didn't feature on the map. This left some of its inhabitants feeling disgruntled. However, its absence may have been a blessing for this peaceful, outlying vale. Nidderdale avoids the footfall of other Dales valleys, yet the wild beauty of its heather moorland, steep-sided river valleys, ancient woodlands and pocket-sized hamlets make it a delight to explore. This enjoyable swim-walk, taking in many of Nidderdale's finest features, is particularly lovely in spring when clusters of ransoms and bluebells carpet its woodland floors and riverbanks.

Designated an Area of Outstanding Natural Beauty (now a National Landscape) in 1994, the dale is often split into Upper Nidderdale and Lower Nidderdale, the two regions lying upstream and downstream of the market town of Pateley Bridge. Whereas Lower Nidderdale is pastoral and gently undulating, the wild and dramatic scenery of Upper Nidderdale includes the spectacular limestone canyon of How Stean Gorge (visited on this route), an elaborate cave system at Goyden Pot (off this route) and a river that plays hide and seek.

The walk begins at Lofthouse, a cluster of stone-built cottages clinging to a steep, winding hill. Fortunately there is parking for several cars next to the village's Memorial Institute. Starting out along a footpath that descends to a stone bridge across the River Nidd, the route follows the water upstream. At Lofthouse, the river can look very different depending on the time of year and recent rainfall; it can even run dry in summer.

The Nidd rises at Nidd Head Spring, on the slopes of Great Whernside (not to be confused with the more famous Whernside, which is, confusingly, the greater of the two), before flowing through the reservoirs of Angram and Scar House. It vanishes at the aptly-named Nidd Sinks, to the north of Lofthouse, the water disappearing underground at Manchester Hole and Goyden Pot into cave systems formed by gritstone overlying more porous limestone. The river then rises again at Nidd Heads, just south of Lofthouse.

If you are in luck and the river is flowing, you soon reach a small cascade. Just beyond it is a multi-ribboned waterfall and a wide pool, sheltered by trees (between ❶ and ❷). After rain the falls are impressive. However, in summer they may be no more than a trickle. Either way, this is a picturesque spot for a paddle and a dip, setting you up for the rest of the walk. The rocks are slippery so take care; aqua shoes, with good grip, would be useful.

After the falls, the continuing footpath narrows, bound by a steep, mossy bank and the sloping, tree-clad riverbank, with knobbly tree roots underfoot. It's not a precipitous drop to the river but you need to tread carefully. As the path rises through a copse, there are a couple more silvery-brown pools

suitable for a swim, guarded by lofty pines. Where the river narrows and flows faster, it has carved out chutes that are fun for swooshing along (between ❶ and ❷). In April and May this pretty woodland glade is a haze of purple, swathes of bluebells stretching out beneath a canopy of new, lime-green leaves.

Beyond the woodland, the route winds through fields along the valley floor as the steep-sided, upper reaches of Nidderdale and surrounding moorland rise to the north. Scaling the slopes to Middlesmoor, through sheep-cropped pastures, an array of stiles and narrow squeezes must be wriggled through. With height gained, panoramic views of the encircling moorland widen, sunlight rippling over the crinkled hills ❸. In summer the heather-covered moors bloom in shades of amethyst, pink and mauve, fading to a warm copper in autumn. The tiny building and tower perched high above Thrope Edge is a shooting house; these wild moors are managed for grouse shooting.

The hill-top village of Middlesmoor ❹ is one of Yorkshire's highest settlements, at 300m above sea level. There are wonderful views of the river valley and surrounding moorland from it. These are best appreciated from St Chad's churchyard, where wooden benches in the churchyard, or stone pews in the porch of the church, also make ideal spots to enjoy a picnic lunch. Cupped in the valley is shimmering Gouthwaite reservoir, created to supply drinking water for Bradford; it is also a nature reserve and SSSI.

From Middlesmoor, the route descends through grazed pastures towards the steep valley of How Stean Beck. Velvety moss and bracken-clad slopes edge How Stean Beck, glittering through the trees of the ancient semi-natural woodland of Cliff Woods ❻. The beck's myriad pools, channels and waterfalls are shaded by ash, birch and hazel; look

for a deep, peaty pool near the start of the trail, or seek out more downstream. In spring the banks are smothered in clusters of white ransoms and carpets of bluebells while yellow marsh marigolds sprout close to the water's edge.

Leaving the woodland, the beck is constricted through How Stean Gorge. This spectacular deep-cut limestone canyon is one of Yorkshire's natural wonders ❼. Often described as a miniature Grand Canyon, or as 'Little Switzerland,' the gorge extends for just over half a mile. The bridge over the beck offers great views up and down the gorge as the water leaps over giant boulders, smoothing the limestone into peculiar shapes as it flows through the narrow chasm.

The gorge itself is managed as a paid-for activity centre, offering a range of outdoor pursuits including gorge walking, ghyll scrambling, caving, rock climbing, abseiling and cave camping. Gorge walkers descend into the ravine by abseiling 13m from a bridge, then forge their way upstream, scrambling over boulders, sliding down chutes and jumping into plunge pools.

The centre's café ❽ is the perfect pitstop for a pot of tea and a slice of homemade cake at the end of the walk; there are fabulous views of the gorge through its floor-to-ceiling windows and glass floor. After refuelling in the café, the route winds back to Lofthouse along a country lane, your soul surely singing after a walk in one of Yorkshire loveliest dales.

❶ Turn right out of the car park. At the war memorial, follow a footpath signed Middlesmoor. Cross the bridge over the river then go through a squeeze on the right into a riverside meadow. You will soon reach some mini falls before a larger cascade that's suitable for a quick dip. Afterwards, continue along the narrow footpath. It is fenced on one side and close to the river on the other so take care. At a small woodland, the path rises. There are some nice pools and chutes where the river narrows.

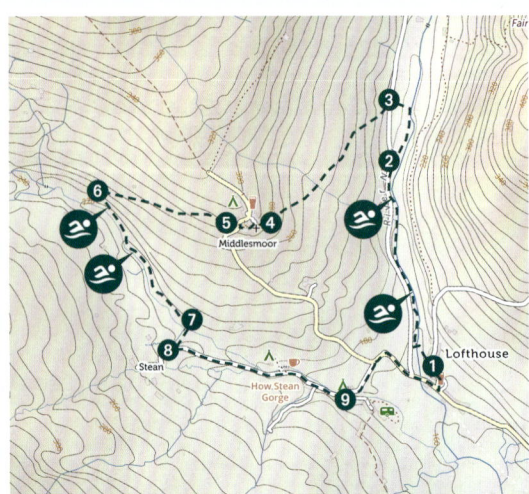

❷ Cross a stile into a field. The footpath runs next to a stone wall and parallel to the beck (on the right). Pass between a tumbling stone wall to another field with a stone wall and a fenced squeeze at the other end. Although the footpath continues towards the farm ahead, there is an informal diversion to reach the road, which runs parallel to the footpath. Follow the edge of the wall (on your right) to a gate that opens onto the road. The gate has an arrow drawn next to it, indicating the diversion from that end.

❸ Cross the road and turn right. Look for a footpath sign to Middlesmoor almost immediately on the left. Climb the stile then veer left, uphill, to another stile. Cross the field diagonally to stone steps and a squeeze then walk, still diagonally, across the field to steps and a squeeze. Continue in the same direction. On reaching a plateau, ignore a metal gate with a 'private' sign. Instead walk beside the stone wall, on your right. Climb a wooden stile then cross a beck and continue over another stile. A waymarker by a lone wooden stile points to Middlesmoor. Follow this, crossing a small stream before reaching another stile. Middlesmoor gradually comes into view. Go through a metal gate and continue, passing through another metal gate.

❹ As you enter Middlesmoor, the route passes a house and the church on the left. It's worth stopping to admire the fantastic views from the churchyard. From the church follow the cobbled road to an unmarked footpath that veers left between houses and a methodist chapel; this path looks like someone's driveway as farm machinery may be parked here. Cross through the farmyard to a footpath opposite and continue to a gate opening into a field.

❺ Walk downhill towards a squeeze in a stone wall next to a gate then continue diagonally across a field towards the valley bottom. Cross a stream and continue to a squeeze and wooden gate towards some trees. Look for a waymarker pointing left and go through a wooden gate to the path above How Stean Beck.

❻ Turn left, following the beck downstream. This is the start of a run of good pools and falls for a dip. The best are near the start, about 20m downstream. After your dip, go through a gate into a field with the beck - now fenced off - to your right. The footpath rises away from the river to a gate. Go through it into another field, then through another squeeze.

❼ Look for a fingerpost on the right. Follow this direction, through a gate, and cross the bridge over

How Stean Beck, with views up and down the gorge. Follow the footpath, with a small stream to your right. The path emerges at a wooden cabin before veering sharp right onto the road.

8 Turn left. The road descends, passing How Stean Gorge Activity Centre. The café here is a good place to stop for refreshments.

9 Afterwards, continue along the lane, turning left to cross the bridge and passing Studfold Campsite on the left. At the junction, turn right towards Lofthouse. Cross the bridge over the river then turn left into Lofthouse, passing the Crown Hotel on the way back to the car park.

Walk 9

CATRIGG FORCE, STAINFORTH FORCE AND THE EEL POOL

Wander through wildflower meadows, with views of Yorkshire's Three Peaks, to one of the prettiest waterfalls in the Dales before returning via the River Ribble

INFORMATION

Well-trodden footpaths and bridleways, riverside paths, meadows and quiet country lanes. Stone step stiles and a hill ascent out of Langcliffe. You may encounter livestock.

DISTANCE: 5 miles
TIME: 2.5 hours
MAP: OS Explorer OL2 Yorkshire Dales, Southern and Western
START & END POINT: Langcliffe village car park (honesty box £2), (SD 823 650, 54.0813, -2.2719)
PUBLIC TRANSPORT: Bus Service 75 (Skipton, Malham, Settle) and DalesBus 11 (Settle, Clitheroe)
SWIMMING: Catrigg Force, Stainforth Force, the Eel Pool and several pools downstream along the River Ribble
PLACES OF INTEREST: Lower Winskill Meadows, Winskill Stones Nature Reserve
REFRESHMENTS: Craven Heifer, Stainforth (BD24 9PB, 01729 822435)
OTHER FACILITIES: Public toilets in Stainforth village hall car park
NEARBY SWIM SPOTS: Janet's Foss at Malham
EASIER ACCESS: Stainforth Force is right next to the lane and packhorse bridge and the Eel Pool is a few metres downstream

The pretty village of Langcliffe sits in an idyllic spot on the eastern side of the Ribble Valley, at the edge of the Yorkshire Dales National Park. Perched on a natural terrace, with attractive stone houses and cobbled streets, it is surrounded by meadows, trees and steep limestone cliffs (from which it takes its name). Narrow lanes radiate out from the large village green, leading onto footpaths and tracks that wind into glorious countryside. This circular walk journeys from Langcliffe to neighbouring Stainforth through hillside pastures and upland hay meadows, with spectacular valley views as height is gained. The return route meanders beside a particularly pictur-esque stretch of the River Ribble, taking in the tumbling falls of Stainforth Force and some enticing river pools for swimming. The highlight, however, is Catrigg Force, on Stainforth Beck. One of the most beautiful waterfalls in the Yorkshire Dales, it is set in a wooded chasm on the moor edge, completely hidden from those who do not seek it out. A dip in this magical cascade is on many wild swimmers' wish lists.

The walk begins from the village car park, next to the old school, where an honesty box is in place near the entrance. The route picks up a path leading onto the back lanes of the village to join a walled, stony track between lush pastures criss-crossed with dry stone walls. Gradually coming into sight is the precipitous limestone crag of Stainforth Scar as the route climbs more strenuously. With height gained, a magnificent panorama unfolds along the valley towards Giggleswick and Settle, with the Settle to Carlisle railway line slicing through its centre and the river glinting through the trees as it snakes along the valley floor.

was bought by the conservation charity, Plantlife, to safeguard it and allow its diverse flora to thrive. The characteristic feature of limestone pavements is their division into blocks, clints and deep vertical fissures known as grykes, which have been eroded by water over time. The grykes provide a moist, shady habitat for a host of woodland plants including several varieties of fern; shining fronds of hart's tongue fern, the greyish-green rigid buckler fern and green spleenwort. In summer, colourful carpets of mossy saxifrage drape the limestone slabs, creating natural, pink-tinged rockeries.

From the track at the far end of the meadows, there are spectacular views northwards to the Yorkshire Three Peaks of Ingleborough, Whernside and Pen-y-Ghent, which looks particularly attractive from this vantage point. Behind you is the dazzling white limestone cliff of Attermire Scar, below which are a collection of large caverns: Attermire, Victoria and Jubilee Caves. All are accessible and well worth a visit another day.

Continuing along the Pennine Bridleway, with Pen-y-ghent directly ahead, the track gradually descends. Ahead, to the north, Stainforth Beck twists serenely through the pastures below, giving no hint at the abrupt change its journey is about to make ❸. A clump of trees and a wooden gate on the right, faintly engraved 'Catrigg Force', indicates its metamorphosis, the waterfall's rumble becoming more audible the closer you get. It is reached through a gate into the woodland and down a flight of steps ❹.

The cathedral-like setting is an awesome sight as water from the beck squeezes through a slot in the towering rock, dropping almost 20m in two stages, first wavering in an upper pool before plunging into a lower basin. This enchanting spot is one of the dreamiest waterfalls in the Dales. It might be tempting to stay here but even on a hot summer's

After a final push to crest the hill the route leads diagonally through the delightful hay meadows of Lower Winskill Farm ❷. If you have time, it is well worth stopping at this working farm to admire these ancient hay meadows more closely; the owners sometimes run tours so do check ahead. Recorded in 16th-century documents, the species-rich meadows are cultivated using wildlife-friendly methods. A nationally rare habitat, these high limestone pastures include a number of different orchids, cowslips, lady's mantle, spring cinquefoil and rock rose, the latter being the sole food source for caterpillars of the rare northern brown argus butterfly.

To the east of the meadows is Winskill Stones Nature Reserve, a protected landscape that includes a striking section of limestone pavement. The rock here was once plundered for use in garden rockeries but following a public appeal, backed by gardens author and TV presenter Geoff Hamilton, the site day the water can be icy as the pool is shaded by a dense canopy of leaves.

Once you have dried off (and, hopefully, warmed up with a steaming flask of tea) the walk continues along the Pennine Bridleway towards Stainforth, where there's a hop, skip and jump across the beck by way of several large, smoothly-hewn stepping stones ❺. The Craven Heifer pub is nearby if you want to stop for refreshments. There are also public toilets in the village car park. Otherwise, an amble through the village brings you to the homeward leg of the walk, which follows the River Ribble as it babbles merrily downstream.

Beneath the village's 17th-century packhorse bridge ❼, the Ribble creates some splendid waterfalls at Stainforth Force where the water tumbles over large slabs of limestone into a rocky gorge. This is a popular spot with families. On sunny weekends and holidays children fish and paddle in the mini rapids that flow below the bridge before the water pours down a waterfall into a deep, smooth-sided, ebony plunge pool, accessed by an old iron ladder. The falls are a magnet for daredevils. Don't be surprised to see teenagers and fearless grown-ups hurling themselves into the swirling cauldron from a startling height.

If you prefer your swimming a little more sedate, the Eel Pool, a few metres downstream, is a long, deep basin where the water slows to pass through a gorge. It is slightly obscured from the main path, with large stone slabs on the near side and a fringe of grass on the other. A beautiful place for a longer swim, bear in mind there is still a flow here and no shallows so you will need to lever yourself off the rocks into the water and be certain you can clamber out the same way. For a more gradual entry to the water, there is a small river beach a few metres downstream, in front of Knight Stainforth Hall

caravan park and campsite, where Stainforth Beck flows into the River Ribble.

Continuing even further downriver brings you to an especially tranquil stretch of the Ribble. The riverside path widens onto buttercup-studded meadows that open out in a peaceful wash of pebbly beaches with several large pools for longer, secluded swims ❽. After a leisurely dip here, the final section passes through sheep-nibbled fields to a weir which collects water for Langcliffe Mill ❾. From the footbridge you can see the fish ladder on the opposite bank. If you happen to be here in late November, it is quite a spectacle to see the salmon leaping to make their way to spawning grounds upstream.

The final stretch of the walk is a gentle stroll back along a country lane to the main road and Langcliffe, where you pass the village green and an unusual war memorial reconstructed from a Victorian fountain.

1 From the car park, follow the track leading to the back lanes of the village. Where the path diverges, keep right onto a walled lane then pass through a wooden gate to enter the upper reaches of a sloping meadow, keeping the wall close to your right. Beyond a copse, a gate opens into another meadow and the route rises more strenuously, offering fine views across the valley. Head towards the trees and scattered stones along a faintly-marked path, to a gate in the corner of the field. Continue to climb the steep path, passing several boulder stones to reach the edge of a wall on your right. Continue for a short distance, keeping this wall to your right before the path widens.

2 Hop over a stone step stile, on the left, to Winskill Meadows and go diagonally across the hay meadows to another stone step stile and onto a track. Bear right then cross over a cattle grid. From here there is a superb view of the Three Yorkshire Peaks. At the fingerpost, take the direction towards "Pennine Bridleway'/ Stainforth," following a track beside a stone wall. To the right are the Winskill Stones, striking limestone boulders which you may wish to visit. Continue to a crossing track.

3 Turn left towards an open gate in the stone wall and a fingerpost marked "Pennine Bridleway/ Stainforth". Follow the descending track to another gate. Immediately beyond this is a small wooden gate on the right, marked Catrigg Force.

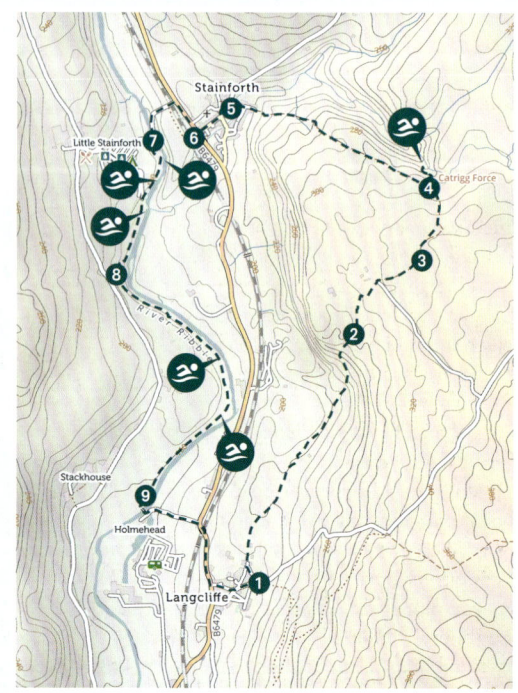

4 Go through this onto a zig-zagging path to a gate into woodland before descending steps to the waterfall. Enjoy your first swim at this secret waterfall. Afterwards, rejoin the main track, following it downhill, eventually entering Stainforth village.

5 Keep right at the village green and cross the stepping stones over Stainforth Beck, following a narrow path beside a house. Then, turn left onto Goat Lane. Follow the road as it curves left, passing the village pinfold. (Just ahead is the Craven Heifer). Turn right onto a street (the Pennine Bridleway) that leads

to the main B6479 road (A car park with public toilets is on the left).

6 Turn right at the main road and walk along the pavement for 100m. Then, cross the road onto Dog Hill Brow, a restricted road that traverses the railway line. Continue to a packhorse bridge. Beyond this, on the left, is a small gate leading to a riverside path.

7 Follow the path as it leads past mini rapids to Stainforth Force. You can dip here or a few metres further along, at the more secluded Eel Pool. After your dip, return to the riverside path, passing a campsite. The path narrows and is closely bounded by trees as it rises steeply to the right along a rockier path to a stone step stile.

8 Cross the stile onto a footpath and continue along this, beside a fence above the river, to another stone step stile. Go over this and take the steps downhill, to rejoin the riverside, following the path as it meanders through narrow meadows with further river pools, all suitable for a swim. After crossing another stone step stile, the route passes through several gated fields to a gate, beyond which is a weir and a footbridge.

9 Cross the bridge then turn left onto a country lane to return to the main road. Cross the road and turn right. Continue for a few metres then turn left into Langcliffe. Keep straight, passing a row of terraced cottages on the left. At the memorial cross turn left, back to the car park.

Walk 10

JANET'S FOSS AND GORDALE SCAR

Take the path less travelled to the amphitheatre of Malham Cove. Plunge into a fairytale waterfall and ascend a towering gorge to a natural Jacuzzi in the rock face

INFORMATION

Rocky terrain and steps in Watlowes Valley, then well-trodden footpaths, country lanes and moorland. You may encounter livestock.

DISTANCE: 6.5 miles
TIME: 3.15 hours
MAP: OS Explorer OL2 Yorkshire Dales, Southern and Western
START & END POINT: Water Sinks Car Park (SD 894 658, 54.0881, -2.1634)
PUBLIC TRANSPORT: Train station at Skipton/Settle then bus to Malham and taxi to start. Bus Services 75 (Skipton, Malham, Settle), 210, 211 (Skipton, Malham). Or services 864, 866, 873 (Ilkley, Malham)
SWIMMING: Janet's Foss, waterfall at Gordale Scar
PLACES OF INTEREST: Watlowes Valley, Malham Cove, Gordale Scar, Malham Tarn
REFRESHMENTS: Gordale Refreshments, Gordale Bridge (BD23 4DL, 07737 237918) serves ice creams, sandwiches, pasties and sausage rolls. The Lister Arms, Malham, (BD23 4DB, 01729 830444), is an elegant 18th-century inn. Or, head to the Beck Hall Hotel, Malham (BD23 4DJ, 01729 830729), for plant-based dining beside a stream.
NEARBY SWIM SPOTS: Catrigg Force and the Eel Pool, River Ribble
EASIER ACCESS: Limited parking at Gordale Bridge for a short walk to Janet's Foss. Or, follow the footpath from Malham.

*A*s you head towards the start of this walk don't be alarmed if you see a string of sightseers snaking up the well-trodden path from Malham village to Malham Cove. This area is a geological wonderland of remarkable limestone features. Its striking karst scenery, including the sweeping amphitheatre of rock that forms Malham Cove, is the result of mildly acidic water eroding the soluble bedrock of limestone. Strange things happen in this extraordinary landscape: streams vanish and reappear, springs seemingly bubble up from out of nowhere, and a subterranean network of caves and sink holes hides beneath the soil.

Instead of joining the crowds on the traditional route up to Malham Cove, this walk follows an alternate path through the limestone canyon of Watlowes Valley, enjoying magnificent views of the awe-inspiring Malham Cove as well as the mighty ravine and cascades of Gordale Scar. The enchanting waterfall of Janet's Foss, with its exquisite plunge pool, is the perfect place for a cooling dip along the way. It is another popular spot so timing your walk to arrive here in late afternoon will give you the best chance of a quiet dip.

Starting just north of the small village of Malham - home to pubs, cafés, a hostel and a National Park Visitor Centre - the walk begins on Malham Moor. The name of the car park, Water Sinks, hints at one of the peculiarities of this landscape; just metres after leaving the south end of the lake, water destined to journey to the North Sea via the River Aire mysteriously vanishes through deep fissures in the limestone, re-emerging south of Malham village at Aire Head Springs and not, as would be expected, beneath Malham Cove -

that is Malham Beck which begins life elsewhere on Malham Moor. You have been warned, things are never quite what they seem around these parts.

From Water Sinks car park, the route almost immediately picks up the long-distance Pennine Way towards Malham Cove. As it approaches the gorge, the path is increasingly hemmed in by exposed and weathered rocks on either side. It eventually emerges at the deep limestone canyon of Watlowes Valley ❷, a dry ravine carved out by glacial overflow from Malham Tarn streaming down to what was once England's highest waterfall at Malham Cove. In 2015 heavy rain from Storm Desmond flooded the valley bottom and water briefly flowed through Watlowes to Malham Cove, meaning it could temporarily lay claim to being the highest waterfall in England once again.

With sweeping views down the dry valley, pause for a moment and take in the splendour of this canyon. The wiggly path through its core is reached via steep, rocky steps before the route rejoins a path, widening out onto limestone pavement, 80m above Malham Cove ❸.

Having soaked up the distant views towards Pendle Hill and the South Pennines, take a closer look at the pavement itself. Blocks of limestone (clints) have been weathered to form deep fissures (grykes). During the summer months, herb robert, spleenwort and mountain pansy grow in the nooks and crannies of the huge slabs of rock, while fresh green fronds of hart's tongue fern unfurl between the crevices. Harry Potter fans will recognise this otherworldly landscape as the place where the young wizard and his best friend, Hermione, camp out in the film version of *Harry Potter and the Deathly Hallows Part 1*.

It's possible to admire the horseshoe-shaped cove from below by descending the 400 stone steps at the far end of the pavement. However, bear in mind that you will need to climb back up to continue the walk. After admiring this unique feature, the route carries on around the cove's ridge line with an impressive side-on view of the cliff face as well as sweeping vistas of characteristic Dales countryside, criss-crossed by dry stone walls. As you head down towards Gordale Bridge ❹, look out for statuesque grey herons patiently awaiting their next meal by the beck. There are a couple of picnic benches and a food truck at Gordale Bridge in spring and summer, though you may wish to wait until after your swim for a treat.

Janet's Foss ❺ is one of the most cherished waterfalls in the Dales and for good reason. Magically situated, in leafy ancient woodland owned by the National Trust, this delightful place has a fairytale quality. According to local folklore, Janet or 'Jennet' was a fairy queen who lived in the small cave behind the waterfall that you can reach by clambering up some slippery rocks by the falls or wading through the pool.

In times gone by the pool of Janet's Foss was used as a natural sheep dip by farmers but you are unlikely to encounter any woolly dippers if you visit today. The lime-rich water has deposited a screen of spongy moss-covered tufa beneath the waterfall, lending the pool a pearlescent quality. To swim here on a sunny afternoon, the foamy white drop of the falls pouring into the turquoise pool, is an unforgettable experience. In spring and early summer the woodland hums with birdsong while, beneath the sun-dappled tree canopy, bluebells and ransoms carpet the steep, wooded slopes.

A brisk walk back up the woodland path and along the lane to Gordale Bridge should warm you up after your dip, perhaps stopping at the food truck for an ice cream. Further along, a path weaves

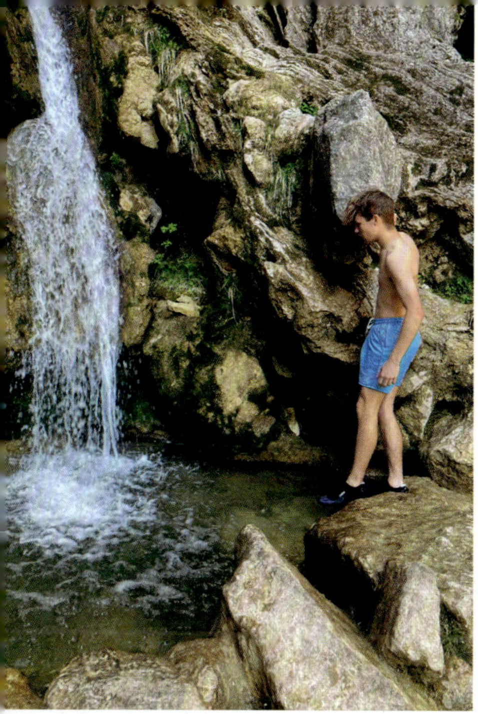
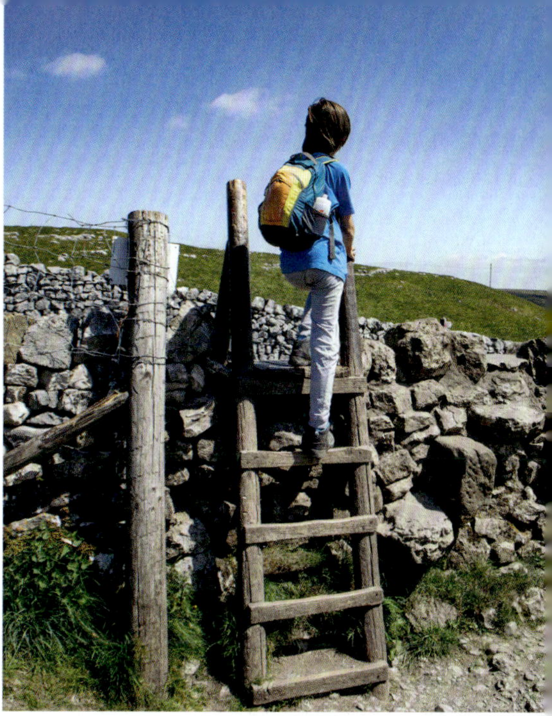
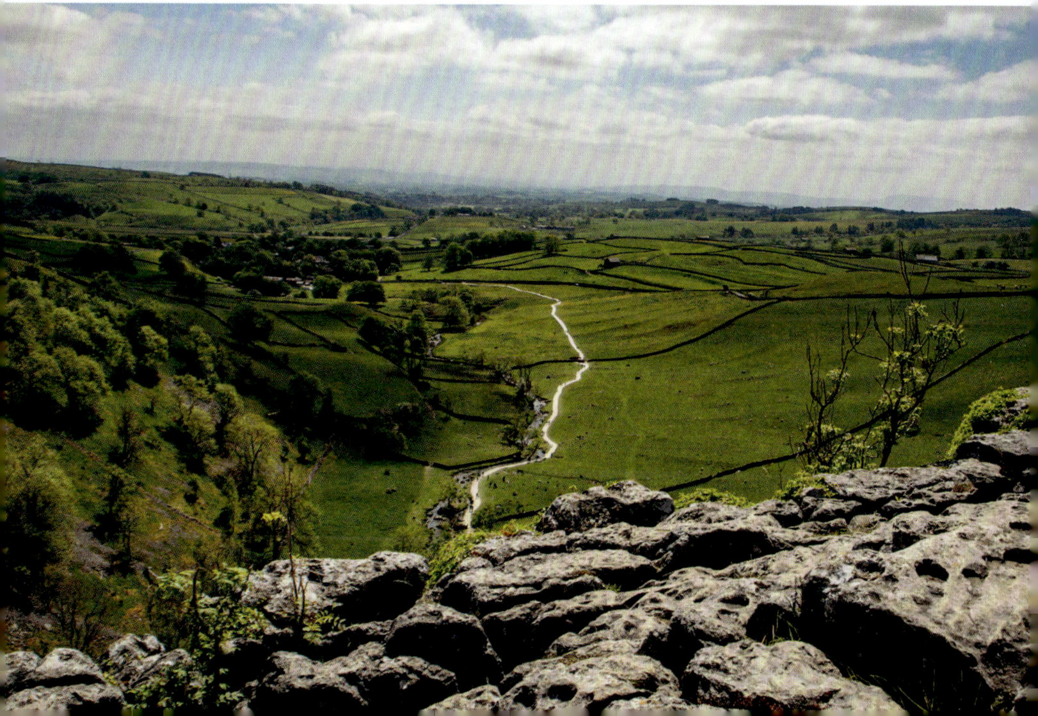

through Gordale Scar campsite, a semi-wild site next to the beck, towards Gordale Scar ❻. Continuing on, the looming grey cliffs of New Close Knotts and Cross Field Knotts edge ever closer as you enter the chasm of Gordale Scar itself.

This magnificent ravine was formed when torrents of glacial meltwater flowed over it, cutting through faults in the rock. Successive ice ages and cave collapses carved it out further, creating the deep gorge that exists today. So awe-inspiring, intimidating even, is this natural feature that it has been immortalised by several English Romantic painters and poets. Artist JMW Turner's 1808 plein air painting, 'Gordale Scar,' hangs in London's Tate Britain and poet William Wordsworth was so moved by a visit that he wrote a sonnet about it: *"let thy feet repair To Gordale chasm, terrific as the lair where the young lions couch."* It is also possible that J.R.R. Tolkien had Gordale in mind when he described Helm's Deep, the scene of an epic battle between men and orcs, in *The Lord of the Rings.*

Like Janet's Foss, the water that flows over the waterfalls here is rich in dissolved limestone, creating a soft tufa screen on the mossy rocks. There is a jacuzzi-sized plunge pool beneath the first waterfall, just large enough for a quick dip in the frothing icy water ❼. Take care scrambling up as the rocks are extremely slippery, and be careful not to damage the delicate tufa. In low water you may spot other hikers scrambling up and above the falls. This walk, however, follows a more surefooted route, returning to Gordale Bridge, and following the path back uphill to the quiet country lane you crossed earlier.

From here the walk continues across the vast, wild moorland of Malham Lings, an area of abundant limestone pavement, deeply riven by rainwater ❿. Although this area feels remote,

remains of settlements, cairns and even a Roman camp indicate that it was an important place for our ancestors. Your only company today, however, is likely to be skylarks performing their aerial acrobatics, and maybe roaming cattle, as you wander back towards Water Sinks.

Beyond the car park lies the shimmering water of Malham Tarn ❶. England's highest limestone lake, 380m above sea level, the tarn is an SSSI and also the centre of a nature reserve managed by the National Trust. Rich in submerged aquatic plants and home to several fish species, and the rare white-clawed crayfish, this glacial lake is also a good place to spot tufted ducks, greater crested grebes and teals. Another of Malham Tarn's claims to fame is that it was the inspiration for Charles Kingsley's 1863 children's classic, The Water Babies. Unfortunately, you can't swim there, due to its precious wildlife habitats. However, it is a beautiful place to unwind after your walk, with spectacular scenery all around.

❶ From the car park, face the road and turn right. Go through a gate, then through another (wooden) gate on the left to join a trodden path. Follow the signpost to Malham Cove. As the path forks, keep following the signed path, the Pennine Way, to Malham Cove (the left-hand path). Continue along the rocky path beside a dry stone wall for a short distance, before continuing along a rock-laid path between the hills. As the path emerges from this valley, it swings right with wide open views ahead.

❷ The path continues around then descends steeply down steps into Watlowes Valley. At the bottom, the path levels out. Follow this through another small valley towards the pavement of Malham Cove.

❸ After admiring the views from Malham Cove, retrace your steps to the path you arrived on and look for a gap in the wall leading uphill on a faint footpath (later this becomes more obvious). Continue to a ladder stile. Climb over this, cross the lane and go through the gate opposite to the path beyond. Follow the path with the dry stone wall on your right.

❹ As the path veers to the right, go through a metal gate and down some steps into a field then head towards a dry stone wall on the other side, which you need to keep on your left. Head towards a country lane, and Gordale Bridge, at the bottom. At the road, turn right and continue to a National Trust sign on the left.

❺ The entrance to the woodland here leads to the waterfall of Janet's Foss, and your first swim. Afterwards, retrace your steps back to Gordale Bridge then continue along the lane. Turn left through a gate on the left into Gordale Scar Campsite.

❻ Follow the winding path through the campsite and into the gorge of Gordale Scar.

❼ To reach the lower waterfall, and small plunge pool, you need to scramble over some wet and mossy rocks so take care as they are very slippery. Afterwards, retrace your steps through the campsite to the gate and return to Gordale Bridge.

❽ Retrace your steps through the fields and along the track to the lane you crossed earlier.

❾ Turn right up the hill to a ladder stile, passing a signpost for Water Sinks on the left.

❿ Climb over the stile to a footpath and follow this across moorland strewn with limestone rocks and cairns. The path is fairly obvious.

⓫ At a fork, follow either path; they join up again at some reedy ponds shortly before a junction, and a signpost for Water Sinks Car Park. Follow this signed path and you will see the car park ahead and Malham Tarn beyond.

GRASSINGTON AND RIVER WHARFE

A ramble across rare limestone pavement to secluded pools, cascades and rapids along Yorkshire's favourite wild swimming river

For many wild swimmers, Yorkshire's River Wharfe is a place of pilgrimage - and deservedly so. As it meanders through the Yorkshire Dales, this picturesque waterway passes through stunning scenery and attractive stone-built villages. Changing character along its journey, it offers contrasting features at every twist and turn - languid, deep sections for a longer swim, narrow gorge cataracts for tubing and countless cascades. This exhilarating ramble includes each of these aquatic adventures and more.

The walk begins in Grassington, the unofficial capital of Upper Wharfedale, and the wider Dales, thanks both to its hosting of a National Park Visitor Centre and to its central location, picturesque setting and cluster of friendly cafés, pubs and independent shops. With its laid-back atmosphere and compact size Grassington feels more like a large village than a town but it was granted a Royal Charter for a market and fair in 1282, giving it town status. The walk passes its cobbled market square, continuing along the main street where you may have to resist the urge to pop into the town's enticing gift shops.

If Grassington looks familiar, that may be because its timeless cobbled streets doubled up as the fictional market town of Darrowby in the 2022 TV reboot of *All Creatures Great and Small*, based on the memoirs of real-life Yorkshire vet, James Alfred Wight. With no modern houses in the town centre, not a lot needed to change but a number of shop fronts were transformed into late 1930s style and The Devonshire pub became the TV show's Drover's Arms.

Leaving the town, the route picks up the long-distance Dales Way path, firstly along a track then across several fields by way of

INFORMATION

Village pavements, a gentle climb onto grassy moorland, well-trodden woodland paths and narrow riverside trails. Some stiles. You may encounter livestock.

DISTANCE: 5.5 miles
TIME: 2.5 hours
MAP: OS Explorer OL2 Yorkshire Dales, Southern and Western
START & END POINT: Yorkshire Dales National Park Visitor Centre car park, Grassington (SE 002 637, 54.0698, -1.9967)
PUBLIC TRANSPORT: Bus Services 72, 72A, 72B (Skipton, Grassington, Buckden), 74 (Wigginton, Grassington), 74A (Hebden, Grassington, Ilkley), 822 (York, Ripon, Grassington), 874, 875, 876 (Ilkley, Hawes)
SWIMMING: River Wharfe, Grass Wood, Ghaistrill's Strid, Grassington Weir and Linton Falls
PLACES OF INTEREST: Limestone pavement, Grassington Moor, Grass Wood ancient woodland, Ghaistrill's Strid
REFRESHMENTS: There are several good cafés and pubs in Grassington, including The Stripey Badger (BD23 5AQ, 01756 753583). This award-winning independent book shop, coffee shop and kitchen is known for its Ploughman's platters but also does delicious afternoon teas.
NEARBY SWIM SPOTS: River Wharfe, Appletreewick
EASIER ACCESS: Linton Falls is a short walk from the National Park car park

stiles and stone steps, passing the site of a medieval village (between ❷ & ❸). The Dales Way trail is well-trodden and signposted and it is only once you have scaled the last stone steps that you need to make sure you follow the correct path. As the Dales Way climbs away to the right, the route forks left. Don't forget to soak up the superb views behind you over Grassington and towards Cracoe Fell as you continue to ascend the sloped path ❸.

Take a moment to observe the unique landscape here as the route traverses sections of distinctive limestone pavement, made up of clints (flat slabs of Carboniferous limestone) and grykes (the cracks in between). These pavements were created during the Ice Age when the scouring action of ice sheets exposed the pavements, their cracks widening with the movement of water through them to create crevices. Today the clints provide ideal habitats for light-loving limestone grassland plants like common rock-rose, small scabious, thyme, bee and pyramidal orchids while the grykes provide

sheltered conditions for shade-loving plants - look out for frilly fronds of green spleenwort peeking out from hollows in the cracks.

Cairns, the embankments of ancient settlements and field systems have also sculpted the terrain here. This area, known as Lea Green, was one of the largest Iron Age settlements in England. Occupied from 200 BC to 400 AD, it only survived the Roman occupation because of its secluded location high up on the moors. The entire area is one of the richest archaeological sites in the UK, much of it intact and still visible due to the relocation of modern-day settlement to Grassington.

As the path edges closer to the dry-stone wall bordering Bastow Wood, there are far-reaching views all around. Leaving the moorland track through a gate, an uphill path cuts across a glorious area of limestone heathland, studded with silver birch trees, towards the entrance of Grass Wood, a nature reserve managed by the Yorkshire Wildlife Trust ❹.

This ancient ash woodland, over limestone scars, is one of the largest areas of broad-leaved wood in the Dales - and utterly beautiful. In springtime the woodland comes alive with birds nesting and raising their young, from elusive mottled-brown woodcocks, chaffinches and green woodpeckers, with their loud, laughing 'yaffle' to returning migratory birds such as pied and spotted flycatchers and wood and willow warblers. The woodland floor is carpeted with bluebells, surrendering later to lily of the valley, betony, St John's Wort and bloody cranesbill. And, on the higher slopes, many species of butterflies and moths can be spotted including, if you are lucky, the rare northern brown argus.

The path twists between the trees to a country lane then drops into Lower Grass Wood, ancient woodland on the fringes of the River Wharfe **6**. There are several routes through the trees but keeping close to the riverbank means you can access the swim spots easily. There are several places along the river to find secluded river pools **7**. On our first trip here, we swam in one shaded pool before discovering another beautiful, wide sunny stretch a little further along, on a meander of the river, with smooth stone slabs for getting changed **8**. The water is the colour of pale ale - and bracing; even on a warm day, the Wharfe can be slow to warm up so be prepared for an invigorating swim.

For the rest of the walk, the path sticks close to the riverbank, widening to a river meadow and an outcrop of rocks, beyond which is Ghaistrill's Strid, a powerful stretch of the Wharfe where the water is squeezed through rocky channels **9**. There is lots of fun to be had here with a chute for tubing and pools below for snorkelling and swimming, plus several smaller - and warmer - rock pools. However, deciding whether to swim

in this stretch of the river requires a good degree of judgement. The Wharfe is unpredictable and water levels can rise in hours. It is dangerous to attempt to enter the water here in flood or high water; if in doubt, it is best to admire this dramatic feature from the water's edge and move on to the next swim spot.

Continuing alongside the river, then through a field grazed by cattle, the path heads towards the town's 17th-century bridge. Beyond is a large, grassy expanse of riverside common with two weirs and a waterfall at Linton Falls, providing the setting for another adventurous dip **11**. This is a popular place with families in the summer months, some of them slithering down the smooth stone slope of the weir on the far side of the river.

The homeward stretch follows a narrow path back to the National Park Visitor Centre. If any of the pubs or cafés in the town centre caught your attention earlier, you can return to them after your walk and reflect on a day full of adventures.

1 From the National Park Visitor Centre car park turn left towards Grassington town centre. At the crossroads, turn right up Main Street. Continue past the shops to a building with a large white clock face on the right - the Devonshire Institute. Turn left onto Chapel Street and continue for around 200m.

2 Just before a farm, turn right onto Bank Lane, following the Dales Way footpath (signed Kettlewell) onto a walled track. As the lane veers right, go through a narrow metal gate on the left, following the Dales Way. Cross the field to a through-stile in a wall opposite. Once over this, bear left, descending to a signed and gated gap stile on the right. Then strike across another field to a narrow squeeze stile, just beyond a fenced and gated section. Cross the next field to the far side where it bears left beside a wall. Pass a gap in the wall and look for another squeeze stile on the right. Go through this and head for another stile a short distance away, onto Lea Green, the site of ancient settlements and an expanse of limestone pavement.

3 Once over the wall, after 70m look out for a faint left-hand fork onto a footpath that diverges from the Dales Way. It is not the first flatter, grassy track you come to but the next one, although both head in a similar direction. Follow this grassy path as it ascends onto the moorland with soaring views behind you and, before long, large slabs of limestone pavement to

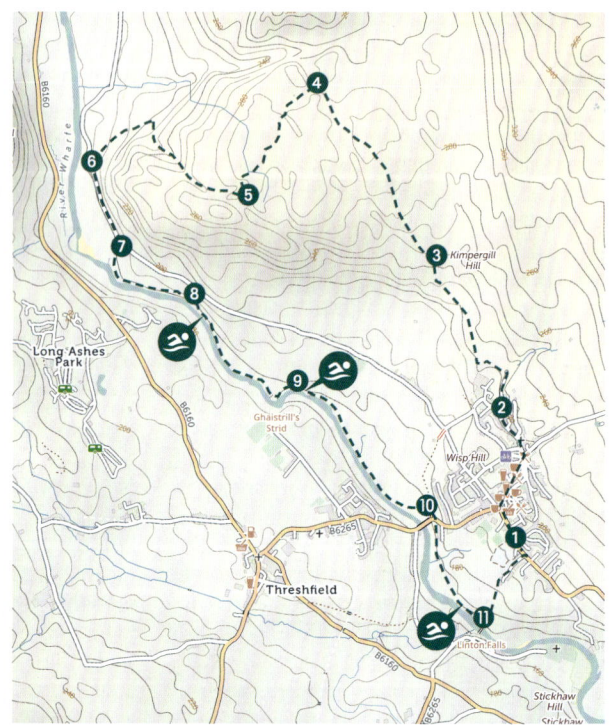

the left and smaller sections to the right. The path becomes rockier and continues to a plateau with 360-degree views, gradually edging closer to a stone wall on the left.

4 Look for a wooden gate on the left and go through this. Follow the ascending footpath straight ahead through heathland and pockets of silver birch. The path undulates, winding through the trees, becoming narrower and rockier underfoot before reaching a wall with a wooden stile. Climb over this to enter Grass Wood Nature Reserve. Follow the wider track downhill to a T-junction and fingerpost.

5 Turn right, following the footpath sign for Grass Wood Lane. Continue downhill along this track. The route veers sharply to the left, eventually reaching a gate onto Grass Wood Lane.

6 Go through the gate and turn left onto the lane. After 500m,

as the road rises, look for a wooden kissing gate on the right into Lower Grass Wood. Go through this.

7 Follow the middle path down to the pebbly riverside. There are several swim spots to choose from. However, for the best of them continue along the rocky riverside path which occasionally rises above the river.

8 Look out for two boulders and some smoothly sculpted steps down to the river on the right. Go down the steps to a beautiful, wide river pool for your first swim. Afterwards, return to the path and continue downstream, passing through a wooden gate into a grassy river meadow. Continue along the riverbank to a footpath sign and pass between some rocky boulders.

9 The river narrows here as the water rushes through Ghaistrill's Strid. You can stop for a dip here

but only if water levels are not high. There are several pools and chutes. Afterwards, climb a tall ladder stile and continue along a short, enclosed path, then over two stone stiles. Follow the paved path then continue past fenced fields on the left, keeping on the riverside path until you reach a gate at the end. Go through this into a field and head towards the bridge. Ascend the path to the left of the bridge to the road.

10 Cross the road and look for a footpath sign opposite, continuing in the same direction into a large river meadow where you will find Grassington Weir and Linton Falls, the last swim spot.

11 Afterwards, continue to the gate in the wall. Go through this and turn left onto a path leading directly back to Hebden Road and the National Park Visitor Centre car park.

Walk 12

HEBDEN, LOUP SCAR AND SCALE HAW FORCE

Stroll beside the River Wharfe, soaking up the dramatic Loup Scar gorge and one of Yorkshire's finest swim spots, plus a dip in Hebden's hidden waterfall

INFORMATION

Country lanes, well-trodden riverside paths, some indistinct footpaths and climbs through grassy slopes. A short, rocky scramble to a waterfall.

DISTANCE: 4.5 miles
TIME: 2.25 hours
MAP: OS Explorer OL2 Yorkshire Dales, Southern and Western
START & END POINT: Hebden, Mill Lane (SE 026 630, 54.0630, -1.9606)
PUBLIC TRANSPORT: 74A (Ilkley, Grassington, Burnsall), 822 (York, Ripon, Grassington)
SWIMMING: River Wharfe at Loup Scar, Burnsall and Scale Haw Force waterfall
PLACES OF INTEREST: Loup Scar, St Wilfrid's Church in Burnsall
REFRESHMENTS: The charming Old School Tea Room, Hebden (BD23 5DX, 01756 753778), is hard to resist with its freshly-baked cakes and scones and vintage afternoon teas. The Red Lion at Burnsall is also en route while the historic Craven Arms at Appletreewick (BD23 6DA, 01756 720270), is a short drive away, with a thatched cruck barn and fireside bar inside and sweeping valley views outside.
NEARBY SWIM SPOTS: River Wharfe, Appletreewick
EASIER ACCESS: The swim spot downstream of Loup Scar can be reached by following the footpath next to the church then walking 300m upstream.

This is a ramble full of variety, taking in a dramatic section of the River Wharfe between Hebden and Burnsall as well as a secluded valley where a beck tumbles entrancingly via a waterfall and plunge pool. Further swim spots along this figure-of-eight walk range from languid, tree-fringed river pools to the striking limestone gorge of Loup Scar. At the latter, the river forms rapids and a cavernous pool into which fearless teenagers plunge from the clifftop above. One of the best swim spots in the Dales is a few metres downstream, a wide, tranquil section of river adjacent to a large grassy bank that's perfect for sprawling out on after a swim. The return leg of the walk climbs above the river, affording superb views over Burnsall and the surrounding countryside, before following a final loop along Hebden Beck to a very pretty waterfall.

Starting from Main Street in Hebden, there is on-street parking near the Old School Tea Room. The village sits on an ancient route used by the Cistercian monks of Fountains Abbey in the 13th century to move their flocks of sheep across Hebden Beck up to higher pastures in Wharfedale, Malhamdale and the Lake District.

During the 18th and 19th centuries, lead mining and cotton joined Hebden's industrial story. The last section of Hebden Beck before its confluence with the River Wharfe was used to power a corn mill in the Middle Ages but in 1791 a three-storey cotton mill was built there too. When more efficient steam-driven machinery came along, the mill could not compete and it closed down in 1870 before being demolished in 1967. Strolling along Mill Lane today, past cattle-grazed meadows bounded by dry stone walls, there is little evidence of this small village's industrial chapter.

Leaving this country lane, the route joins the Dales Way towards a suspension bridge and stepping stones across the river ❷. Until the 19th century the stepping stones were the only way to cross the river here, a precarious passage only possible when the water was low. Locals tell stories of people slipping on the stones and losing their lives in these fast-flowing, unpredictable waters. The stones are still very slippery so take care! After the closest bridge, at Burnsall, was largely destroyed in the floods of 1883, it was decided that a proper bridge crossing was needed at Hebden;

the ensuing suspension bridge was built by Hebden blacksmith William Bell, mainly from materials recycled from the lead mines. Opened in 1885, and quickly dubbed the swing bridge by locals alarmed at how much it swayed, the bridge still stands, and still wobbles, today.

Around half a mile downstream, the river makes a dramatic twist and the water has scoured out lofty limestone banks to form the steep crags of Loup Scar (between ❷ and ❸). There is often a small gathering here as daredevils leap into the plunge pool below. Downstream, the path opens out onto a sublime stretch of grassy riverside with beaches and meadows, spangled with wildflowers in summer and punctuated by smooth slabs of cream limestone. It is an enticing swim spot with a wide, deep pool the colour of Yorkshire tea, and a rope swing dangling from a tree on the root-tangled banks opposite.

The riverside path continues, passing the terrace of the Red Lion pub, in Burnsall. The story goes that the pub has a cheeky resident ghost who turns off the beer taps from time to time - so be warned if you are hoping to quench your thirst here. Beyond Burnsall Bridge a grassy river meadow stretches out, encircled by a loop in the Wharfe. It is often busy with day-trippers, particularly with families in the summer, the children paddling and playing in the shallows ❸.

With its idyllic location, flanked by the Wharfe, Burnsall is hailed as one of the Dales' most pictur-esque villages. It was originally an Anglo-Viking settlement and the parish church of St Wilfrid's contains rare Viking and Anglo-Saxon carved stones. A small exhibition inside the church tells their story.

After crossing Burnsall's historic packhorse bridge, and descending a stone staircase to a meadow, look out for an old notice etched on the side of the bridge, referring to some 17th-century repairs – and their cost **4**. There are beautiful views from here back towards Burnsall and St Wilfrid's Church, with the fells as a backdrop as the route follows the river upstream through rippling meadows. Pretty purple harebells fringe the stony path in summer and gnarled trees cling to the vertiginous river bank as it enters Skuff Wood.

The craggy limestone outcrop of Wilfrid Scar **6** is, like the nearby church, named after one of the greatest English saints. St Wilfrid of Ripon is reputed to have preached from this crag in the 7th century, baptising converts to Christianity. Wilfrid founded monasteries at nearby Ripon and at Hexham, in Northumberland, and became Bishop of York. Leaving the craggy slopes behind, the route joins Burnsall Lane, a quiet country road, flanked by moss-smothered dry stone walls and soaring, wide-open scenery.

A short beck-side ramble leads back to Hebden and the next leg of the walk which visits the picturesque waterfall of Scale Haw Force. These hidden falls are only a short distance from the village yet remain off the radar for many visitors. A steep scramble down a grassy bank and a careful walk upstream lead to this tumbling white curtain as it cascades down a sheer rock face into a refreshing plunge pool **9**. Hazel trees cling to the steep-sided riverbanks, and wagtails can often be seen bobbing up and down on the rocks.

It is best to get changed on the grassy bank leading up to the falls as there is not much room for manoeuvre further upstream. After a dip in the pool, hop over the stepping stones to climb the hill towards the craggy scar ahead. In summer lush, green ferns smother these slopes, sprinkled with the pink spires of foxgloves. This can make

it tricky to locate the exact footpath but keeping the crags in sight then veering right gets you onto the right path.

Descending sheep-grazed pastures back into Hebden, there are lovely views of the surrounding fells and meadows, criss-crossed with dry stone walls. After passing a cluster of stone cottages and some pretty beck-side gardens, the route crosses a small bridge over the beck to the start of the walk, hopefully with enough time to pop into the Old School Tea Room for a well-deserved coffee and a slice of cake.

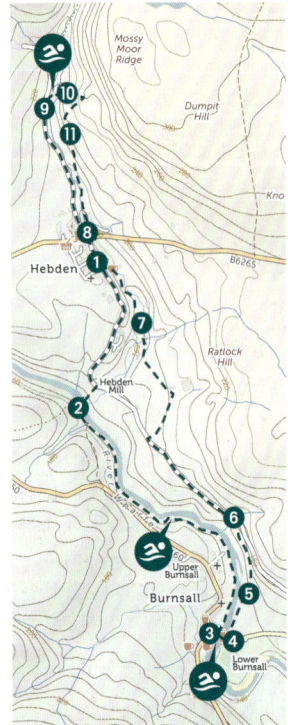

area next to a large, deep pool, perfect for a swim. After your dip, rejoin the riverside path and continue to Burnsall Bridge, passing the Red Lion pub on your right.

3 The stretch of river on the other side of the bridge is a popular place for paddling and swimming and you may wish to stop here too. Otherwise turn left across the bridge.

4 Look for a footpath sign on the left, signed Scuff Road. Go through the squeeze in the wall, down steep stone steps into a field with the river on your left. Cross this field and go through another gated squeeze. Follow the field edge and look out for a ladder stile ahead with fingerposts.

5 Next, choose your path carefully. Do not take the steep path up the field towards a dry stone wall. Instead take the path that ascends gently uphill, rising above the river to a fence on the left. Continue along this path, as the views widen over Burnsall. Go through a wooden gate into Skuff Wood. Follow a level gravel path, with views over the river and beyond. The path eventually curves right at the wooded ravine of Wilfrid Scar to a gated squeeze onto a country lane.

6 Turn left onto the lane and head towards Hebden. Just after a 'bend in the road' sign turn right onto the driveway of Ranelands Farm. This becomes a footpath through the farmyard. Go through

a metal gate between some barns and cross the field ahead diagonally to another metal gate in the corner, leading onto a track through a field with the beck and a footpath sign on the left.

7 Cross a small stone slab over the beck and continue along a stone-flagged path. Cross a wooden bridge over the beck, with a cascade to the right. Continue along the footpath, through a wooden gate, keeping the beck on your right and passing the remains of an old mine. Climb over stone steps in the wall and follow the obvious gravel and cobbled path to a metal gate onto Mill Lane. You can end your walk here or stop for refreshments at the tea room before continuing to Scale Haw Force. For Scale Haw Force, follow Mill Lane to the main B6265 road.

8 Cross the road carefully and follow the lane opposite, with the beck and stone bridge to your right. Pass some cottages on the left before emerging back into open countryside. Pass through an open wooden gate and look for a green shed on the right, beyond the stone wall. Just after this go through a gate and follow a footpath on the right, signed towards Edge Top.

9 Follow the grassy path towards the beck and Scale Haw Force, which you will hear. Look for the stepping stones. A vague path zig zags down to the beck. Follow this and walk upstream on the grassy bank to reach the falls. After your dip, return to cross the stepping stones.

1 Park along Main Street and follow this south, as it morphs into Mill Lane, to leave the village. As the lane bears left look for a Dales Way footpath and gate on the right and follow this, crossing a field to the river (there is pebble beach and swim spot about 300m upstream if you want an early dip). Cross the river via the bridge or the stepping stones.

2 Turn left onto the riverside path and continue through a couple of gates to the limestone gorge of Loup Scar. Just ahead is a grassy

10 Follow the path that rises left up the hill, heading towards the crags. At a clearing, turn right, just before a large oak and a sycamore tree. Go through a gap in the wall to a fork in the path. Keep right, following the grassy path towards a dry stone wall, with splendid Dales views ahead. Keeping the stone wall to your left, continue to a step stile into another field and continue, with a stone wall to your right.

11 Pass through another stile at the end of the wall. The grassy path gradually descends towards the beck. Pass through a small gate and look for a metal bridge. Do not cross this, instead follow the narrow path beside the beck, to your right. Pass through another small wooden gate, past a small enclave of cottages and beck-side verandas. Cross the bridge then turn immediately left to cross the main road back to Main Street.

Walk 13

NIDD GORGE

A short stroll through ancient broadleaved woodland, never straying far from the River Nidd as it meanders through this sheltered, sun-dappled gorge

INFORMATION

Woodland walk along well-trodden forest tracks, uneven riverside paths and steps. Can be muddy.

DISTANCE: 1.75 miles

TIME: 1 hour

MAP: OS Explorer 297 Lower Wharfedale and Washburn Valley

START & END POINT: Nidd Gorge car park, Ripley Road (SE 330 584, 54.0211, -1.4973)

PUBLIC TRANSPORT: Trains to Knaresborough. Buses to Knaresborough include Services 1, 1A, 1B, 1C, 1D (Harrogate), 8 (Harrogate, Wetherby), 21 (Boroughbridge), 74 (Wigginton, Grassington), 82, 83 (Ripon, York), 182 (Ripon), 825 (York, Fountain's Abbey). Service 182 stops at Scotton Drive, very close to the start of the walk.

SWIMMING: River pools along the River Nidd

PLACES OF INTEREST: Knaresborough Castle, Knaresborough Viaduct

REFRESHMENTS: There are several cafés in Knaresborough. Try The Ugly Duckling Tearoom (HG5 9AX, 01423 868090), a riverside spot popular with walkers and cyclists.

NEARBY SWIM SPOTS: Knaresborough Lido, River Nidd, is a wide, shallow swim spot next to the Watermill Café. Or River Nidd at Conyngham Hall, accessed from Conyngham Hall car park.

EASIER ACCESS: There is a small beach and swim spot by the Burgess Bridge

Ancient deciduous woodland cloaks the steep-sided ravine of the Nidd Gorge, a deep sandstone valley carved out during the last Ice Age. The River Nidd twists and tumbles for three miles through this imposing canyon, its shoreline flanked by hazel, alder and oak trees and several secluded, sandy beaches with enticing pools for swimming.

Ribbons of green on the doorsteps of Knaresborough and Harrogate, the main trails through the gorge are popular at weekends, though the narrow riverside paths are often quieter. Early evening or first thing in the morning are the best times to visit with more chance of having the place to yourself on the fleeting forays this pocket-sized walk lends itself to.

Despite the walk's short length, however - it focuses on the best sections of river for swimming and paddling – a multitude of paths and tracks lace the woodland, giving many options for longer strolls. Venturing upstream, for instance, leads to the Nidd Viaduct, a series of graceful arches that once carried North East Railway Line trains from Leeds to Thirsk and is now part of the Nidderdale Greenway, a Sustrans cycle path. Downstream is Knaresborough with another imposing viaduct as well as a castle, and a host of independent shops and cafés.

Leaving behind the hum and clatter of cars on Ripley Road, the walk starts at the northern edge of the gorge's woodland, following a broad, leafy track. Strolling here, you're immediately doused in melodious birdsong; listen out for the joyful trilling of song thrushes, chiffchaffs, goldfinches and robins as you amble downhill, towards the river. The gurgling waters of the River

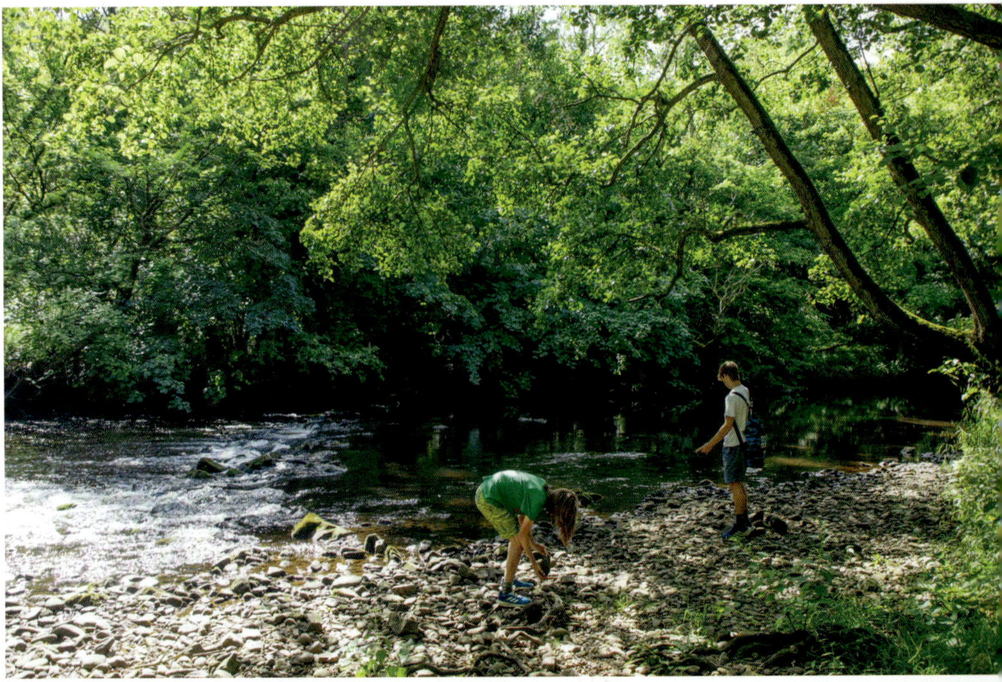

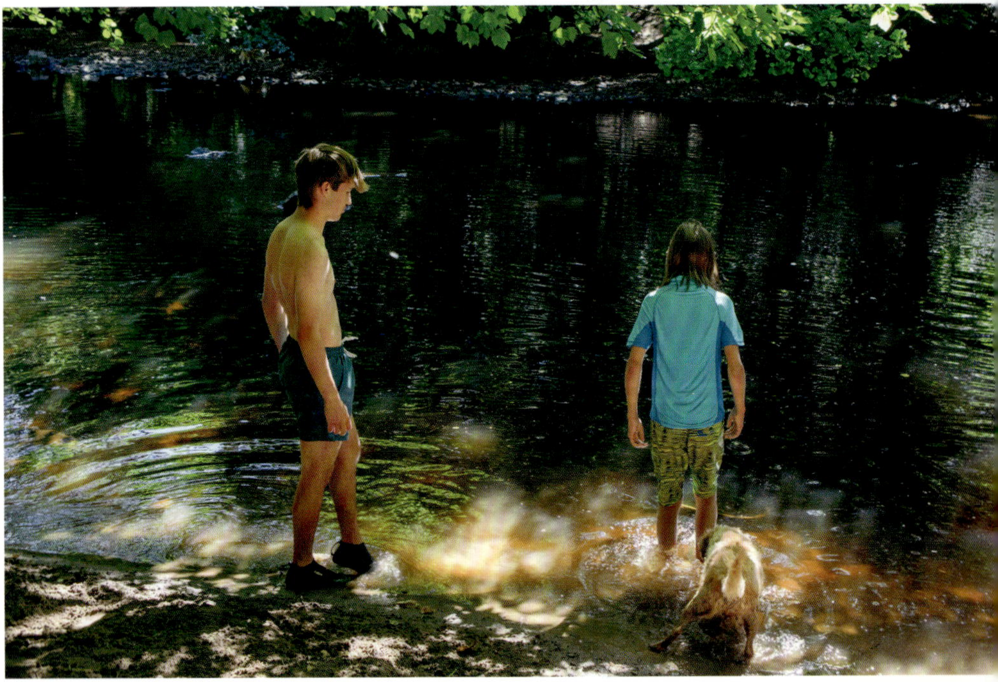

Nidd glint through the trees as you go, offering a tempting glimpse of what is to come.

Burgess Bridge is the only crossing of the river along the entire gorge. However, the route sticks to the main forest track for now. The 114-acre gorge is made up of five woodlands: Coal Pits Wood, Bilton Banks, Spring Wood, Scotton Banks and Gates Wood. Coal Pits Wood, on the river's south bank, hints at past industry; coal deposits were worked here in the 18th and 19th centuries though today any industriousness is restricted to the rootling and rustling of roe deer, badgers and foxes.

As the track rises, it cuts a path through mixed deciduous woodland, fringed with stands of conifers, sitka spruce and Corsican pines. These lofty trees were planted in the 1960s but are now subject to a programme of thinning to encourage the re-establishment of natural flora such as celandine, wood sorrel, wood anemone and bluebells, whose green foliage and flowers peak out amongst patches of sunlight on the woodland floor in late spring. Also shrouded by trees is the site of an Iron Age hill fort at Scotton Banks. Now overgrown, local legend tells of its use by Colonel Fairfax's Roundheads, who apparently mounted cannon within the fort's defences during their 1644 siege of Knaresborough Castle.

From here, the track drops down to the river, where a small beach slopes into a calm river pool. It's possible to take a dip here ❷ but more secluded swim spots can be found by following the river upstream along the narrow riverside path. Along this magical stretch of trail, the gnarly knuckles of tree roots protrude and tiny streams tumble over gleaming woodland mosses

into the river, making the route uneven and muddy in parts.

The path tails off as it runs into craggy cliffs and diverges up a steep set of steps, arriving back on the forest track for only a few metres before descending to the river again ❸. Hidden among the crags is Jack Carter's Cave. It is said that Jack was a Civil War soldier who hid in a cave here; as hiding places go it is certainly a good one since there is no evidence of it now, despite it being featured on OS maps.

As the route rejoins the riverside, it ribbons alongside the rippling water to a sandy beach with a rope swing and a fun place for a dip ❹. Floating here, beneath a canopy of leaves in the magical surroundings of the gorge is a restorative experience. Look out for grey wagtails and dippers bobbing in the water beside you and keep an ear out for the creaking song of the siskin.

Further along is another wide, sandy beach, this one with a shallow entry into a calm river pool. Greenery has colonised the trees here, garlands of ivy draping around the thick trunks or dangling decoratively over the water. From here Burgess Bridge is visible a little further upstream ❺. It is worth taking a detour onto the bridge as it is an excellent vantage point from which to soak up the scenery up and down the gorge.

If you want to explore further, you can cross the bridge and join the riverside path in either direction. The walk towards the Nidd Viaduct is particularly attractive, passing through riverside meadows and more pools. Otherwise, a forest track winds up through the trees, back to the starting point of this sensory woodland trail.

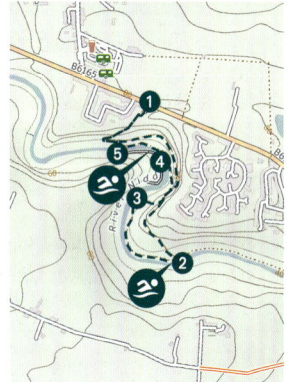

1 From the car park, follow the broad forest track downhill as it zig zags towards the river. The route curves round, past a stone wall and a footbridge, along the river's north bank, gradually climbing above the river. Stay on this track and go over a crossroads of paths to descend to the water's edge.

2 To the left of a fingerpost is a small beach where you can take a dip. Afterwards return to the fingerpost and continue along the uneven riverside path, past a bench. Pass a small island in the river. Just after it is another possible swim spot. However, the best swim spots are a little further along.

3 The path leaves the river up a steep set of steps to rejoin the forestry track. After a few metres, go down the steps to rejoin the riverside path. The path becomes rocky and can be muddy.

4 After a few metres you reach a wide, sandy beach with a rope swing. This is a good place to stop for a swim or paddle, particularly if you have children in tow. Afterwards continue along the path; this rises gently above the water then returns to it. There is another wide, sandy beach here, not far from the footbridge, where you can also dip.

5 After your swim, continue to Burgess Bridge then turn right up the steps then a left to join the forest path back to the car park.

Walk 14

RIVER OUSE AT BENINGBROUGH

A gentle stroll through splendid 18th-century parkland to a wide, sandy beach and further swim spots along the meandering River Ouse.

*N*ine miles north-west of York, Beningbrough is a popular day trip for visitors to the city, who come here to visit the elegant Baroque mansion of Beningbrough Hall and its beautiful gardens. This National Trust-owned estate is also cherished by locals who enjoy walks on their doorstep through glorious 18th-century parkland, fairytale woodland trails, idyllic riverside paths and meadows with sweeping views across the park. The house sits on the banks of the River Ouse and a walk through the grounds, with a dip or two in the river, makes for a gentle and accessible swim-walk. The walk is best done in summer as the river can flood the beaches and surrounding 'Ings' (water meadows) in the wetter months, making the route impassable. The first of the swims is at a popular 'beach' at the confluence of the rivers Ouse and Nidd, with a couple more secluded beaches upstream. If cool, thirst-quenching refreshment is on your mind as you finish the walk you will be delighted to know that this swim-walk passes through the gorgeous riverside beer garden of the historic Dawnay Arms on its return.

The walk starts from the pretty village of Newton-on-Ouse, with on-street parking near the village green. A gentle stroll along aptly-named Cherry Tree Avenue is particularly dazzling in spring when the cherry blossom is in full bloom. Passing the 12th-century All Saints church, the route arrives at the gatehouse to Beningbrough Hall ❷ before following a tree-lined avenue to the house. After a glimpse of the red brick hall through the trees, its full Baroque splendour soon comes into view. The house was built in 1716 by York landowner John Bourchier to replace the modest Elizabethan manor he had unexpectedly inherited aged just 16. After more than 100 years of ownership under the

INFORMATION

A level walk along a tarmac driveway to Beningbrough Hall then riverside and woodland paths. Can be muddy after rain. Liable to flooding. You may encounter cattle.

DISTANCE: 4 miles
TIME: 1.45 hours
MAP: OS Explorer 290 York
START & END POINT: Newton-on-Ouse, roadside parking near village green (SE 511 600, 54.0336, -1.2204)
PUBLIC TRANSPORT: Bus Service 80 (Raskelf, York)
SWIMMING: Two stretches of the River Ouse at Beningbrough
PLACES OF INTEREST: Beningbrough Hall and Gardens
REFRESHMENTS: The Dawnay Arms at Newton-on-Ouse (YO30 2BR, 01347 848345) is an obvious place to stop as the walk passes through its inviting beer garden, overlooking the river. Equally welcoming is the Blacksmith's Arms (YO30 2BN, 01347 848249), also in the village.
NEARBY SWIM SPOTS: River Ure, Aldwark Toll Bridge
EASIER ACCESS: There is a small car park at the Beningbrough Lane entrance to Beningbrough Hall with a 0.75 mile walk to the first swim spot.

Yorkshire to admire these beautiful native wildflowers, which thrive in pockets of ancient woodland such as this. Artfully carved wooden benches provide seating along the route, with different aspects of the hall visible through the trees. A further loop in the path to the left circles medieval pike ponds that were dug out, lined with clay and used to keep fish to supply the hall's kitchens.

Bear in mind the paths through these woods can get very muddy after rain so if you prefer, you could stay on the driveway instead and rejoin the walk at the end of the gated woodland trail ❹. The mixed deciduous copse extends across the driveway where, in autumn, purple-staining blackberries provide a handy foraged snack as the route winds through the trees, picking up a riverside path beside the Ouse. Vegetation is abundant along the riverbank, with pretty purple wood cranesbill spilling across the footpath.

Bourchiers, the estate passed to the Dawnays, an old Yorkshire family with strong links to Parliament, the church and army. However by 1916, its owner, Guy Dawnay, an army officer, decided to sell the estate, opting for a career in investment banking instead. The last private owners were the Chesterfields of Holme Lacey, who offered the estate to the Treasury to pay death duties on Lady Chesterfield's death, in 1957. It was acquired by the National Trust the following year.

At a grassy triangle you will no doubt find yourself reaching for your camera to snap away at the attractive vista of the tree-lined avenue as it sweeps towards the grand country house. A little way further along, the route detours briefly from the main driveway, along a short woodland trail. If you are lucky enough to be visiting in springtime, you will be treated to the heady scent of bluebells, their delicate purple bells radiating out in a haze of violet beneath the tree trunks ❸. This is one of the best places in North

As the Ouse meanders sharply to the right, at its confluence with the River Nidd, it has created a wide, sandy cove: a fantastic spot to cool off with a dip ❺. The beach plays host to locals and visitors alike on a hot summer's day so expect company. Having said this, we have been here on warm days and had the place to ourselves so you might find the same in anything less than tropical weather. The river has a shallow entry, gradually getting deeper further out, and there is sometimes a tree swing here where daredevils can leap into the deep water. Avoid swimming too close to where the two rivers meet, however, as there are strong currents and turbulent eddies. You are also likely to encounter some river traffic here so make sure you are visible to passing boats and paddle boarders; it might be a good idea to use a tow float. The jetty opposite was in use until recently, connecting the villages of Nun Monkton, Moor Monkton and

Beningbrough via the 'Bryan Ferry' riverboat. It is sad that this closed in 2023 as it was run by a team of enthusiastic volunteers for the benefit of locals and visitors and was the continuation of a long tradition: an ancient ferry crossing was first recorded here in 1174, when the priory of Benedictine nuns was founded at Nun Monkton, and until 1952 a small passenger ferry operated, where villagers rang a loud bell to cross the water between Nun Monkton and Beningbrough.

The yellow flower brightening up the riverbank in summer is Tansy, often mistaken for Ragwort, and the sole food source for the Tansy beetle. This eye-catching iridescent green beetle is nationally rare and its home here, on the banks of the River Ouse, may be its most northerly habitation. In order for the beetle to survive, the clumps of aromatic Tansy need to be close enough together to walk between as the beetles rarely fly. As you pack up your swim things and continue along the path, you will notice an abundance of one particular plant - Himalayan Balsam. Its bright magenta flowers may look attractive but this gargantuan runaway weed colonises riverbanks in late summer, squeezing out native species such as Tansy, which end up too far apart for the beetles to find. The Himalayan Balsam's explosive seed pods pop out at speed, sending seeds into the river, and dispersing them up and downstream.

As you wander upstream, along the narrow riverside path, there are fleeting glimpses of the hall and parkland. After passing a red-brick Victorian water tower **6**, used to bring water to the hall and, at one time, to an ice skating pond, the route opens out into unfenced, cattle-grazed parkland. As the path forks, most people tend to take the right-hand fork which leads back to Newton-on-Ouse, however, by sticking with the riverside path, you will discover two more sandy beaches along this stretch - tranquil spots for a second - and third - swim. Entry to the water is shallow, deepening towards the opposite bank. In high summer, be mindful of weeds in the shallower parts of the river and also keep an eye out for passing river traffic. The meadow is an idyllic spot to enjoy a picnic before wending your way back to Newton-on-Ouse. The rest of the footpath cuts across the lower slopes of private gardens that stretch right down to the water's edge. This is private property so keep to the footpath, which is clearly marked and eventually arrives at the bottom of the Dawnay Arms' beer garden **7**. Beyond here, the footpath continues to the road and back to the village. However, a refreshing drink in the garden of this 18th-century inn, with the silvery-grey river sliding by, is a perfect end to this enjoyable swim-walk.

1 From parking near the village green, continue south along Cherry Tree Avenue, past the church on the right and the Blacksmiths Arms on the left, to Beningbrough Hall entrance gates.

2 Follow the driveway through parkland. This is a shared road so cars will pass by, hopefully at slow speed. The road curves left with your first glimpse of Beningbrough Hall through the trees. At a triangle of grass, continue straight ahead, not towards the hall, and look for a gate on the left, signed 'larch walk'. This short loop is well worth taking in spring when the bluebells are out.

3 Go through the gate and follow the permissive path for about 200m, to another gate into woodland on the right. Pass through this gate. There are several attractive, carved wooden benches along the trail and a frame that captures the landscaped parkland and hall. The path can get muddy. To the left are Medieval fishponds which you can walk around.

4 The path eventually returns to the main driveway. Cross this and go through the gate opposite, back into woodland with a large bench on the right. Follow the narrow trail through trees to a gate and information board. Go through the gate and continue, passing through two more gates. The path narrows as it weaves through the woods to

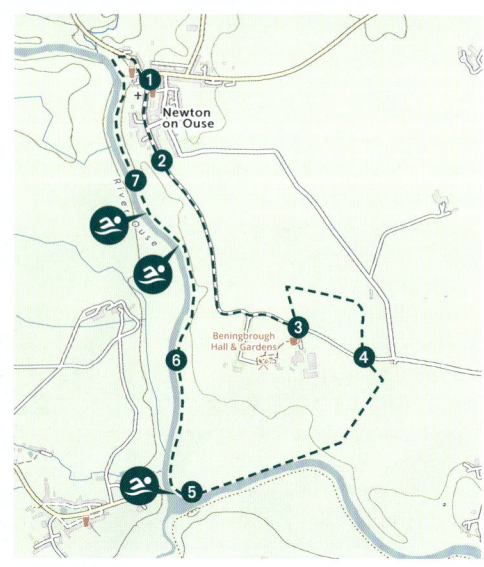

another gate. Beyond here you get glimpses of the River Nidd on your left. To your right are views across parkland to Beningbrough Hall.

5 The path soon widens to reveal a wide sandy beach at the confluence of the Rivers Nidd and Ouse. This is your first swim spot. Keep away from the confluence as currents can be strong and flow may be fast. Boats also use this stretch so make sure you are visible. After your swim, continue along the path.

6 Keep left of a brick building and go through a wooden gate before continuing between an avenue of trees to open parkland grazed by cattle. Keep close to

the riverside footpath, which passes two sandy beaches quite close together. Both offer easy access to the water for a swim.

7 After your swim, walk on to a wooden stile and continue along the narrow trail that passes through the lower reaches of private gardens. Although this is a footpath, it is private land and there is no access to the river here. After going down and up some wooden steps, the footpath enters the beer garden of the Dawnay Arms where you might like to stop for refreshments. Otherwise, continue along the path. Just before a wooden bridge, turn right to rejoin the road back to the village and your car.

DOUGLAS RIDGE AND UPPER RYE FALLS

Embrace the moodiness of the moors on this remote loop into wild country around the head of the River Rye and find a sylvan valley far from the madding crowd.

INFORMATION

A moorland walk on gravel tracks with a short section of uneven and possibly boggy open-access land beside the river. Ends with a short stretch of walking on a quiet moorland lane

DISTANCE: 4 miles
TIME: 2 hours
MAP: OS Explorer OL26 North York Moors Western Area
START & END POINT: Spacious grassy verge next to the Osmotherley - Hawnby road (SE 497 952, 54.3500, -1.2361)
PUBLIC TRANSPORT: This remote walk requires a car to get to the start
SWIMMING: Waterfalls along the Upper River Rye and at Stonymoor Sike
PLACES OF INTEREST: Nearby are the Hambledon Drove Road and Mount Grace Priory
REFRESHMENTS: Hawnby Tearoom, Hawnby (YO62 5QR, 01439 798223) is a much-loved pitstop for walkers. Also in the village is The Owl at Hawnby (YO62 5QS, 01439 330180), an elegant former drover's inn where you can soak up panoramic views from its splendid terrace after your walk.
NEARBY SWIM SPOTS: Small roadside waterfall on Blow Gill
EASIER ACCESS: Use moorland tracks rather than following the river downstream after the first falls

The River Rye starts life as a series of rivulets in a remote corner of the Cleveland Hills, a range of fells that curve around the north-western edge of the North York Moors National Park. It is not long before these gushing head-waters collect to form a series of small waterfalls that tumble through an idyllic wooded valley below Snilesworth Moor. This delightful walk combines a classic moorland hike, along access tracks, with an amble beside the river as it babbles along the valley floor, guarded by gnarly old oaks, rowan and silver birch - and a smattering of ferns in summer. This hidden vale is a serene spot that feels a long way from civilisation and is one of my family's favourite places to spend time in the great outdoors, paddling, dipping and picnicking. We often do this walk in wintertime as, once you are down in the valley, it feels quite sheltered. The three waterfalls are all small but have scoured out decent plunge pools for a cooling dip, and the shallow river is perfect for younger children to paddle and play in.

Parking for the walk is on a large, grassy clearing off the Hawnby to Osmotherley road and the scenery soars, right from the start. To the south are the whaleback massifs of Arden Great Moor and the plateau of Black Hambleton; the highest point on the Hambleton Drove Road, this is part of an ancient highway from Scotland to the south of England. Now part of the Cleveland Way national trail, it is the best-preserved drover's road in Yorkshire. It is an exhilarating walk for another day, highly recommended for its superb panoramas over the Vales of York and Mowbray, and particularly beautiful when the heather is in bloom.

Starting out along a well-laid sandy track on the lower fringes of Douglas Ridge, the walk follows one of many access routes that

slice across the swathe of heather that carpets the moorland slopes. These upper reaches are a haze of purple, amethyst and violet in late summer; at other times these atmospheric, wild uplands can feel exposed and bleak ❶. The only sounds punctuating the solitude are circling skylarks, the evocative calls of curlews performing their territorial displays and the clatter of startled grouse.

Although remote, this area is one of the largest grouse moors in the UK, owned and managed by the Snilesworth Estate. The grouse butts along the way are used during the shooting season, in early autumn, and you may notice patches of heather that have been burned, creating a patchwork of heathers varying in age and height. This scorching happens between October and mid-April across vast stretches of the North York Moors to remove old growth and provide new green shoots to feed red grouse, deer and livestock. Not everyone is happy with this practice; in the opposite camp, conservationists argue that burning grouse moors, particularly when it is carried out on blanket bog, degrades peatland habitat, reduces biodiversity and increases the risk of flooding. It is a complex, ongoing debate.

Veering right onto another well-laid track, ever-widening views of the valley open up ahead, where the River Rye, at this point a gushing moorland stream, starts its journey. From here the water flows through clear upland becks, carving out steep-sided dales before the land flattens and the river slows and broadens, swallowing up the rivers Seph, Dove and Seven to join the River Derwent in the Vale of Pickering. As it tumbles through the wooded valley north-east of Douglas Ridge, the Rye creates some delightful cascades and waterfalls.

The first of these is reached by descending to the valley floor. The waterfall is tucked away beside the track ❷. If one cascade isn't enough, you'll find another small waterfall just a few metres away, flowing from Stonymoor Sike before its confluence with the River Rye. Both have small plunge pools - perfect opportunities to cool off. Take your pick or dip in both. In high summer, the grass between the falls is smothered in waist-high ferns so, rather than beating your way through, it is best to continue a short distance along the track and access the second waterfall by way of a small bridge; this takes you to the opposite side of the stream and back to the waterfall.

The next leg of the walk crosses the streams at the watersmeet and follows the River Rye downstream. There is no footpath so it is a scramble over open-access land beside the babbling water, navigating between weathered trees and lush ferns, and crossing wooden boardwalks, to reach the next waterfall. Look out for a large stone with a flat surface, ideal for laying out a picnic ❹. This is an idyllic spot to linger, surrounded by mini falls upstream and a wider waterfall with a small plunge pool downstream.

Climbing back out of the dale along a wide, gravel track, the effort is sure to warm you up after your dip. There are expansive moorland and valley views and, to the east, beyond a patchwork of grazed pastures and mixed woodland plantations, you can

spot the 295m spike of the Bilsdale Transmitting Station looming tall on Bilsdale West Moor ❺.

Skirting the entrance to Snilesworth Lodge, the track rises steeply then flattens, flanked by an avenue of pines and cherry trees and the boundary wall of Snilesworth Lodge. After picking your way across a small section of moorland, which may be boggy, it is a short amble along a quiet moorland road back to your car, with soaring views of the surrounding fells. A pint of Timothy Taylor, or a glass of Yorkshire Wolds apple juice, on the terrace of the Owl at Hawnby - or a cup of tea and a slice of homemade cake at the Hawnby Tearooms – is the perfect way to round off this swim-walk, and reflect on a grand day out on the moors.

1 From the parking area look for a sandy track between two conifer plantations with a metal barrier just beyond. Follow this track onto moorland to the west of Douglas Ridge. After less than a mile turn right at a T-junction as views across the valley open up ahead.

2 After another half a mile, turn sharp left along a track which descends to the valley bottom and the first waterfall (River Rye), right next to the track on the right. There is another small waterfall with a plunge pool on Stonymoor Sike, a few metres away. If vegetation is abundant the bridge upstream of the falls is the best way to reach the second waterfall.

3 After your dip, head to the confluence of the two streams and cross Stonymoor Sike (you may need to remove your shoes). Now on open-access land, you need to beat your own path as there is no footpath. Keep the River Rye to your right and, beyond some trees, carefully cross a wire fence. Then climb left

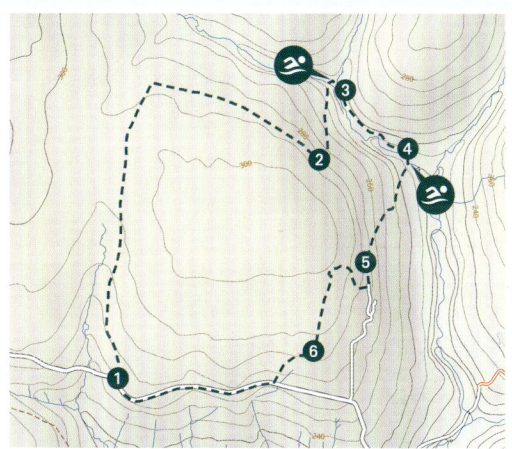

towards a stone wall and pick up a narrow path that runs parallel to it. As the wall curves away to the left, descend towards the stream and a riverside meadow (this may be smothered in vegetation in high summer). Cross one boardwalk over the stream then another to a tumbling stone wall that runs alongside the stream.

4 Cross another two boardwalks over the stream onto a grassy area

with a large boulder on the slopes of the hill. There are several small cascades upstream and a broader waterfall with a pool downstream. Afterwards, follow the gravel track up the hill.

5 At a T-junction turn left and follow the track towards a wooded area, leading to Snilesworth Lodge. Just before the lodge entrance, the track rises steeply to the right, curving round and passing a logging area on the left. Follow the track round, passing between an avenue of trees and a stone wall. Continue to the end of this track to another entrance to Snilesworth Lodge on the left.

6 Deviate right here, across a small stretch of open-access land, towards a conifer plantation and follow the perimeter of the fence (on your left) onto the lane. Turn right and follow this lane back to where you parked your car.

Walk 16

NUNNINGTON AND RIVER RYE

A ramble through bucolic meadows following the dramatic meanders of the River Rye, dipping in shaded river pools and returning beside the picturesque River Ricall.

INFORMATION

A level walk along riverbanks, tracks, lanes and field margins. Some stiles. Can be muddy in places after rain.

DISTANCE: 5.5 miles
TIME: 2.25 hours
MAP: OS Explorer 300 Howardian Hills and Malton
START & END POINT: Nunnington village car park, Station Road (SE 665 790, 54.2029, -0.9828)
PUBLIC TRANSPORT: Ryedale Community Transport operates RyeCat, a rural bus service - Service 177 (Malton, Nunnington - limited days and times)
SWIMMING: Several river pools along the River Rye
PLACES OF INTEREST: Nunnington Hall, Caulkey's Bank
REFRESHMENTS: The family-run Old Yard Coffee Shop, Nunnington (YO62 5UR, 01439 741274) serves coffees, cakes, ice creams and sandwiches in the courtyard of Nunnington Studios, a cluster of independent galleries and shops. The National Trust-managed Nunnington Hall Tearoom (YO62 5UY, 01439 748283) has a riverside tea garden and a useful kiosk window for busy summer days.
NEARBY SWIM SPOTS: River Seven at Sinnington (9 miles), Oulston Reservoir (10 miles)
EASIER ACCESS: There are some more accessible pools near the start of the walk

ippling wooded hills, scenic river valleys, honey-stone villages and historic country houses characterise the Howardian Hills. This part of North Yorkshire, a designated National Landscape, also boasts myriad tempting places to eat, drink and stay, including gastropubs such as the award-winning Star Inn At Harome, just off the route. A short distance away is Malton, Yorkshire's food capital, where artisan producers, independent shops and cafés circle the market square.

Nunnington, however, is the starting point for this swim-walk. Tucked away on the banks of the River Rye, in the north-east fringes of the Howardian Hills, the village is a good jumping-off point for excursions to the limestone ridge of Caulkey's Bank, with its superb views towards the North York Moors National Park to the north, and across the lowlands of the Vale of Pickering to the east. The village is also home to the National Trust-owned Nunnington Hall, a 17th-century manor house known for its organic walled garden, delightful flower meadows and traditional fruit orchards. It also contains one of the world's finest collections of miniature rooms in its attic, and hosts excellent art and photography exhibitions.

The walk starts from the north-west corner of the village, joining the riverside path as it meanders between low-lying pastures. The majestic River Rye rises in the moors of the Cleveland Hills and embraces 532 miles of streams, becks and twisting waterway on its journey to join the Derwent, near Malton. This serpentine river gives its name to the Ryedale district of North Yorkshire and is also the source of several legends, many of them featuring dragons, or worms as they're known locally (from the Old English, *wyrm*, and Old Norse *ormr*, meaning snake or serpent).

One old folk tale, dating back to Saxon times, is particularly attached to Nunnington. The story goes that, on a fine St Barnabas Day one summer, the harvest had been gathered and a feast was being held, the culmination of which was the crowning of the Barnabus Queen, Frances Mortain. During the procession, a huge, fire-breathing dragon appeared, snatching Frances and whisking her off to its lair on nearby Loschy Hill. Nobody dared tackle the terrifying creature except Sir Peter Loschy, a visiting knight, and member of King Arthur's court. On hearing of the maiden's plight, Sir Peter set out to slay the dragon with his faithful mastiff in tow. A hideous fight ensued; each time the knight cut the dragon, it managed to heal itself. It was only when Sir Peter hacked the dragon into pieces, carried away by the dog to bury, that the creature finally died. Though Frances was saved, that wasn't the end of the story. The dog was so pleased to have helped his master that he jumped up, licking Sir Peter's face. Unfortunately, the dragon's blood was poisonous, and both man and dog died. The pair are said to be buried together in the churchyard of All Saints and St James', Nunnington's church.

Inside the church an effigy of a knight with an animal at his feet is thought, by some, to depict Sir Peter. Others believe it is Sir Walter de Teyes, lord of the manor in the late thirteenth century. You can visit the church and decide for yourself.

Either way, you'll find Nunnington a peaceful place today. The Rye's flourishing valleys and clear waters are known for their beauty, flora, fauna and tranquility - and this section of the river ❶ is home to an abundance of wildlife, including herons, swans and kingfishers. If you visit in the early morning, you may even catch a glimpse of otters; they're known to frequent this stretch. These playful mammals are great swimmers, with long, streamlined bodies and webbed feet, and they can close their ears and nostrils under water. They are protected by law and it is illegal to hunt, trap or disturb them so if you do spot one, keep your distance.

This stretch of the Rye is also a fishing hotspot; look out for ring patterns on the water as brown trout feed on flies. The river is shrouded by over-hanging willows and alders and you may spot several ladders, placed there by anglers. There are some secluded pools for a dip but if people are fishing, move on to the next swim spots.

Beyond a footbridge the Rye takes a sinuous detour away from the footpath before circling the deciduous woodland of Plump Wood. Here, the track is edged with blackthorn and brambles, providing foraged snacks of ripe blackberries in early autumn. As the route rejoins the river, you'll spot a beach by the footbridge. This is a good entry point into the water for a swim beneath the bridge, where the water is deeper ❹.

The meadow above the river is awash with butterflies in the summer and you may spot brown hares, or just their long black-tipped ears, bounding across the fields. After drying off, the

route continues along a footpath, passing a deep pool that's good for a longer swim, just before an old, brick railway bridge ❺. There are several shaded pools with beaches along this stretch. The depth of the water depends on recent rainfall but the pools are generally more suitable for paddling and dipping than swimming. It is a pleasure to bathe in any of these pools on a summer's day, gazing up at a canopy of sycamore and hazel as dragonflies and damselflies flit around you. If you are lucky, you may see the aquamarine flash of a kingfisher darting across the water.

Further along the river the water spools out in a dramatic loop, just before a pocket of private woodland, and the riverside path emerges onto a track at Harome Siding ❼, part of the former Pickering to Gilling railway line. After passing old railway cottages, the route diverges through arable fields, following the River Ricall. In spring and summer, this stretch of water is festooned with mats of flowering water-crowfoot ❽, and there's a good chance of spotting dippers and pied wagtails. You might also catch a glimpse of barn owls or common buzzards circling the open farmland, hunting for prey such as small birds, rabbits and earthworms. Leaving the river to skirt Crook House Farm, the walk then leads back into Nunnington, trailing field margins.

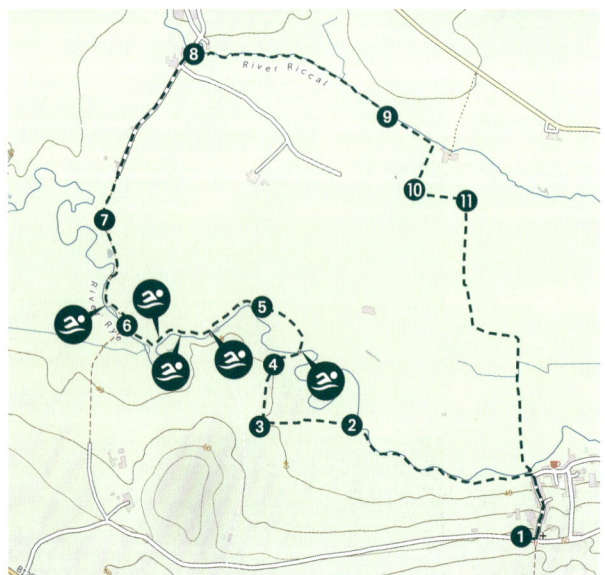

Continue along the footpath beside an arable field. The river is obscured behind trees on the left. Cross another wooden bridge over a small stream and continue. There is a deep pool suitable for a swim next to the old railway bridge. Afterwards, pass under this brick bridge, past more secluded river pools with shingle beaches, hidden behind the trees.

6 Pass a ford on the left. Shortly afterwards the path diverts left into woodland, edging the riverbank. There are more pools here. The path re-emerges into the field, passing a footbridge on the left, with a metal gate ahead. Go through the gate, past a sharp meander of the river, and continue along a grassy path beside a private woodland until you come to a gate.

7 Go through this gate and turn right, onto a gravel track passing a couple of railway cottages on the left. The rough track soon becomes a lane. Just after a house on the left, look for a fingerpost and stile on the right (just before the bridge).

8 Cross the stile and follow the footpath across the field with the River Ricall to your left. Cross another stile into a field and continue along the riverside path. Cross another stile into another arable field, passing a wooden bridge on your left (leading to Harome). Take care keeping to the narrow riverside path as it can be overgrown.

1 From the village car park, turn left then left again onto Church Street. Continue down the lane to the north-west corner of the village. Go through a kissing gate on the left, signed High Moor Lane, and follow the riverside footpath through a field, gradually departing from the river. Go through two gates and two fields. Pass a metal footbridge on the right. There are some nice pools along this stretch, although anglers fish here so move on if they are present. Continue along field margins, beside the river.

2 Look for a wooden footbridge on the right. Cross this then turn left along a grassy path, hemmed in by a fence on the right and Low Moor Plantation on the left. At the end of the path bear left before some trees, then immediately right with Plump Wood on the right.

3 At a fingerpost (signed Harome) turn right, onto a gravel track with Plump Wood still on your right.

4 At the end of the woodland, go through a gate on the right into a riverside meadow to re-join the River Rye. There is a swim spot and beach by a wooden bridge. Afterwards, cross the bridge and continue straight to the field boundary. Follow the field margin around, with the boundary to your right, and head towards a gate.

5 Go through the wooden kissing gate and cross a wooden bridge.

9 Eventually you reach a wooden gate. This may have a 'bull in field' sign on it. Go through this gate, into a field, then continue through another gate and on towards a farmhouse, following the field margin around to the right and then beside an avenue of trees, to a gate on the left.

10 Go through the gate into a field, then through a second gate. Head to the corner of the field and pass through another gate.

11 Turn right and continue along the field margin to the entrance of another field. The footpath runs through crops, or ploughed earth, depending on the season, eventually joining a gravel track. At the track, turn left and follow this all the way back, over a farm bridge, to the start of the walk.

Walk 17

KIRKHAM ABBEY AND HOWSHAM MILL

Swim beside the glorious ruins of a 12th-century abbey and explore a tiny island with a Gothic Georgian watermill, on this picturesque stretch of the River Derwent.

*M*edieval monks had a talent for discovering beautiful places to build their monastic houses, and Kirkham Priory surely counts as one of the loveliest. Just outside the compact hamlet of Kirkham, or Kirkham Abbey as it is known locally, the ruined priory stands on the fringes of the Howardian Hills National Landscape, on a graceful bend of the River Derwent. Tucked within the deeply-incised Kirkham Gorge, it overlooks a sylvan valley formed by the outflow of a glacial lake during the Ice Age. Today the river is bounded by steep slopes of deciduous ancient woodland and small pastures - a bucolic frame for the atmospheric, English Heritage-managed ruins.

The former Augustinian priory was founded in around 1122 by Walter L'Espec, a soldier and nobleman who also established a Cistercian abbey at Rievaulx, 20 miles away. Meeting the same fate as many religious houses, Kirkham Priory was all but destroyed 400 years later, during Henry VIII's dissolution of the monasteries. The remains of its ornately carved gatehouse, in particular, point to the magnificence of the priory in its heyday.

Less well-known is the vital role the building played during World War Two, when it was used by the military to test equipment in preparation for the D-Day landings. Troops climbed the cloister walls using clambering nets, to prepare them for scaling defences in Normandy - the priory's proximity to the river also meant it was an ideal testing ground for amphibious vehicles – and top-secret visits were made to the site by the prime minister, Winston Churchill, and King George VI. Today the ruins are a popular place for picnicking families in summertime.

INFORMATION

A fairly level walk along woodland and riverside paths, tracks and lanes. Sometimes muddy or overgrown. You may encounter livestock.

DISTANCE: 7 miles
TIME: 3 hours
MAP: OS Explorer 300 Howardian Hills and Malton
START & END POINT: Kirkham Abbey car park (SE 734 658, 54.0828, -0.8781)
PUBLIC TRANSPORT: Nearest train station Malton, six miles away, then a taxi, or the RyeCat rural bus service - Service 184 & 185 (Malton, Kirkham Abbey, Howsham - limited days and times), Yorkshire Coastliner X40, 840, 843 & 845 to Whitwell On The Hill then 0.75-mile walk, crossing the busy A64.
SWIMMING: River Derwent, Kirkham Abbey and Howsham Mill
PLACES OF INTEREST: Kirkham Abbey, Howsham Mill
REFRESHMENTS: The Stone Trough, Kirkham Abbey (YO60 7JS, 01653 618713), is en route, serving pies and ploughman's lunches overlooking Kirkham Priory.
NEARBY SWIM SPOTS: River Rye, Nunnington
EASIER ACCESS: The River Derwent is next to Kirkham Abbey car park but there is no 'shallow' end. Otherwise try Pool Bridge Farm, near York, or Chaloner Pond, Haxby (both fee-charging).

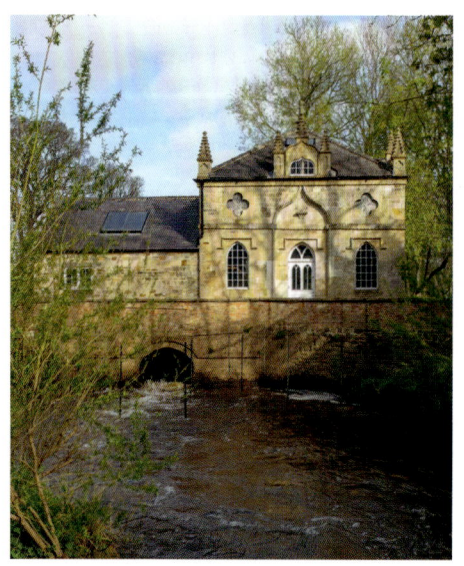

Setting out from this dreamy setting in a southerly direction, the walk crosses Kirkham's old stone bridge, offering an excellent vantage point from which to admire the riverside ruins. While you may feel the urge for a swim, it is best to resist temptation as this is a beautiful place to linger at the end of the walk.

From the bridge you will also spot the scenic York to Scarborough railway line; purposefully constructed to hug the riverbank it follows the sharp meanders of the River Derwent from here to Malton, saving its builders the expense of tunnelling into the Howardian Hills ❶. Winding uphill through Oak Cliff Wood, the path opens onto a narrow country lane, following a field headland with sweeping views across the Vale of York, before re-entering the same woods ❷. In spring the path is fringed by the frothy white heads, and telltale

scent, of ransoms. Further along, the clear-cut, narrow track opens onto a field with a well-placed log bench offering the chance to pause and soak up the views ❸. Descending to a quiet country lane, intersected by the railway line and Howsham Crossing (between ❹ and ❺), the walk then passes through arable fields and grazing pastures, following the riverside path downstream.

It is possible to walk the entire length of the River Derwent from Kirkham to Howsham, but the path becomes overgrown in late spring and summer. This route, instead, takes in a half-mile stretch of river as far as Howsham Bridge and then bears with the overarching greenery for just a short distance ❻. The haze of pink that festoons the riverbank looks pretty but it is the thuggish Himalayan Balsam. This leggy plant is a relative of the popular garden annual busy lizzie, but it is an invasive species, growing rapidly on riverbanks and smothering other vegetation. Each plant can produce up to 800 seeds which are scattered widely as the seed pods propel their charges up to seven metres away.

Across the water is Howsham Hall, a Jacobean pile and former prep school that's said to be cursed; it was built using stone and timber from Kirkham Priory, considered an act of sacrilege at the time. Downstream, the rumble and tumult of white water cascading over Howsham Weir is deafened by the thrashing of a pair of Archimedes screw turbines **6**.

Through the trees you can glimpse Howsham Mill, perched on a small island in the river. This dainty Georgian watermill **7** was built, in Gothic Revival style, as a folly within Howsham Hall's parkland but there had long been a flour mill on the site. Restored from ruin in 2007 by the Renewable Heritage Trust, it is run entirely by volunteers and used as an education centre. The Trust also installed the two Archimedes' screw turbines, which now supply hydroelectricity to the National Grid.

Above the weir is a languid river pool, perfect for a leisurely swim **7**. The riverbank is steep here so access to the water is via a metal ladder by an overhanging tree at the far end of the island. Keep an eye out for the blue-green flash of kingfishers; these elusive birds may be spotted hovering above the water before darting below the surface to scoop up small fish on which they feed. Equally evasive are otters, which also inhabit the island. These semi-aquatic mammals favour clean rivers with an abundance of food and overgrown riverbanks such as these, where they can raise their cubs.

After a Swallows and Amazons-style swim adventure, the walk carries on towards Howsham

village. This quaint hamlet has a single string of cottages but it once had two; in 1770 the then-owner of Howsham Hall, Nathanial Cholmley, had the opposite row removed to improve the outlook from his stately pile. The remaining houses now look onto woodland he had planted.

The village church, St John's, was built for another member of the Cholmley family, Hannah, in 1859 **9**. With its unusually ornate bell tower, it is considered one of the finest examples of the work of Victorian architect George Street, noted for his many Gothic Revival-style English churches as well as London's Law Courts. It is worth popping in to look at the church's elaborate interior and cinquefoil-cusped chancel arch.

After passing the church, the route leaves the village along a footpath abutting pastures and arable fields towards Howsham Wood, where it follows tree-lined footpaths and forestry tracks for just over a mile **10**. In springtime these woods are carpeted with wild flowers: primroses, wood anemone, ransoms and a dazzling display of intoxicatingly scented bluebells. Opening out onto a quiet country lane, the walk then continues back to Kirkham Abbey with glorious valley views and the chance to stop off at the Stone Trough pub, perched up high on the outskirts of the hamlet.

Back in the centre of Kirkham, a wide grassy bank upstream of the weir edges a broad, graceful stretch of the river **11**. Here, the silvery-brown water slides smoothly past the priory ruins. The riverbank is steep; the best place to get in and out of the water is next to an overhanging tree, using the gnarled tree roots as handles and foot holds. On a sunny, summer afternoon, this silky section of the River Derwent is a beautiful place to swim, dive, bathe and picnic, with the romantic ruins of the priory as a backdrop.

1 From the (free) car park, in the centre of the hamlet, cross the bridge and level crossing and continue uphill to a public footpath sign on the left. Enter Oak Cliff Wood and follow the clear-cut path to a clearing opening out onto a tarmac lane.

2 Turn left then look for a gate and public footpath sign on the left. Go through the gate and follow the field headland, which re-enters the woods. The path continues through the woodland for half a mile to a metal gate into a field.

3 Turn right and follow the footpath around the field margin and downhill, passing a log bench. Continue to the gravel track and bear right, crossing a cattle grid.

4 At the end of the track turn left onto Riders Lane, eventually reaching Howsham level crossing. Cross the track if it is safe to do so and continue past cottages on the right.

5 After a few metres, look for a public footpath sign pointing left across a field. Follow this (obvious) path through the crop field. Go through two wooden gates and two fields. Then cross a wooden bridge over a beck then head towards a wooden gate.

6 Go through the gate and turn right onto the riverside footpath, following the river downstream to a wooden gate. Pass through this and continue to a wooden bridge over a

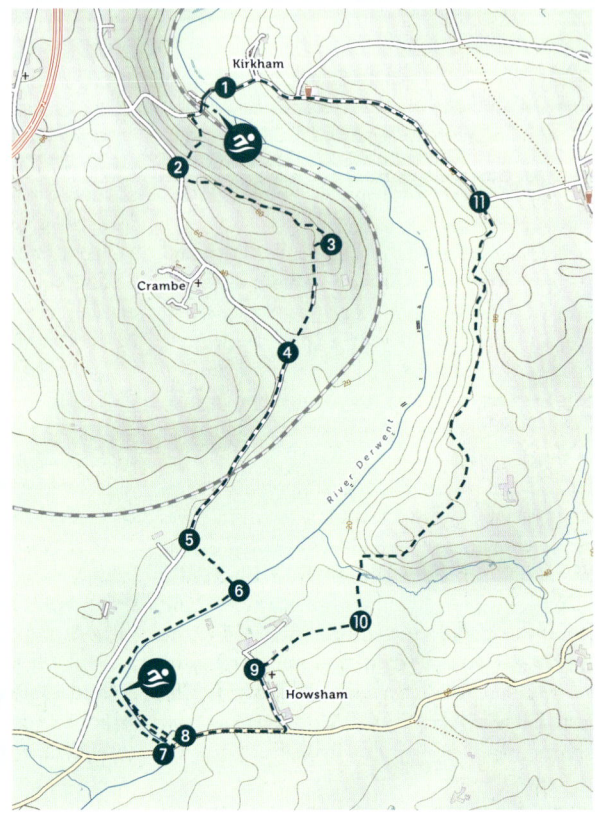

small beck to the right. The footpath runs beside the beck, parallel to the river for a short distance. You will soon hear the gushing waters of Howsham Weir, which you can glimpse through the trees. Descend wooden steps to cross the beck. Go through a gate into a meadow and continue towards Howsham Bridge.

7 At the field end, go through the gate and turn left, crossing the stone bridge. Once over the bridge

turn right, in the direction of the river, following the footpath beneath the bridge onto a path towards Howsham Mill. Cross the wooden bridge over the beck on the left then cross a decorative bridge onto an island. Turn right at the river and continue to Howsham Mill. The swim spot is beyond the mill, towards the woodland. You will see a tree and a rope swing on the left. There is sometimes a metal ladder into the river but it may be submerged, depending on water levels. After your swim, retrace your steps, passing beneath the stone bridge, back to the road.

8 With the parking area behind you, do not cross the bridge but cross the road and turn right, passing the entrance to Howsham Hall. Continue to a sign saying 'Howsham Only', and turn left at this junction, into the village. Go past a row of cottages and the church, all on your the right.

9 After the church, look for a public footpath sign on the right at the entrance to Church Farm.

Take this footpath, passing a house on the left. Go through a wooden gate into a field and continue to the next gate. Go through this and walk along a fenced path to another wooden gate leading onto a footpath beside an arable field. Continue to a footpath sign and cross a wooden stile into another field. At the field end, look for a metal gate on the left and a footpath sign.

10 Go through the gate and bear right then almost immediately left to follow a permissive path with the hedge on the left. Walk towards a wooden gate. Go

through this, past a pond on the right, and continue uphill to a gate at the top of the field. Go through the wooden gate and turn right onto the forest track through Howsham Wood. At a junction, with a green metal bench on the left, the track veers right to a metal gate next to a wooden gate. Go through this and continue to the end of the track.

11 Turn left onto the lane with views across Kirkham Gorge to your left. Pass the Stone Trough pub on the right and continue downhill to Kirkham Abbey and the River Derwent for a final swim.

Walk 18

SALTBURN AND CATTERSTY SANDS

An exhilarating walk from Saltburn's Victorian splendour to a hidden, dune-fringed beach, taking in coastal cliffs and relics of the area's ironstone-mining past.

INFORMATION

A clifftop walk along coastal paths. Some steep sections. Steps at Saltburn and Cattersty Sands. Well-trodden inland footpaths.

DISTANCE: 6 miles
TIME: 3 hours
MAP: OS Explorer OL26 North York Moors Western Area
START & END POINT: Cat Nab car park, Saltburn (54.5849, -0.9675)
PUBLIC TRANSPORT: Train station at Saltburn. Bus Services X4, X4A (Whitby to Middlesbrough)
SWIMMING: Beaches at Saltburn and Cattersty Sands
PLACES OF INTEREST: Saltburn Pier, Saltburn Cliff Tramway, Valley Gardens, Saltburn, Guibal Fanhouse, Land of Iron, Skinningrove
REFRESHMENTS: The Seaview Restaurant at Saltburn (TS12 1HQ, 01287 736015) serves imaginative seafood dishes (including a signature crab brioche) with wonderful coastal views. Enjoy slices of lemon drizzle and Yorkshire tea in china cups at the Victorian-themed Valley Gardens Tea Rooms, also in Saltburn (TS12 1JS, 01287 626792).
OTHER AMENITIES: Toilets at Cat Nab car park
NEARBY SWIM SPOTS: The beautiful cove of Runswick Bay, or head north to Marske-by-the-Sea
EASIER ACCESS: Saltburn Beach is a short walk from the car park. Park in Skinningrove for a short walk to Cattersty Sands

*O*nce a smugglers' haunt, Saltburn-by-the-Sea became a celebrated Victorian spa resort, while today it has a bohemian ambience. Known as the surfing capital of the North, it draws surfers from far and wide. The wide expanse of shingle and sand here is backed by some of the highest cliffs on the east coast of England, providing a dramatic backdrop for swimming as well as surfing - and high-rise hikes along clifftop paths.

As well as these natural attractions, Saltburn has all the attributes of a traditional seaside town - golden sands, cheerful beach huts and seafront cafés. Its impressive pier, the most northerly Victorian pier in the UK, extends 200m into the sea. Built in 1861, it was originally more than twice this length; despite bearing the brunt of violent storms and a constant pummelling from the North Sea it was a ship that shortened it, in 1924, when the pier was sliced through by the SS Ovenberg in bad weather. Other local highlights of Victorian engineering include the town's cliff lift. A funicular railway, this transports visitors from the town to the seafront and is the oldest working water-balanced incline tramway in Britain.

The town's heyday as a seaside resort began in 1861, in large part thanks to Quaker entrepreneur Henry Pease. Pease had had a vision in which he saw a town rising from the clifftop above the small village that existed at the time around the Ship Inn, down on the shore. Over the next 20 years his vision was brought to life, with a railway, hotel, chapel, pier, cliff tramway and seaside villas all built, and pleasure gardens created in the sheltered glen that ran between the clifftop resort and the Ship Inn.

The glen's three ancient valleys are steep-sided wooded denes formed by melting glaciers at the end of the Ice Age. The most

accessible of these is Valley Gardens and Rifts Wood. The pleasure grounds' Italian gardens are still there, along with a lovely Victorian-themed tea rooms and a miniature railway (added in the 1940s). You could easily spend a day exploring this secluded valley, cut through by tumbling Skelton Beck, though it's also tempting to head straight to the beach where you may bump into the Saltburn Mermates, a friendly group of sea swimmers who meet all year round for an early morning dip.

The walk starts at Cat Nab car park ❶, down on the shore, close to where Saltburn village first sprang up. Tucked away in the secluded valley of Saltburn Gill, beneath lofty Hunt Cliff, Old Saltburn had just one row of cottages, for fishermen and farmers, and the Ship Inn. Dating back to 1500, this ancient pub was a hub for smugglers. Its landlord in 1780 was Scottish-born John Andrew, Saltburn's most famous smuggler he came from a wealthy family and combined his life of criminality with the role of respected community member, the duality earning him the nickname 'king of smugglers'.

After a heart-pumping climb onto Hunt Cliff, the reward is far-reaching views across the town

and north towards Redcar. Between AD 367 and AD 385 the Romans made use of this towering promontory for one of their coastal signal stations, protection against Anglo-Saxon raids from Germany and Denmark. During excavations in the early 1900s, only the southern section of the fort was discovered, the rest having succumbed to the North Sea.

Part of these cliffs are now a Wildlife Trust nature reserve due to their importance as a habitat for kittiwakes, who nest on the clifftops and ledges from February to August. Keep an eye out for these pretty birds as they return to their nests with food for their young, or soar on thermals. Recognisable by their 'kittiwake' call, they can be distinguished from other gulls by their ink-dipped wing tips. In autumn and winter terns, the gulls and gannets take their turn on the cliffs instead. It is quite a spectacle to watch the gannets, driven by their insatiable appetites, dive into the water at 60mph to catch fish.

In spring and summer, carpets of wild flowers brighten the coastal grasslands; three species of orchid jostle with sea plantain, wild carrot and shrubby spiny restharrow. As you wander further along the path, look out to sea to spot grey seals, harbour porpoises and even minke whales; all are frequently sighted here.

The narrow path soon runs parallel with a train track and it's a battle for space on the cliff top ❷. The Whitby, Redcar and Middlesborough Union Railway was opened in 1872 but, as passenger numbers dwindled, it became unviable and, in 1960, it was dismantled with some of the concrete used to form sea defences. However, when a potash mine was sunk at nearby Boulby, in the 1970s, the line was restored. You may encounter a passing freight train carrying potash along the track from Boulby, the UK's only commercial potash mine.

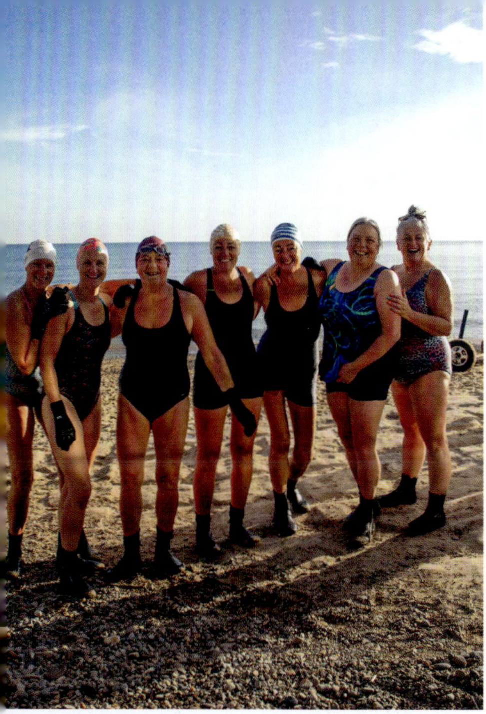

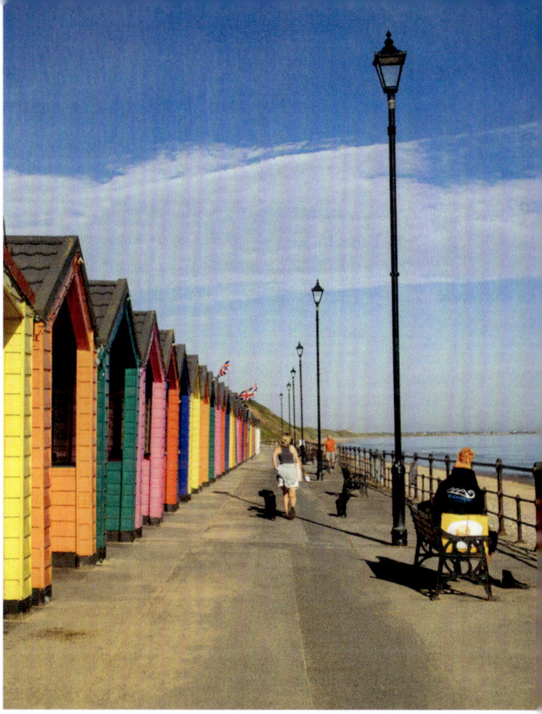

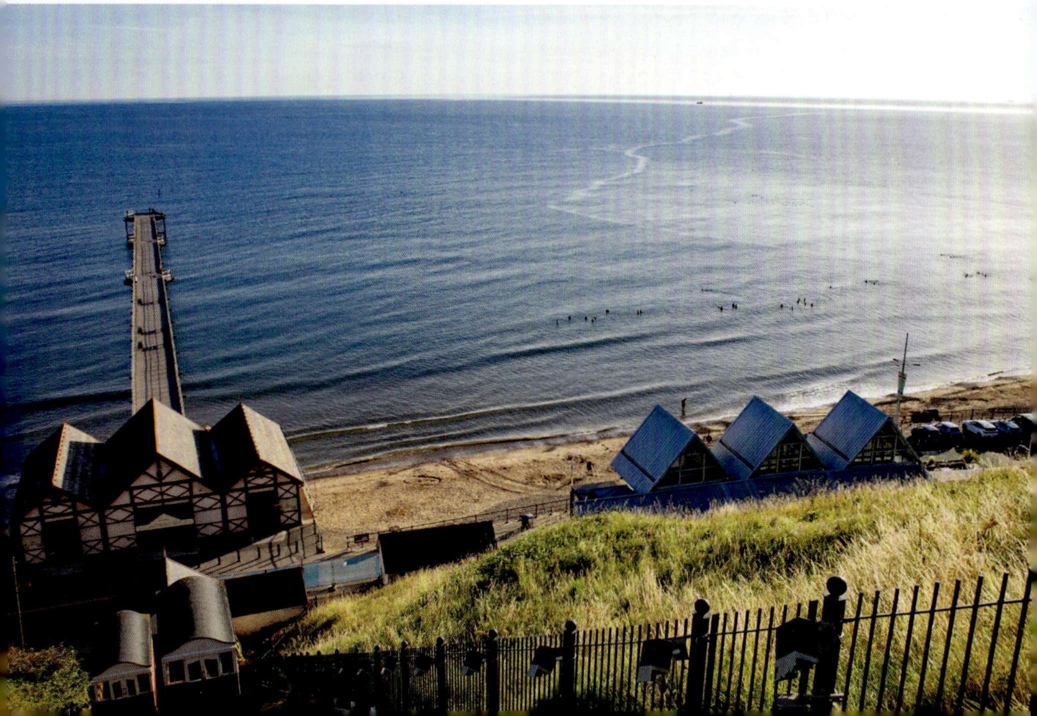

As the path widens, a striking iron sculpture frames the landscape. Perched on a small mound, near the railway line below Warset Hill, the charm bracelet sculpture 'Circle' was created by artist Richard Farrington (between ❷ and ❸). The ten figurative 'charms' hanging on metal rods from a steel hoop represent the social, industrial and natural history of the area. A wooden bench provides the perfect opportunity to take in the gorgeous coastal scenery - with the promontory of Hummersea Scar in the distance and Warsett Hill and the ruined Guibal Fanhouse to the right.

Fortunately, it is not too far before the unspoilt golden crescent of Cattersty Sands comes into view ❸. Sheltered by tall cliffs, and a rocky pier at its southern end, this is one of the most beautiful beaches along this coastline, cherished by locals and anyone who stumbles upon it. Steps lead down to the beach through grassy dunes and marram grass, interlaced with scrambling dog roses in summer then plump, red hips in autumn. When the tide is out, the dune-fringed sands seem to go on forever, and splashing about in the waves, beneath the dramatic coastal cliffs, is an unforgettable experience.

Despite the coastline's wild beauty, there is a long history of ironstone mining in the valley just beyond the beach, a history brought to vivid life at the Land of Iron attraction at Cleveland Ironstone Museum, in Skinningrove. This former mining village sits just beyond the pier and its museum recounts how the area once supplied a third of the world's iron and steel; indeed, Skinningrove Jetty was built, in around 1886, to load pig iron from Skinningrove Works onto ships bound for Grangemouth in Scotland.

The return leg of the walk rejoins the Cleveland Way, diverging onto a footpath towards Warsett Hill and the Guibal Fanhouse, beyond the train track. Named after its Belgian inventor, the fanhouse was used to ventilate Huntcliff Ironstone Mine until 1906 ❺. One of the best remaining examples of its kind in the UK, it is possible to crawl into the fanhouse through a tunnel at the back of the building to emerge in a large pit in the interior.

After circumnavigating Warsett Hill ❻, there are far-reaching views of the north-east coast towards the industrial heartland of Teeside as the route returns to Hunt Cliff ❽ and back to Saltburn. At the latter the sea shore and a cooling swim beckon ❿. The sea may be bouncy or smooth as you plunge into the bracing swell of the North Sea, with Old Saltburn nestled beneath rugged cliffs on one side and the town's seaside charm standing proud on the other. At high tide, the water comes right up to the slipway. Steer clear of swimming too near the pier, and where Skelton Beck flows into the sea, as there can be rip currents.

After an exhilarating dip, Saltburn has a host of places to eat and drink, whether it is tea and cake, ice creams or fish and chips you're craving.

1 Leave Cat Nab car park, cross the road and turn right along the promenade, towards the Old Ship Inn and Old Saltburn. Go past the pub and, at the bus stop, take a left turn onto a footpath. At a fork, follow the Cleveland Way up a steep, stepped path. Continue along the clifftop path, passing the site of the Huntcliff Signal Station.

2 After a short distance the path runs adjacent to the railway line. A National Trust sign and a circular metal sculpture marks Warsett Hill, the mound to the right. You can also see the Guibal Fanhouse.

3 Cattersty Sands soon comes into view. A stepped path winds through the dunes to the beach where you can enjoy a swim. Afterwards, retrace your steps and return to the Cleveland Way. Continue along the

path you arrived on, following the contours of a ravine, crossing a small, often dry beck.

4 Look for a stile in the fence on the left. It is the stile opposite Warsett Hill, with the fan house in the distance, not the first stile you arrive at. Cross the field. The path is not always obvious unless there are crops with a trodden route. The footpath runs directly ahead. However, you need to bear right, towards the fanhouse, to cross the railway track safely.

5 At the wooden gate, stop, look and listen for passing trains then carefully cross the track. You can explore the Guibal Fanhouse to your right. Afterwards, walk across the field to a gap in the hedge, leading to the lower reaches of Warsett Hill.

6 Head towards the hill and join a well-defined dirt path that circumnavigates the mound. There are great views ahead. Follow the obvious path through a couple of fields.

7 At a stile, cross the train track again. Then turn left, onto a path, following the field headland. The path becomes a gravel track at a rustic fingerpost. Continue past a stone cottage and along the track, with views of Saltburn ahead.

8 At a public footpath and a public bridleway sign you can choose either; both paths lead you back to Saltburn. This route, however, takes the footpath, past a row of white houses, towards Hunt Cliff and a National Trust sign for Old Saltburn. Rejoin the path you started out on, taking you back to Saltburn for a final swim.

ESK VALLEY RAIL TRAIL

Hop on board for a scenic train ride through the leafy Esk Valley then return along riverside paths with a choice of secluded swim spots.

INFORMATION

A fairly level walk, including a train ride, then woodland and riverside paths (possibly muddy), gravel tracks and narrow country lanes.

DISTANCE: 3.5 miles
TIME: 1.5 hours plus 10-minute train journey
MAP: OS Explorer OL27 North York Moors Eastern Area
START & END POINT: Grosmont Station (NZ 827 052, 54.4360, -0.7260)
PUBLIC TRANSPORT: Train station at Grosmont, Bus - Arriva North East 96 (Whitby)
SWIMMING: River Esk at Beggar's Bridge, East Arncliffe Wood and Grosmont
PLACES OF INTEREST: Grosmont Station and Engine Sheds, Grosmont
REFRESHMENTS: Delicious cakes, excellent coffee and light lunches at the Old School Coffee Shop, Grosmont (YO22 5QW, 01947 895758). The Horseshoe Hotel, on the route at Egton Bridge (YO21 1XE, 01947 895245), has a riverside beer garden along with a farm shop. Good food and real ales.
OTHER AMENITIES: Toilets at Grosmont Station
NEARBY SWIM SPOTS: Goathland waterfalls, River Esk, Lealholm
EASIER ACCESS: The River Esk is a short walk from the car park at Grosmont

The charming station at Grosmont is the starting point for this leisurely amble. One of several vintage-style stations along the 24-mile long North Yorkshire Moors Railway, this pale blue and cream, 1952-themed station is where the heritage steam railway meets the Esk Valley Railway, a community line that brings visitors from Whitby and Middlesbrough inland. After a short ride on the Esk Valley line, through the picturesque Esk Valley to Glaisdale, it is an easy walk back to Grosmont with several opportunities for a dip along the way. You could, of course, make this an out-and-back walk.

If you are familiar with the steep road out of Grosmont, you would be forgiven for thinking that the village's name stems from the French words, 'gros,' as in 'big,' and 'mont,' as in 'hill'. However, this is only part of the story. Grosmont acquired its grandiose name following the arrival of monks from the Grandimont order, in Limoges, in the 13th century. After land was gifted to the order, a priory was established here in around 1200 and remained until the dissolution of the monasteries in the 1530s. Unfortunately there is no trace of this religious building today.

Grosmont's real heyday, however, came in 1836, with the arrival of George Stephenson's railway line from Pickering to Whitby. One of its builders' major feats was cutting a 110m-long tunnel through the rock at Grosmont – now one of the oldest railway tunnels in the world. It was while digging through this tunnel that ironstone was first discovered; the population of Grosmont subsequently swelled with the opening of ironworks, clay pits and brick works. At one time, three blast furnaces and a huge chimney towered above the village and hundreds of workers produced 1,000 tonnes of pig iron (crude iron obtained directly from the blast furnace) each week.

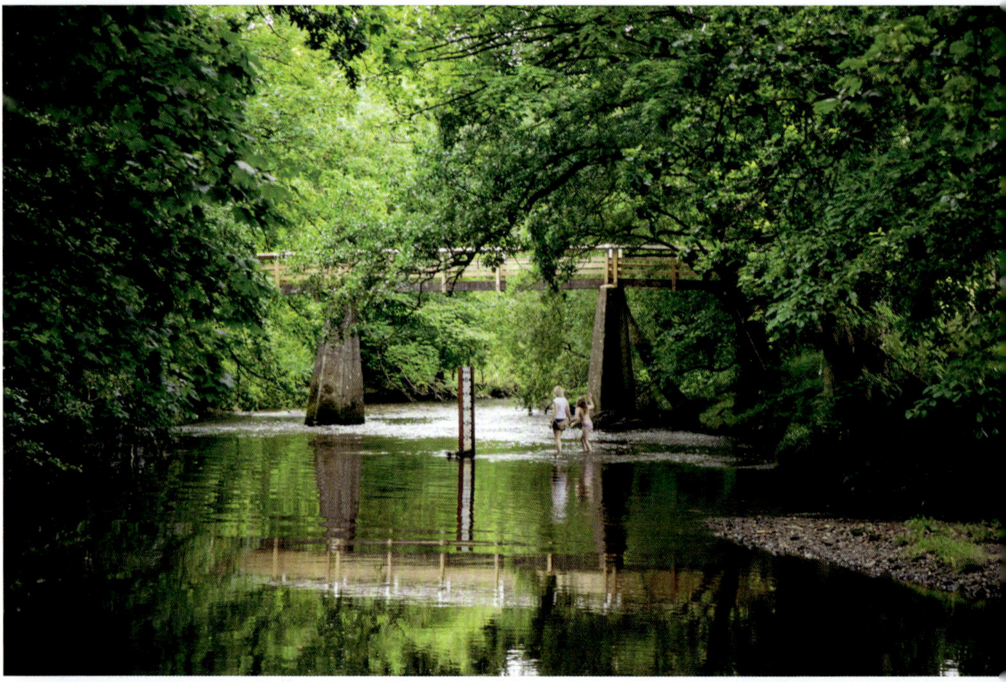

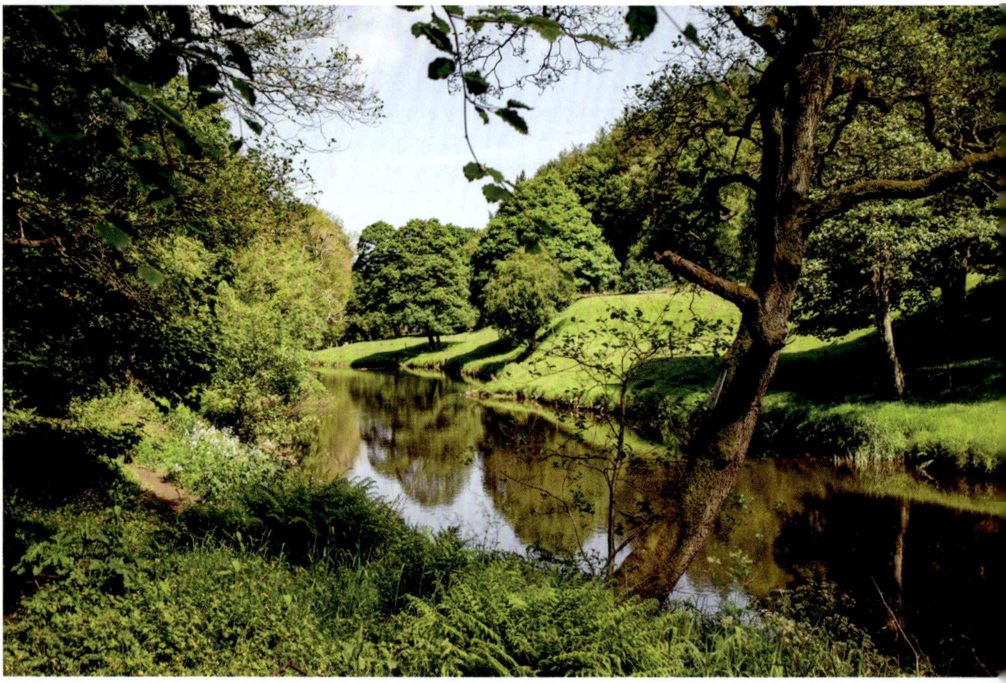

Relics of the ironworks, including the stone and brick base of one of the furnaces, can be seen in the station's overflow car park, where there is also a miniature model of the works.

These days the tunnel leads to the station's engine sheds, where the steam and diesel locomotives are maintained and restored; there is a public viewing platform for those keen to observe the work on the engines. Also in the vicinity is the Old School Coffee Shop, serving cakes and scones as well as a savoury menu. However, with a train to catch, it might be wise to leave any feasting until the end of the walk.

The train journey to Glaisdale is short - just 10 minutes - and passes through rolling hills and wooded river valleys, never far from the tumbling Esk ❶. After alighting at Glaisdale Station, take time to admire Beggar's Bridge, the graceful 17th-century packhorse bridge just beyond the brick railway bridge. According to legend, two young lovers - Tom Ferres, son of a poor sheep farmer, and Agnes Richardson, daughter of a wealthy Glaisdale landowner - were prevented from marrying because of Tom's lowly status. On the eve of his departure to seek his fortune at sea, Tom's attempt to cross the flooded river to say farewell to Agnes was thwarted. After returning a wealthy man, years later (allegedly gaining his riches through piracy), Tom married his beloved Agnes and had the bridge built so that future lovers were never kept apart by the river.

A few metres upstream of Beggar's Bridge there is a secluded beach area where you can paddle or take a dip ❶. The river here has a shallow entry but is deeper as you swim downstream and there is sometimes a rope swing near the bridge. After cooling off in the river, the walk continues into East Arncliffe Wood. This beautiful ancient woodland connects Glaisdale to the hamlet of Delves, just above Egton Bridge. Much of the woodland path is flagged with medieval stone setts – the remains of a monk's trod, a kind of stone causeway worn smooth over time by the hooves of packhorses journeying between Guisborough Priory and Whitby Abbey. The path, which also forms part of the Esk Valley Trail, can be sludgy and the stones slippery, particularly in wetter weather, so take care.

Sturdy walking boots may now be the order of the day but this sylvan spot once housed a thriving clog-making industry. The woods' plentiful supply of coppiced beech, ash, alder and sycamore - all used for clog soles – meant the industry prospered here, the clogs made by hand while the wood was green then left to season in open conical pyramids. After being finished by a master clogger, the clogs were transported to the towns of the West Riding and Lancashire; between the 1840s and 1920s trade in clogs was brisk among people working in mills, mines, ironworks, workshops and even on farms, where labourers claimed they stopped them slipping on slick stones. A pair might have been handy for the next part of this walk!

The woodland path initially hugs the riverbank before rising steeply away from the water along

The woodland path opens out onto a country lane which runs down towards Egton Bridge, passing The Horseshoe Hotel and Farm Shop, where you might like to stop for a drink ❸. The stepping stones across the river here will keep the kids entertained and, in season, look out for gooseberries in the farm shop; Egton Bridge is home to the oldest surviving gooseberry show in the country. Established in 1800 and held in August each year, it assesses champion growers over six categories - heaviest red, yellow, green and white berries, heaviest twin berries and heaviest dozen. The show's hand-written rules date back to 1823 and needless to say, competition is fierce.

those stone trods. At the start of the trods, look out for a secluded clearing by the side of the Esk. This deep pool of silvery-brown water, just above the weir, can be reached by clambering down the riverbank onto a small gravel beach ❷. Named Dead Man's Pool, it is unclear how this sublime spot got its cheerless name but it has inspired several artists, including pioneering photographer Frank Meadow Sutcliffe, whose sepia-toned image of it forms part of the Philadelphia Museum of Art's collection.

The Esk is the only major Yorkshire river to flow directly into the sea, at Whitby (all the others flow into the North Sea via the Tees or the Humber). Revered as a clean watercourse, it is a haven for wildlife so keep an eye out for kingfishers, dippers, herons and otters.

After enjoying a dip here, the onward path climbs steeply through the woodland, past a legendary boulder bearing a huge cleft. This ancient wishing stone once had a yew growing out of it and it is said that if you walk around the stone three times, your wish will come true ❷. It's definitely worth a try! Around it rare species of Tunbridge filmy fern and hay-scented buckler-fern thrive in the damp and shaded woodland conditions.

The original village of Egton lies a mile up the steep hill above Egton Bridge but the walk continues roughly along the river, leaving the river along Barnard's Road, an old toll road to Grosmont that's now a permissive track ❹. Until the 1940s anyone using this route had to pay a charge to the Egton Estate, whether horse or tractor, motorcycle or hearse. Beside the path the River Esk drifts in and out of view, creating riffles over rocks and stones, and some deeper pools, as it winds through the valley.

Towards the end of the track, the route rejoins the river, veiled by a curtain of shrubs and trees. Several grassy paths and wooden steps lead down to the narrow riverbank, offering the chance of one last swim ❺. The river here is a mix of riffles and deeper pools. The flow can be fast in places so take time to find a safe spot to enter and exit the water. We have had lots of fun here on warm summer days, floating on our backs and swooshing downstream with the current. After drying off, the road at the end of the track leads back to Grosmont, hopefully in plenty of time to explore this captivating moorland village.

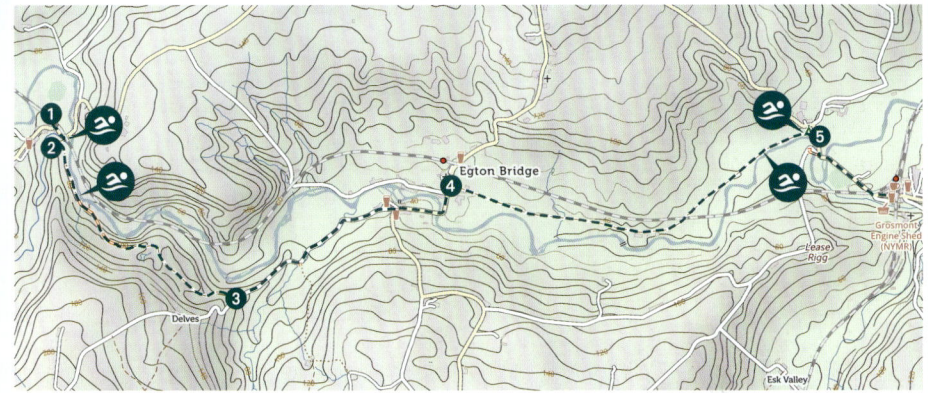

1 Starting at Grosmont Station, take the train on the Esk Valley Railway Line to Glaisdale station. Follow the exit then turn left down the hill and under the railway bridge to the packhorse bridge. If you want to swim here, cross the main bridge and continue along the road for a few metres to a parking lay-by on the left, and a small beach. Afterwards retrace your steps to a metal footbridge across a beck on your left, just after passing beneath the railway bridge. Cross the bridge and continue up the steps.

2 Turn left onto the Esk Valley Walk as the path rises above the river. Continue for around 500m to stone trods and cross a small stream. Just beyond the trees to the left, there is a swim spot at a gentle meander of the river, above a weir. After your dip, rejoin the path and continue along the trods. Look out for the ancient wishing stone, a large boulder with a wide cleft, on the left. Make a wish!

3 At the end of the track, go through the wooden gate. Turn

left onto a country lane, passing a house on the left and a stream on the right, then cross a ford or a footbridge depending on the water level. Pass the Horseshoe Hotel on the left, possibly stopping off here for a drink, or something to eat. Continue along the road, between a row of houses, then cross Egton Bridge. Follow the road as it bears left.

4 Look for a Coast to Coast footpath sign on the right (Grosmont 1.5 miles) just before the 'school' sign. Follow this track along the old toll road, Barnard's Road. Pass under a bridge and a little further along, just after a gate, there are several grassy tracks down to the river for another swim.

5 After your swim, continue to the end of the track and turn right. Cross the bridge over the Murk Esk and continue back into Grosmont.

Walk 20

WATER ARC AND THOMASON FOSS

Enjoy moorland views and a pair of enchanting waterfalls hidden in a woodland dell, with only the bleating of sheep and hooting of steam trains for company.

*H*ome to no less than four delightful cascades, the popular moorland village of Goathland has waterfalls at its heart. Many people seek out Mallyan Spout, the highest fall in the North York Moors National Park, at 21m high. However, the outlying waterfalls of Thomason Foss and Water Arc Foss are equally worth a visit, and are often quieter. These pretty cascades leap over rocky ledges on the Eller Beck, creating enticing plunge pools for a secluded wild swim. Elsewhere, the walk also takes in gorgeous moorland views, steam trains, the tiny hamlet of Beck Hole and an opportunity to visit pint-sized Birch Hall Inn.

Starting out at Darnholm, a small hamlet to the north-east of Goathland, the route passes a cluster of houses. A blue plaque on the gatepost of one of them may catch your attention ❶. It is dedicated to Alfred John Brown (1894-1969), a walker and outdoor writer who was devoted to the Yorkshire Dales and Moors and whose books *Tramping through Yorkshire* and *Moorland Tramping* were bestsellers in the 1930s. Brown and his half-French wife, Marie Eugenie, were hoteliers here in 1945, running the Whitfield House Hotel for the benefit of outdoorsy folk seeking solitude and quiet in the days when Goathland was celebrated as an exclusive moorland spa town.

A stone bridge crosses the railway line that carries steam trains along a heritage route from Pickering to Whitby. The North Yorkshire Moors Railway is one of the busiest steam railways in the world, and another of Goathland's attractions. The station was built during the 1860s and its platform and stone buildings, with their ruby-red paintwork, have altered very little over the

INFORMATION

Well-used tracks and indistinct footpaths. Steep, precipitous path down to Water Arc Foss. Uneven riverside path to Thomason Foss, country lanes. You may encounter livestock.

DISTANCE: 3 miles
TIME: 1.5 hours
MAP: OS Explorer OL27 North York Moors Eastern Area
START & END POINT: Darnholm, Goathland (NZ 829 017, 54.4048, -0.7231)
PUBLIC TRANSPORT: Coastliner 840 (Whitby to Leeds)
SWIMMING: Waterfalls of Water Arc and Thomason Foss
PLACES OF INTEREST: Goathland village, North Yorkshire Moors Railway, Allan Tofts prehistoric rock art
REFRESHMENTS: Enjoy tea and a slice of cake at Goathland Station Tea Room (YO22 5NF, 01751 472508), a converted 1922 goods shed. Goathland Tea Rooms & Gift Shop (YO22 5AL, 01947 896446) is a traditional café, serving soup, sandwiches, jacket potatoes and homemade cakes both indoors and from its pretty tea garden. Along the route, the Birch Hall Inn at Beck Hole (YO22 5LE, 01947 896245), is a charming riverside pub (cash only).
SWIM SPOTS NEARBY: Mallyan Spout pools, Nelly Ayre Foss
EASIER ACCESS: Small pool for paddling and dipping on the Eller Beck, upstream of Water Arc Foss.

years. Unsurprisingly, it is a popular film location, doubling up as Hogsmeade Station in the first Harry Potter movie among other appearances.

After fording the Eller Beck, the route climbs onto bracken-cloaked Goathland Moor. This wild and remote moorland feels miles away from the hubbub of Goathland's village centre. The North York Moors is home to one of England's largest expanses of heather moorland, the tops taking on a bruised purple hue in August and September when the plants flower. Growing together to form a thick carpet, the heather provides a rich habitat for bees, moths and butterflies. Wandering across the moors above Hawthorn Hill Farm, there are glorious views back to Goathland and Fylingdales beyond, the railway line winding through the valley, and sending the occasional puff of steam curling through the trees.

To the north of Cass Hill is Allan Tofts, an ancient site that includes a field system, burial cairns and prehistoric rock art ❷. This entire area is crossed by paths, tracks, holloways and post-medieval sheep beelds (shelters) - evidence of how well-inhabited these now-peaceful uplands were thousands of years ago. These days, you are more likely to bump into sheep rather than people on your walk since a common right to graze the village greens and moorland was granted around Goathland by the Duchy of Lancaster; the 10,000-acre Goathland Estate is the duchy's largest rural holding.

From the moor, the route gently descends towards the valley floor. A green bench beneath a holly bush (between ❸ and ❹), is a popular spot for trainspotters; if you time your walk well, you might see a steam train puffing along the track below, on its way to Goathland.

Although not long, the descent to Water Arc Foss, is steep, following a rocky path that zig-zags

down to the falls, so great care should be taken ❹. If you prefer a dipping spot with easier access, continue along the path you arrived on, following the beck upstream to a small cascade and pool beneath a footbridge and the railway bridge. Beyond the footbridge, a footpath then leads back to the crossroads at Darnholm; a good option if you want to shorten the walk.

The double-tiered waterfall of Water Arc ❹ is in an enchanting setting with several cascades tumbling into a pair of pools. The water flows over rocky ledges dripping with lush, green ferns and velvety moss. There is a deeper plunge pool beneath the second set of falls, under the arches of the railway bridge.

After swimming here, careful navigation is required to pick up the right path. The only safe way is by following the path directly beneath the railway bridge, a route which involves clambering onto a rocky ledge to reach a path high above the beck. This runs parallel to the railway line, with the beck flowing through the valley below and the rush and rumble of Thomason Foss echoing through the trees. Narrow trails lead down to join the main, uneven path to the falls.

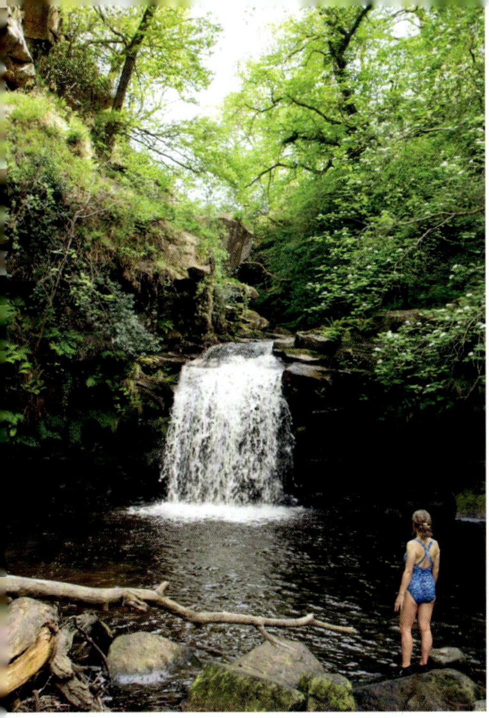
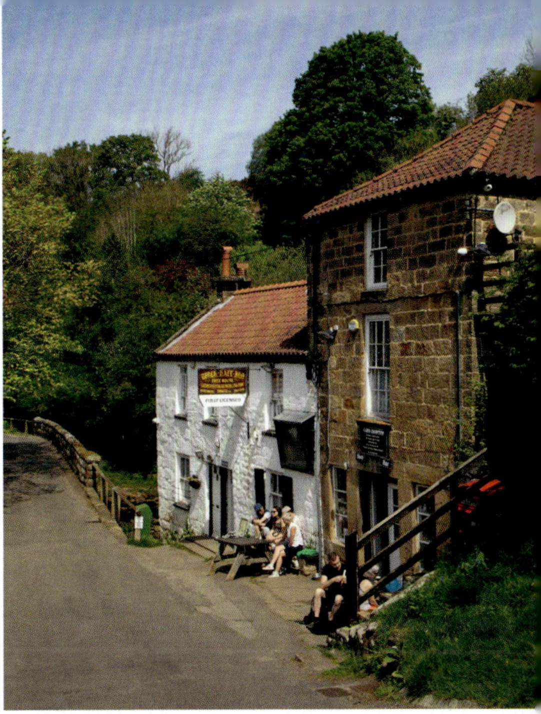
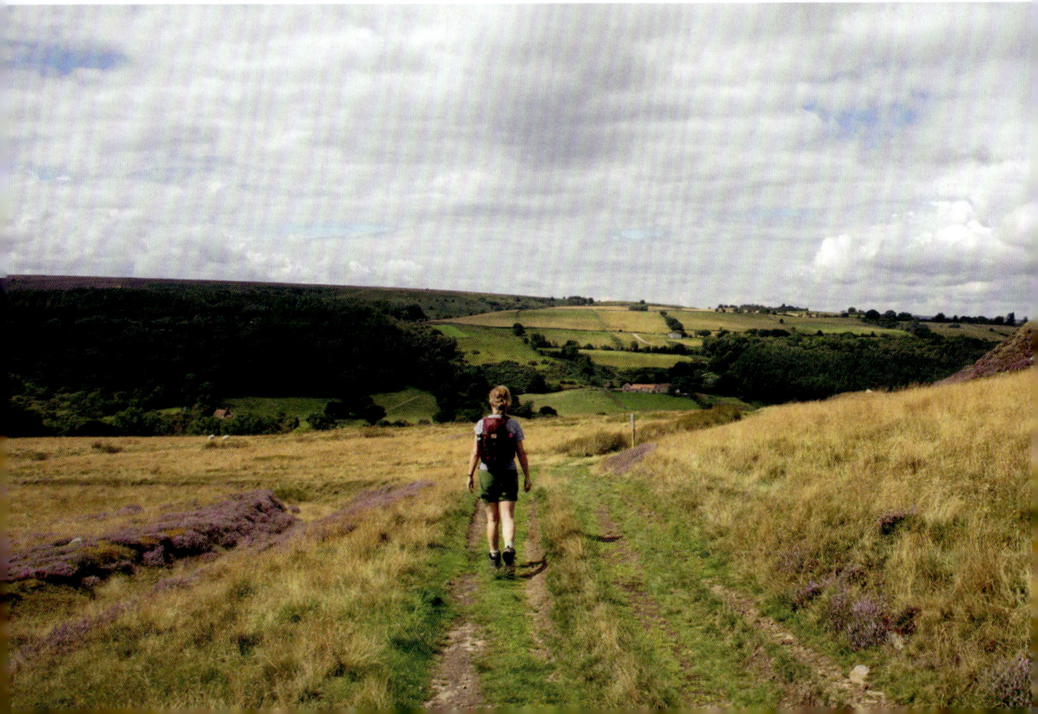

gigantic worm once made its lair at Beck Hole. With scaly skin and a mouth like a dragon, the worm inhabited the deep holes around the beck, preying on cattle, sheep and young maidens. In an attempt to kill the beast, a young girl named Kitty was tied to a tree as bait and, in the battle that ensued, the worm was slain and the girl was rescued by a brave Danish knight.

Today Beck Hole is a place where the past is tangible and traditions live on. Tucked in the corner of the village, on the other side of the bridge, is the cash-only Birch Hall Inn, one of the smallest pubs in Britain ❻. Its two age-old bars sit either side of a traditional sweet shop, which opened in the 1860s to sell supplies to the Whitby Iron Company workers and their families who lived in the village at the time. There's a pretty beer garden overlooking the beck and a simple, no-fuss menu including butties, pies, stotties and the pub's signature Beck Hole beer cake. Remember to check ahead for opening times.

Nestled in a wooded ravine, Thomason Foss tumbles over Eller Beck before joining West Beck to form the River Murk Esk ❺. A picturesque waterfall in a dreamy dell, its cascades pour into a fabulous plunge pool and there are several smaller pools downstream. As you enjoy a tranquil dip, look and listen for some of the birds that inhabit this stretch of water. Dippers, recognisable by their white throat and breast, are often spotted bobbing up and down on the rocks, bravely walking into and under the water in search of insects - the original swim-walkers! Grey wagtails nest near the water, creating homes in crevices and hollows, and dining on ants, midges and snails they find in shallower water.

Clambering back out of the ravine, a woodland path winds through the trees towards Beck Hole. This hamlet of around half a dozen cottages lies at the foot of a steep hill in the wooded valley of the Murk Esk, a tributary of the Esk. The name 'Beck Hole' comes from an old Norse description of a 'deep valley through which runs a stream' and, despite its small size, the hamlet lays claim to a fearsome legend. According to the tale, a

The village also has several clay pit quoits pitches where the local club, which dates back to the 19th century, still play this traditional game, throwing heavy metal hoops over a post. One of the oldest longsword-dancing teams in England is also based nearby; the Goathland Plough Stots perform their own dance, dating back to the 19th century, on each January's Day of Dance and on other occasions through the year. Any concerns that such age-old rituals might die out are put aside when you see that the local primary school has its own junior sword-dancing team.

With the walk all but over, there is just the tree-lined hill out of Beck Hole to conquer. If you treated yourself at Birch Hall's sweet shop, you will be glad of the sugar-boost as you tackle the steep climb back to your car.

1 From roadside parking on Beck Hole Road, walk towards a crossroads (in the direction of Goathland) then turn left towards Darnholm, passing a 'no through road' sign. (If arriving by the Coastliner bus, follow signs for Darnholm from the bus stop in Goathland and follow the directions from here). Pass several cottages, cross the railway bridge, and the ford over Eller Beck, then bear left. Follow the track for a few metres to a NYM footpath sign, pointing to a stony path on the left. Follow this path, crossing a wooden bridge, then climb steep, wooden steps onto open moorland.

2 At the top, continue straight ahead, keeping the fence to your left. The path soon joins a stone track which passes behind Hawthorn Hill Farm. Head straight across the moor in a westerly direction, passing behind another house and following obvious tracks.

3 At a large mound on the right look for a grassy footpath on the left and continue downhill along this to a stone wall and Hill Farm holiday accommodation. Keep to the footpath, with the stone wall to your right. Pass the entrance to the accommodation then join a track bearing left, passing close behind an old stone house on the right. Continue beside overarching trees and shrubs to a green bench on the right.

4 The footpath in front of the bench leads down to Water Arc Foss, your first swim. The path can

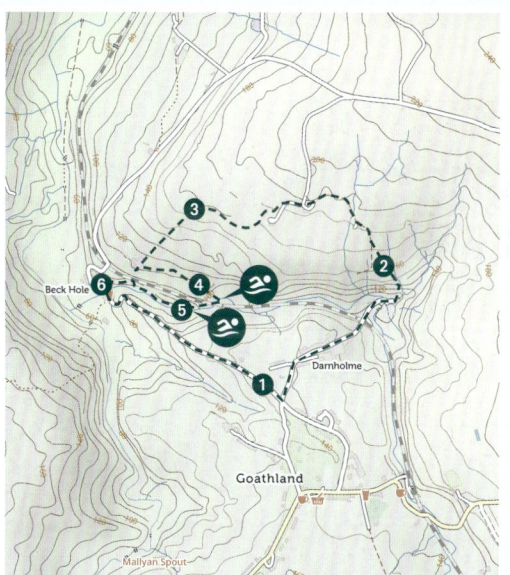

be obscured by bracken in summer. Steam trains cross the bridge here. The footpath to the waterfall veers left. It is a precipitous, zig-zagging descent so take great care. (If you have young children with you, it is best to continue along the path you arrived on to a footbridge above a smaller pool, perfect for paddling). After your swim retrace your steps but instead of returning to the path back to the green bench, climb onto a rocky shelf beneath the railway bridge. You will need to crouch as you duck under the bridge then clamber onto a higher path along a short, rocky, tree-rooted incline. Do not attempt to descend to the beck and climb what looks like another way onto the same path. There is a sheer drop on the other side.

5 The path opens onto a narrow trail high above the beck with the fenced railway line immediately to the right. After about 50m the path dips to avoid the roots of an oak tree. There are faint tracks here: pick your way down towards the water along the best tracks, passing a tumbledown wall. The beck-side path, which doubles back to Thomason Foss, is below. Follow this upstream, crossing a boardwalk, to reach the falls. After your dip, return to the beck-side path, which can be muddy. The gradually rising path to Beck Hole is easy to follow.

6 At the end of the path turn left, crossing the bridge to Birch Hall Inn, which is worth visiting. A steep climb uphill from here leads back to your car.

157

GOATHLAND TARN, SIMON HOWE AND NELLY AYRE FOSS

Glide across a glittering moorland tarn, tread ancient pathways to a prehistoric stone circle and dip in a secret waterfall.

icture-postcard Goathland has been celebrated for its natural beauty since the mid-19th century, having gained a reputation among the Victorians as a mini spa town. Tucked away in the eastern fringes of the North York Moors National Park, it is cosseted by undulating moorland scenery and dramatic scars, interlaced with streams, becks and rills. Mallyan Spout, the highest and best-known waterfall in the North York Moors, pours over a steep-sided 20m drop into West Beck, on the outskirts of town. Much of this wild swim-walk entails a remote hike across open moor, however, following rugged footpaths to the prehistoric cairn and standing stones of Simon Howe. It takes in three delightful swim spots - a shimmering moorland tarn, the secluded waterfall of Nelly Ayre Foss and Mallyan Spout itself, as well as some of the loveliest views in the national park. Panoramic views abound so it is worth choosing a clear, dry day; the abundance of rills rushing off the moors also means the route can be boggy in wetter weather.

While it may have been the Victorians who discovered Goathland's charms en masse, following the arrival of the railway, its popularity endures. Its pulling power soared in the 1990s, when Goathland was used as the setting for the fictional 1960s village of Aidensfield in the TV drama, Heartbeat, and again in the noughties when its characterful stone station buildings were used as a location in the first Harry Potter film,

The fact that Goathland is still a magnet for visitors today is partly due to its excellent public transport connections; it lies on the epic 840 Coastliner route, voted Britain's most scenic bus route, and Goathland's train station is part of the North Yorkshire Moors heritage railway line, which runs between Pickering and Whitby.

INFORMATION

Some indistinct paths over occasionally boggy, heather-covered moor. Steep scramble down to Nelly Ayre Foss and a narrow, rocky beck-side path to Mallyan Spout.

DISTANCE: 5.5 miles
TIME: 2.5 hours
MAP: OS Explorer OL27 North York Moors Eastern Area
START POINT & END POINT: Goathland verge parking (NZ 826 006, 54.3946, -0.7295)
PUBLIC TRANSPORT: Coastliner 840 (Whitby to Leeds)
SWIMMING: Moorland tarn, Nelly Ayre Foss, Mallyan Spout pools
PLACES OF INTEREST: Simon Howe, Mallyan Spout, Wheeldale Roman Road
REFRESHMENTS: For homemade cakes and light snacks head to The Coach House Coffee Shop, part of Mallyan Spout Hotel (YO22 5AN, 01947 896486). Step back in time at Goathland Station Tea Room (YO22 5NF, 01751 472508), a retro-style cafe in a converted engine shed, or enjoy modern British dining at the Homestead Kitchen (YO22 5AN, 01947 896191), a welcoming, award-winning restaurant where elegant dishes are rooted in supplies from local farms and gardens.
NEARBY SWIM SPOTS: Thomason Foss and Water Arc Foss
EASIER ACCESS: The tarn is about half a mile from the road

of heather moorland in England and Wales and puts on a glorious show of purples, pinks and lilac from August to September. Three main types grow here; bell heather and cross-leaved as well as ling, the most common variety with tiny pink flowers.

The ancient funerary monuments of Two Howes sit on a prominent ridge-top position to the left of the path, from where the concrete pyramid of RAF Fylingdales, is just visible over on Snod Hill. This top-secret radar base was built during the Cold War and still provides a continuous ballistic missile early warning service to the UK and US governments. It also tracks objects orbiting in space.

You can take a short diversion to visit the Two Howes, however the walk continues straight ahead with Simon Howe gradually coming into view. Burial mounds and well-preserved settlement sites dating to the early Bronze Age are a distinctive feature of the moors. Simon Howe ❸ must be one of the most atmospheric of these sacred sites our ancestors left behind, beautiful reminders of their presence that we can see and touch today, giving us a physical and spiritual connection with the past.

The variety of stones around the cairn at Simon Howe date from different times. The prominent cairn and low wall are modern additions made by walkers, but the circle of standing stones and the main row of stones date back much further; finds at this site show that it has been occupied for 5,000 years. The views from the cairn are splendid and it is easy to appreciate its long-standing appeal, whether as a place to live or as a more momentary spot to pause while out walking.

From here, the route joins the Lyke Wake Walk across Howl Moor, the path marked by a handwritten sign. 'Lyke' comes from corpse and 'wake' is the watching over the corpse; the route remembers the many corpses carried over the moors on old

Starting out on the western fringes of the village, the walk ascends along a grassy bridleway towards Two Howes Rigg, with ever-widening views of Goathland and the surrounding moorland. Just beyond the first hillock is a sparkling moorland tarn ❷, cupped in a bowl of upland hills and circled by swallows and skylarks in summer. If you are here in August, when the heather is in bloom, the water glistens mauve from the purple flowers reflected in the oval pool. The tarn is spring-fed and the grassy shore is spongy but if you follow the shoreline around to the south-west corner, there is a gradual slope into the water, which can be surprisingly warm on a summer's day. Swimming in this glassy pond affords panoramic views over the valley as well as close encounters with damselflies and dragonflies, their slender bodies skimming the surface of the tarn as you glide through the water.

After your swim, it is a matter of picking the best path through ankle-deep heather towards Simon Howe. This twiggy purple shrub cloaks the uplands of the North York Moors, covering around a third of the national park. It is the biggest stretch

coffin routes and the ancient burial mounds encountered. This legendary walk stretches 42 miles, from Osmotherley to Ravenscar; anyone who completes its full length in 24 hours gains membership of the New Lyke Wake Walk Club.

Despite the Lyke Wake Walk's popularity, you need to pick your way carefully across remote Howl Moor along rutted, peaty tracks that descend the moor. Opposite is the valley of Wheeldale Beck, which eventually merges with Wheeldale Gill to form West Beck and tumble down to Goathland. The dale is best known for the Wheeldale Roman Road or Wade's Causeway. This excavated mile-long stretch of flagstones cutting across Wheeldale Moor is thought to be part of a route that ran between the Roman fort at Cawthorn Camp to another fort at Lease Rigg. According to local legend, however, Wade was a local giant who built the road for his wife, Bell, so she could herd her sheep to market. Although off the route, which leaves the Lyke Wake Walk at Wheeldale Lodge, it is worth returning another time to explore this remote valley with opportunities for bouldering at Hunt House Crag and Skivick Crag.

The next swim spot is at Nelly Ayre Foss **5**, a secluded waterfall hidden in a copse at the bottom of a wooded slope. The final descent is a short scramble down a steep bank, to shaded falls bounded by large stone slabs - useful for getting changed - and a deep plunge pool, with further pools downstream. The plunge pool beneath the falls is reached by clambering down the stone slabs encasing it and then sliding into the water; this requires a certain level of agility. It is such a sequestered setting, with sunlight filtering through the canopy of leaves and water cascading over rocky ledges that bathing here, then lounging on the rocks with a flask of tea, feels like discovering a secret world.

Emerging from this cloistered setting, a faint footpath keeps close to a stone wall, weaving between ferns and tussocky ground before opening out onto a country lane. The permissive path opposite climbs up to the escarpment of New Wath Scar, a steep-sided ravine carved out of sandstone above West Beck with far-reaching views all around **7**. Keep an eye out for wildlife; common lizards are just that, frequently spotted in the North York Moors, basking in sunny spots like the top of gate posts, so watch where you put your hands!

At a junction a set of steps leads down to a peaceful stretch of West Beck. There are some tempting pools here, along with a rope swing. The dramatic chute of Mallyan Spout is about 500m further downstream in a beautifully lush setting **8**. The rocky path passes directly below the falls as they plunge more than 20m into the beck, spraying mist all around. There are a couple of deep, wide pools for further dips before a final, steep, climb to the Mallyan Spout Hotel and the Coach House Coffee Shop.

1 From verge parking near the Mallyan Spout Hotel look for the public bridleway sign in front of a tree enclosed by a stone wall (if arriving by bus, the Coastliner bus stops near the Mallyan Spout Hotel). Follow the grassy path for a few metres to a junction. Bear left, following the bridleway as it rises onto moorland. Just after the first hill, you will see a tarn, your first swim spot.

2 Head clockwise around the tarn to its south-west corner to access the water. After your swim, choose your onward path carefully. Do not follow the bridleway you arrived on but follow the trodden path immediately above the tarn, passing a small cairn on the left. This uneven path can be wet and boggy after rain. A small stream which feeds the tarn runs to the right of it. Continue along the rugged path, navigating a rising route past the two burial mounds of Two Howes (off to the left) with Fylingdales in the distance. After passing Two Howes, the path forks to rejoin the bridleway you left earlier. Take this path, heading towards the cairn of Simon Howe.

3 After admiring the views from Simon Howe, take the path to the right of the howe, signed Lyke Wake Walk. Follow this rutted route as it crosses Howl Moor. Pass a couple of small piles of stones on the left and keep sight of a stone wall rising up the hill opposite. The path becomes very rocky as it descends the moorland. Straight ahead is Wheeldale Lodge.

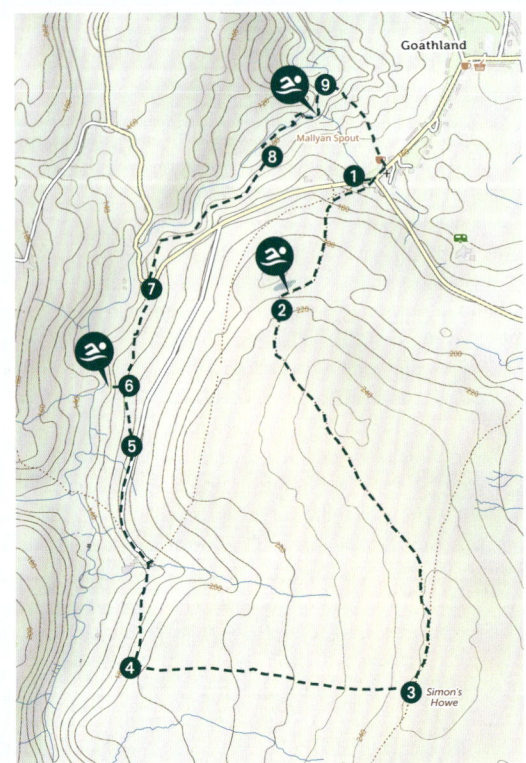

4 At the end of the rocky path, turn right onto a narrow lane then right again at the way marker. Follow this stony lane with a stone wall on your left. Continue past Hunt House. Keep to the lane, ignoring a track veering off left.

5 At a weathered green public footpath way marker, follow the path across the grass towards a copse. The path down to Nelly Ayre Foss, the second swim spot, is at the end of the fence. It can be obscured by bracken in

summer. The last short section is a steep scramble using tree roots as handles, so take care. Climb into the plunge pool carefully from the flat stone slabs surrounding it. After your dip, clamber back up the path.

6 Turn left, following a perimeter fence to join a path, bordered by another fence on the left then a stone wall and rowan trees. Follow the footpath (faint tracks) past a stone house, then pass through a wooden gate onto a lane.

7 Cross over and follow a permissive path (with a sign about erosion control) uphill. Go through a gate and onto the escarpment of New Wath Scar, high above the gorge of West Beck.

8 The path descends to a junction. If you want to shorten the route here, turn right to get back to the road where you parked your car. Otherwise, turn left, down steps to the beck, and a plunge pool and rope swing. Mallyan Spout waterfall is 500m downstream.

9 After visiting Mallyan Spout, return to the road by way of the steep steps that emerge next to the Mallyan Spout hotel. Turn right back to your car.

Walk 22

RAVENSCAR, STOUPE BECK SANDS AND BOGGLE HOLE

Soak up spectacular seascapes and swim in secluded coves on this history-steeped coastal hike, seeking out fossils and folklore along the way.

T he coastal village of Ravenscar was designed as a seaside resort to rival Scarborough and Whitby - or so its Victorian planners thought. Having spent a small fortune laying out roads, marking 1,000 building plots and digging a drainage system for this chic new holiday destination, The Peak Estate Company's grand scheme ended in bankruptcy in 1911 - for one main reason. Instead of the sandy beaches the investors had been promised, what they discovered on their first visit was a wild, clifftop location with limited access to the rocky shore below. Ravenscar, thereafter, became known as 'the seaside town that never was'.

The area's distinctive landscape is due to the Peak Fault, a geological anomaly that occurred 70 million years ago. This raised rocks to the south more than 180m higher than those to the north, bringing more resistant rock to the surface. For the Romans, this offered an excellent vantage point on which to build one of their coastal signal stations (roughly where the Raven Hall Hotel stands today). It also provides the ideal habitat for a colony of grey and common seals, which shelters behind a shelf of hard rock on the stony beach below.

A steep cliff path descends roughly through the line of the fault but this walk begins by heading out along the clifftops instead. Starting from the visitor centre, Ravenscar's imposing setting can be fully appreciated. The broad curve of lofty cliffs that sweeps round to the quaint fishing village of Robin Hood's Bay is what makes this dramatic location one of the most spectacular stretches of Yorkshire coastline, and the views here are sensational.

Making use of the Cleveland Way coastal path, this swim-walk passes the site of one of Britain's earliest chemical works, before

INFORMATION

Clifftop paths (may suffer from erosion), steep steps to coves, some indistinct footpaths inland. Cyclists use the gravel Cinder Track. You may encounter livestock.

DISTANCE: 6 miles
TIME: 3 hours
MAP: OS Explorer OL27 North York Moors Eastern Area
START & END POINT: On-street parking on Raven Hall Road, Ravenscar (NZ 980 016, 54.3989, -0.4918)
PUBLIC TRANSPORT: Bus Service 115 (Scarborough to Ravenscar)
SWIMMING: Coves at Stoupe Beck Sands and Boggle Hole
PLACES OF INTEREST: Peak Alum Works, Cinder Track, WWII radar station is just off-route
REFRESHMENTS: Tuck into cream teas and light lunches at Ravenscar Tearooms, Ravenscar (YO13 0LU, 01723 870444), right next to the Cinder Track. The nautically-themed Quarterdeck Café, at Boggle Hole Youth Hostel (YO22 4UQ, 01947 880352), has a terrace overlooking the beach.
OTHER AMENITIES: Toilets at the Quarterdeck Café, Boggle Hole
NEARBY SWIM SPOTS: Whitby, Scarborough North Bay or South Bay
EASIER ACCESS: There is a small car park above Stoupe Beck Sands but the steps down to the beach are steep. Limited roadside parking above Boggle Hole.

dropping down to the beach at Stoupe Beck Sands. The path then ribbons round to Boggle Hole, a small cove steeped in myths and legends, with a fossil-strewn sandy beach. The return is through undulating meadows, and along the Cinder Track, an old coastal railway line that used to run between Scarborough and Whitby. To swim at Boggle Hole, you will need a low or outgoing tide so aim to arrive there at least three hours before low tide.

From the visitor centre at Peakside, the route joins the Cleveland Way. Ahead is a wide-angle vista across Ravenscar's terracotta rooftops, with the crescent of Robin Hood's Bay beyond. Descending through woodland, the path emerges onto a route fringed with ferns and brambles, the latter laden with blackberries in late summer. The shimmering horizon of the sea - silvery grey on an overcast day or sapphire blue beneath a summer sky - gradually comes into view as the path dips down. Continuing along a wider gravel track, still on the Cleveland Way, the path narrows, hugging the cliff edge as it leads round to the well-preserved Peak Alum Works ❷.

The remnants of the works' stone buildings show how the extraction process worked in this once burgeoning industry. Alum was an essential fixative for dyes in the 16th century. Initially imported from Italy, until a Papal monopoly cut off supply during the Reformation, production switched to the northeast of England, as fossils found on the Yorkshire coast were similar to those of the alum quarries of Europe. One unexpectedly high-value commodity in this process was human urine; the works required 200 tonnes of this each year, mixing it with leachate to provide ammonium. Public urinals were, hence, installed in Hull specifically for this purpose, and barrels of the stuff were also imported from London and Newcastle, hauled up the cliff by tramway. The stench can only be imagined.

This part of the coast is also a good place to listen out for the mournful wail of seals, and to view them, too, if you've packed binoculars. Hundreds of seals come to breed on the rocks below - common seals in June and July, grey seals in October and November.

Continuing along the clifftop path, the views soar. A set of steep steps lead down to the clear waters of Stoupe Beck Sands ❹. This secluded, sandy beach forms part of Robin Hood's Bay and it is often quiet, even at the height of summer. The sandy beach in the middle is the best spot for a swim, with rocks either side for rockpooling. At low tide (check tide times), it is possible to walk between Ravenscar and Stoupe Beck Sands then onto Boggle Hole and Robin Hood's Bay.

You may encounter seals here, bobbing along from Ravenscar. Meeting a seal in its natural environment is a wonderful experience, however, always be mindful not to cause distress to these curious creatures. If you find yourself in the water with them, swim away slowly and quietly. Keeping a minimum of 100m, preferably 200m, away from them is recommended. They may look cute but they have a powerful bite.

After drying off, the walk continues towards Boggle Hole. Along its route, the Cleveland Way (and much of the Yorkshire coast) is suffering from coastal erosion and land slippages; you might notice the ground has cracked and shifted in places and there are sometimes diversions in place.

Before long, the path drops down to the slipway of Boggle Hole, lying at the end of the steep wooded valley of Mill Beck. Boggle Hole Youth Hostel ❻, set in a former watermill, is on the opposite side of the water and there's a small beach. It is a sheltered cove with carved-out hollows eroded by the sea – a spot well-used used

by smugglers in the 18th century to hide contraband, including rum and tobacco. Its curious name comes from local dialect for hobgoblin, a reference to mischievous, tiny folk they believed lived in the sea caves here. It was said that these boggles had magical healing powers and mothers would bring their sick children to the 'hob holes', hoping the boggles would cure them of their ailments.

The beach has a rocky, seaweed-strewn foreshore, giving way to a wide expanse of caramel sand. It is perfect for rockpooling and one of the best places on the Yorkshire coast for fossil hunting; the chance of spotting ammonites is high so keep your eyes peeled. The sea makes for an exhilarating swim at low or a receding tide but take care with the tide times to ensure you don't get cut off when you are on the sands or swimming. At high tide the water laps the slipway, joining Mill Beck and flooding the sands. The youth hostel café is the perfect place to refuel before the return leg of the walk.

Leaving Boggle Hole, the landscape becomes more pastoral as the route weaves through sheep-nibbled meadows and skirts pockets of woodland. A brick railway arch signals the Cinder Track ❾. Taking its name from the cinders the track was built on, in place of the usual crushed stone, the railway was in use from 1885 until 1965 but is enjoying new life as a 21.5-mile off-road cycling and hiking trail ❿.

The Cinder Track runs all the way back to Ravenscar, with several well-placed benches along the way to pause and admire the sea views. A spur off the main route leads to the old Brickworks Alum Quarry, just before arriving back at Ravenscar, if you're keen to explore more of the area's industrial heritage. Otherwise you can find out more about the wider area at the National Trust Visitor Centre, in Ravenscar – washed down with tea and scones at its friendly café.

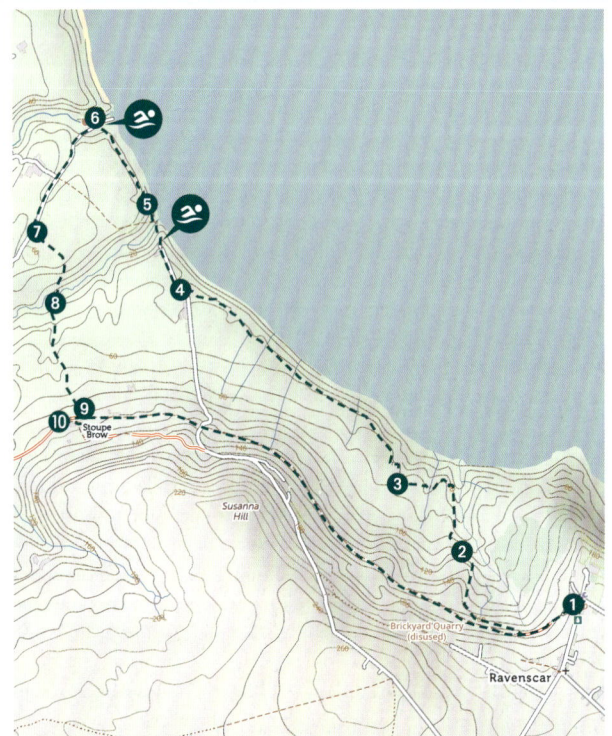

4 Turn right onto a lane, past Stoupe Bank Farm and a small car park on the left. Descend the stone steps to Stoupe Beck Sands and your first swim. Afterwards, return to the path, crossing a wooden footbridge and climbing some steep steps.

5 The path opens out with superb views towards Robin Hood's Bay. It is partially eroded so take care, particularly if it is wet. Descend the stepped, wooded path to a lane, with Boggle Hole Youth Hostel and café straight ahead.

6 Turn right down the slipway to the beach. Make sure to check tide times. You need at least three hours before high tide to swim here safely. After your swim, walk up the hill, passing parking bays on the left.

7 After a further 300m, look for a gate in the hedge on the left, leading onto a footpath through a field with great views towards Ravenscar. Towards the end of the field, follow the path into a wooded copse on the right, crossing a stile into a field with trees on the hillside ahead. Go across this field, through a wooden gate then cross the wooden bridge over Stoupe Beck.

8 Go through another wooden gate, into a field. Keep the trees and fence close to your left and continue along the faint path. Ignore a metal gate on the left. Go through a metal gate ahead, which

1 From roadside parking on Raven Hall Road, turn left onto Peakside, signed Cleveland Way, and go past the visitor centre. At a fork in the track, signed Alum Brickworks and Cinder Track, keep straight on, along the Cleveland Way. The path soon enters woodland, before descending to a junction.

2 Turn left at the Cleveland Way sign. At a footpath sign on the right follow the route for the Cleveland Way and Peak Alum works along a gravel track, past the alum works, which you can explore. The path continues, descending some steps to a gate. Go through the gate, cross a field to another gate and cross a wooden platform over the beck.

3 Turn right at the signpost and follow the hedge-lined path to a wooden bridge over a beck, down some steps and across another wooden bridge to a gate. Go through the gate, down a cobbled path and through another gate. The path ends at stone wall and gate.

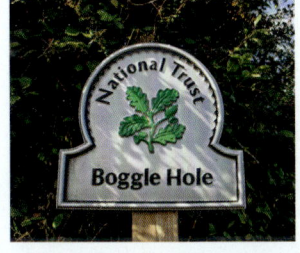

may be open, and follow the track into a large meadow. Go through another gate, or cross the stile, and continue straight ahead with the hedge on your left. Head towards a wooden gate and a brick railway arch.

9 Hop over a stile, go under the bridge and bear right, following footpath signs through a farm to a gate which leads onto the Cinder Track.

10 Turn right. Follow the Cinder Track for almost two miles back to Ravenscar. As you approach Ravenscar, look for a National Trust sign pointing to the Alum Brickworks Quarry on the right; detour off here if you would like to explore them. Afterwards, return to the track and continue to the visitor centre and parking.

FLAMBOROUGH COVES AND CAVES

Explore smugglers' coves and sea caves then swim to a secret beach beside a natural amphitheatre while puffins and gannets wheel around you.

Coastal clifftop paths, some steep climbs and uneven terrain. Rickety steps down to Thornwick Bay. Some pavement walking on the shortened walks.

DISTANCE: 7.5 miles (with 5.5 mile and 3 mile options)
TIME: 3.15 hours
MAP: OS Explorer OL301 Scarborough, Bridlington and Flamborough Head
START & END POINT: Flamborough village (TA 228 709, 54.1193, -0.1214)
PUBLIC TRANSPORT: East Yorkshire Buses Service 14 (Bridlington to Flamborough)
SWIMMING: Coves of Thornwick Bay, North Landing and South Landing
PLACES OF INTEREST: Flamborough Head, Danes Dyke, RSPB Bempton Cliffs
REFRESHMENTS: Thornwick Bay Cafe (YO15 1BD, 01262 850430) serves snacks and drinks (seasonal only). Boathouse Burger and Grill, North Landing (YO15 1BJ, 01262 673563) serves takeaway Flamborough crab sandwiches and more from the Old Lifeboat House. Headlands Restaurant and Café Bar at Flamborough Head (YO15 1AR, 01262 851020) serves crowd-pleasing classics.
OTHER AMENITIES: Toilets at Thornwick Bay café, North Landing and Flamborough Head
NEARBY SWIM SPOTS: Danes Dyke, Bridlington Bay
EASIER ACCESS: There are car parks at each of the coves but access is still steep. South Landing has a slipway.

lamborough Head is Britain's only northern chalk sea cliff, and is home to one of the most important seabird colonies in Europe. In spring and summer the bluffs throng with tens of thousands of breeding gannets, puffins and gulls while the chalk grassland above is carpeted with flowers, attracting butterflies and rare moths. You may even catch sight of dolphins or seals in the water. Alongside this striking seascape and wonderful wildlife is an abundance of coves, smugglers' caves and sea stacks, making this swim-walk an adventurous day out.

To get the most out of this walk, you'll need to familiarise yourself with local tide times; at low tide you will be able to swim to a secret beach from Little Thornwick Bay and explore the caves both there and at North Landing on foot. At high tide the sea floods the caverns, though it's still possible to swim from small, sandy beaches. Confident sea swimmers can swim in the caves but take extra care as tidal streams off Flamborough Headland are strong; a good knowledge of tides and weather is needed. There are options to shorten this walk at North Landing and Flamborough Lighthouse, walking back to the start along roads. Whichever walk you choose, start out around two hours before low tide for maximum enjoyment.

The name Flamborough comes from 'Flaneberg', possibly stemming from the Saxon word 'flaen' meaning arrow (which the spear-like headland resembles) or from another word meaning 'place of the flame'. The latter would be quite apt, as each year Flamborough holds a fire festival commemorating the Viking invasion of the coastline. Though it's not directly on the route, fans of Viking history might want to seek out Danes Dyke, a 2.4 mile-long flat-topped earthwork and ditch that dates from the Iron Age and slices the headland from north to south. It is most obvious at Danes Dyke, two miles south of South Landing.

The walk itself starts on the fringes of Flamborough village, soon joining a bridleway through fields towards the sea. As you pass the Haven holiday village ❷ there's a reminder of the precarious nature of this coastline in the form of The Friendly Forester, a Liverpool lifeboat rescued from the scrap heap by the owners of the site 34 years after she was taken out of service, and now safely docked beside a children's play area; an information board tells of her dramatic rescues around the Flamborough headland. Opposite is Thornwick Pools, reed-fringed wetlands that attract a wide variety of waders including buff-breasted sandpipers, spotted redshanks, dunlins, curlews and little egrets.

Beyond the cliffs, glimpses of the sparkling sea come into view. Perched on the rugged headland is the Thornwick Bay Café, a traditional, family-run snack bar that's been serving day trippers for almost half a century.

The impressive chalk cliffs encircle two pebble and shingle coves ❸. The more sequestered is Little Thornwick Bay, reached by steep, rickety steps behind the café. On a calm, summer's day the water here is transparent as it laps over pebbles and rocks. At low tide you can walk through an arch to the left of the cove and swim round to a secret beach. When conditions are right, it is hard to believe this is the North Sea, as you float in the clear water, strands of seaweed tickling your legs. On a blustery day, however, this tiny cove is wild and windswept; you only need to look at the sea stacks and arches to see what effect the elements have had on this coastline.

At low tide you can walk behind the headland dividing the two coves to a natural amphitheatre

and barnacle-cratered rock pools. It is a wonderful place to spot wildlife on a lazy summer evening, the setting sun casting a warm glow over the cliffs; we have watched bottlenose dolphins breaching out of the water and spied the slick heads of seals bobbing in the sea.

Just to the south-east, the larger Thornwick Bay is shrouded by grass-topped chalk cliffs that have eroded to create sea caves perfect for exploring at low tide. Always be sure of the tide times and swell before doing so; they change daily and the only time to venture safely into the caves is at slack water. If conditions are calm, you can snorkel around these awesome caverns.

After drying off, there is plenty more to enjoy along the route as you pass through Flamborough Cliffs Nature Reserve. In early summer, yellow bird's-foot-trefoil, common-spotted orchids and pyramidal orchids all thrive in the thin alkaline soil, seemingly untroubled by sea spray and biting easterly winds. This is a breath-taking stretch of coastline, unrivalled in the abundance of seabirds that depend on the ledges and crevices of its sheer cliff face. Fulmars, kittiwakes and razorbills all flock here but the highlight for most is the nesting

WALK 23 FLAMBOROUGH COVES AND CAVES

puffins, who return here from mid-May to July. Spending entire winters at sea, they return to nest in burrows here to raise their fluffy pufflings.

Mesmerising displays of delicate pink thrift, a favourite source of nectar for butterflies, adorn the cliff edge as the path ribbons around the headland and North Landing becomes visible beyond a gorse-lined gully. You will probably spot one or two cobles hauled up onto the sand and pebble beach here. These Yorkshire fishing boats are reputedly based on the Viking longboat, and were designed to be dragged up and down beaches in areas with no harbour.

Flanked by dramatic chalk cliffs, with turquoise water and a sand and pebble shore, North Landing is a beautiful place for a swim ❺. Tide times will determine your adventures here. North Landing is renowned for its extraordinary caves; on the south side of the bay is Robin Lythe's Cave, a cathedral-like cavern with a domed ceiling and a main (seaward) entrance where you can step out to watch the waves break. Named after a smuggler, this colossal cave was used to land and store contraband. It can only be accessed at low tide; an hour either side of low water is the only time you should enter the cave. At slack tide it's possible to swim back to shore from the seaward entrance but beware strong currents, check the tides and weather and be mindful of your party's swimming abilities.

If you want to shorten the walk here, you can return to Flamborough along North Marine Drive ❻. Otherwise the main route continues, climbing to chalk grassland and soaring cliffs with panoramic views of North Landing and the crinkled coastline behind. In late spring the chalk wall of this rock face is nicknamed 'seabird city' because of the huge number of sea birds it harbours. There are some fascinating sea stacks along this stretch and, as the

path veers inland, Selwicks Bay and Flamborough lighthouse come into view ❼. If you're up for another swim, Selwicks Bay is a sand and pebble beach with more caves and inlets to explore, as well as rock pools brimming with tiny marine life at low tide. The second set of steps is a marginally easier descent.

The active lighthouse here dates to 1806. The older lighthouse, several metres inland, was built in 1674 as a business venture and is the earliest known lighthouse still in existence in the UK. Curiously, however, it was never used due to lack of donations from passing ships. You can also shorten the walk here and if you do so, you will pass the chalk-white lighthouse on your route back to Flamborough ❽. Before doing so, don't miss a quick detour to High Stacks, an isolated pebble cove with a spectacular sea arch known locally as the Drinking Dinosaur. Just south of the lighthouse buildings, hundreds of common seals can often be spotted sprawled out on this shingle beach ❾.

The onward path towards South Landing is easy to follow, abutting the field headland on one side with steep drops on the sea-facing side, so take care with young children and dogs. This secluded beach lies at the end of a narrow, wooded gully, flanked by lofty chalk cliffs that continue beneath the sea to form part of the largest underwater chalk reef in Europe ❿. A wide band of weathered chalk cobbles gives way to a sandy shore and, at low tide, a secret underwater world of anemones, limpets, crabs and starfish is revealed in the myriad of rock pools.

The sandiest part of the beach, the best place to enter the water for a swim, is directly ahead of the slipway. After enjoying a relaxing dip here, there is one final push up the hill from the beach, past the lifeboat station and Living Seas Centre, back to Flamborough village.

❶ From roadside parking walk along North Marine Drive, signposted North Landing, to a bridleway on the left, just past the last house. Follow the field headland to a wooden fence circling a holiday park.

❷ Bear right and just before the exit of the site, turn left onto a bridleway, passing a stationary lifeboat on the left and a nature reserve on the right. At the fingerpost pass through a wooden gate and turn left onto the 'adventure trail'. At a gap in the fence on the left join a path and head towards Thornwick Bay Café.

❸ Steps down to Little Thornwick Bay are to the left of the cafe. After your swim, return to the cliff top.

❹ Just after an information board, turn left onto a track signed Private Road, then follow the permissive path diagonally across the field to join the coastal footpath.

❺ Go through a small wooden gate into a Yorkshire Wildlife Trust (YWT) reserve and continue on the coastal path. North Landing gradually comes into view. Cross a wooden bridge over a small ravine and stream and climb the wooden steps to North Landing car park. Keep left of a low wooden barrier and head towards the cafe. Use the slipway to reach the beach. An hour either side of low water is the only time you can safely walk into the caves.

❻ After exploring, you now have options. To continue, follow the main directions. Or follow North Marine Drive back to Flamborough village make this a three-mile circular walk,

7 Follow the footpath in front of the café onto the grassy cliff top and continue around the headland. Pass between two large stone pillars with Flamborough lighthouse visible in the distance. The path then skirts the golf course, with a great view of Selwicks Bay ahead. Climb some wooden steps. A steep path on the left leads down to the cove if you want another swim. There are also (less steep) steps down at the other end of the beach.

8 To continue to South Landing follow the main directions. Or, for a shorter 5.5-mile circular walk follow Lighthouse Road past the old lighthouse, for 1.4 miles to the crossroads then pick up directions from point 10 below.

9 Rejoin the coastal path from the lighthouse onto the headland. Continue straight ahead to High Stacks to admire the large seal colony from above. Afterwards, continue along the clifftop path. Take care with children and dogs as the path is close to the cliff edge in places and can be muddy. After skirting a couple of ravines, South Landing comes into view. A sculpture trail leads off to the right but the coastal path continues ahead, passing two benches.

10 A few metres further along, a set of wooden steps descend to the slipway and beach. After a final dip in the sea, return to the slipway and climb the hill alongside a ravine, passing the Living Seas Centre on the right, to the crossroads *(Pick up directions here for the shortened 5.5 mile route).* Cross the road onto South Sea Road North and continue towards the playing field, keeping this on your right as the road bears left to a junction. Turn right at the junction and continue back to where you parked on North Marine Drive.

Walk 24

SPURN POINT OUT-AND-BACK

A world's end kind of walk, along a strip of sand dunes beneath wide open skies, taking in wildlife, wild flowers, wartime heritage and secluded beaches.

*W*ild, windswept and constantly shifting, Spurn is unique, a remote tip of land that stretches for three and a half miles but is as narrow as 50m wide in places. Curving between the North Sea and the Humber Estuary this iconic, finger-like peninsula is forever at the mercy of the elements, created by longshore drift washing away sand on its east side and depositing it on its west.

What makes this striking landscape so compelling is its remote location. There's a real end-of-the-world feel and, if you are craving solitude and tranquility, this is the place to find it, beneath wide, open skies, surrounded by the sound of lapping waves.

If it feels peacefully empty, though, it isn't. Spurn is a wildlife-rich blend of beach, mudflats, dunes, salt marsh, grassland, native sea buckthorn scrub and saline lagoons. One of the best bird observatories in the UK for bird migration, myriad birds arrive here throughout the year, from tiny goldcrests and Arctic geese to whooper swans, merlins, peregrines, redwings and fieldfares, as well as a huge variety of wading birds. This is also a great place to spot harbour porpoises, seals and bottlenose dolphins. On our last visit, the Yorkshire Wildlife Trust (YWT) ranger had just sighted a humpback whale. So bring your binoculars!

Wandering along wildflower-fringed paths, there are miles of sandy beaches hidden behind the dunes for a secluded sea swim. Spurn's exposed location means it has strong tidal currents and swimming near the tip is not advised. It is best to choose a calm day, with little or no wind, for a safe swim from the beaches between the groynes. Although the walk is mostly linear, there is much to take in besides the beauty of the natural surroundings,

INFORMATION

A level walk along tarmac and sandy tracks, a stretch of sandy beach and meadow footpaths. Check tide times.

DISTANCE: 7 miles
TIME: 3 hours
MAP: OS Explorer 292 Withernsea and Spurn Head
START & END POINT: Spurn Point Discovery Centre car park (TA 417 154, 53.6163, 0.1411)
PUBLIC TRANSPORT: Bus Service 71E (Hull, Easington, Spurn Discovery Centre)
SWIMMING: Beaches between the groynes
PLACES OF INTEREST: Spurn Lighthouse, chalk meadows, relics of WWI battery
REFRESHMENTS: Spurn Discovery Centre café (HU12 0UH, 01964 650144) serves a locally sourced menu with ever-changing views of the Humber through its huge glass windows. Or try the Crown and Anchor at Kilnsea for good value pub classics and sunset views over the estuary (HU12 0UB, 01964 650276)
FACILITIES: Toilets at the Discovery Centre and a toilet block at the tip of Spurn
NEARBY SWIM SPOTS: Easington Beach
EASIER ACCESS: You can park right next to Easington Beach for a swim just north of Spurn

including military and maritime heritage, so the return leg doesn't feel repetitive. Enjoy the delights of the sea-facing side on the outward stretch and detour through the flower-filled meadows of the estuary on your return.

You will need to check tide times as there is a half-mile 'wash-over' section of sand that is covered by water at high tide, cutting off the peninsula from the mainland - effectively creating Yorkshire's only island. Do not attempt to cross this stretch until the tide has completely receded as strong currents and soft sand mean it can be dangerous. You should consult Spurn tide times on the YWT website before your visit.

Before setting out, you might want to pop into the Spurn Discovery Centre, to find out more about the wildlife and heritage of Spurn. There is also a small shop and a light-filled café with superb views over the Humber Estuary. The centre also runs events throughout the year including Spurn Safaris, military safaris, photography trips, bird-spotting excursions and sunrise and sunset tours.

The walk begins on a footpath running parallel to the road onto the point (no cars are allowed beyond here), passing the meeting point for the Spurn Safari ❶, which transports visitors to the tip in an ex-military Unimog. Beyond is Spurn Peninsula, where the boulder clay cliffs of the Holderness coast end and the promontory begins. As one of the world's fastest eroding coastlines, the peninsula is forever in a state of flux. The route cuts across the foreshore, strewn with pebbles, shells and driftwood, with groynes and the relics of military pillboxes at the far end ❷. The wash-over is one of the narrowest stretches of the peninsula, and it gets inundated at high tide. It was created by a huge tidal surge in 2013 that destroyed a large amount of sand dune and the road leading to

the point. There is a shelter for anyone who gets caught out.

A growing sense of wilderness permeates the walk as you look across the estuary and beyond the sand dunes to the empty beaches on the opposite edge. The sandy track is fringed with wild flowers, including spiky, silvery-mauve sea holly, orange-berried sea buckthorn and marram grass, all of which help to stabilise the dunes. On the seaward side, look out for paths through the dunes onto the sands where you can take your pick of the beaches for a swim in the sea ❸. It can feel exposed but choose the right day and there is lots of fun to be had splashing in the billowing waves, with not a soul to disturb you.

Strands of seagrass wreath the mud flats: it is the only flowering plant that can survive in seawater and pollinate while submerged. The species that grows on the peninsula is dwarf eelgrass. Back in 1936 Spurn's seagrass meadow was the size of 700 football pitches but now only five per cent of that remains due to pollution, coastal development and bait digging. The Yorkshire Wildlife Trust (YWT) is spearheading a project to restore 80 hectares of seagrass meadow by gathering, germinating and replanting seagrass seeds, raising the profile of blue carbon capture in a bid to help manage the climate crisis.

Bee-friendly restharrow and the pink and white parasols of sea bindweed flutter in the breeze on the fringes of the track. The beautiful wildflower meadows of the Chalk Bank lie on the estuary side ❸. In 1849 a huge storm penetrated the peninsula and further storms created a channel, leaving Spurn in a vulnerable state. It was thought the whole promontory would wash away, leaving the Hawke Roads anchorage exposed to the full force of the North Sea. To prevent this, the port authorities filled the breaches using chalk, hence the name, Chalk Bank. The embankment is now an important habitat for passage and wintering waders, such as dunlins, oystercatchers and sanderlings, and the hides provide discreet lookouts for birdwatchers.

Spurn's iconic black and white lighthouse soon comes into view. This award-winning 39-metre beacon was built in 1895 and guided sailors around the coastline for 90 years before it was decommissioned in 1985. It is open at weekends for tours with 360-degree views over land and sea from the top.

Not far from here, a side track leads to the relics of World War One bunkers and a railway ❹. There is also a fascinating timeline display board, charting Spurn's military history right back to the Napoleonic Wars. In the Victorian era Spurn was celebrated as a tourist attraction and a particularly captivating photograph, dating to 1870, shows Victorian families paddling in the water here. Under the ownership of the Constable family, of nearby Constable Burton Hall, Spurn was under military control as a defence complex from the outbreak of World War One to 1959, when it was taken over by the YWT.

Beyond the lighthouse and jetty ❺, Spurn's tip is within striking distance. It may feel an anticlimax to be greeted by a line of brick buildings and houses but a lifeboat has been stationed at Spurn since before the RNLI was even formed, in 1824. Crew members and their families used to live in the houses, though nowadays they operate on rotating shifts, using the houses as a base. For a dramatic finale to this outward leg you can clamber onto the hilly terrain to explore gun emplacements, bunkers and tunnels or drop down to the sands to circumnavigate the point (just beyond ❻). Standing on Spurn's tip it is possible to watch the sun rise over the North Sea and set over the Humber Estuary,

enjoying the kind of end-of-the-earth feel very few places provide.

Returning along the main track, the route branches off into the chalk meadows ❼. Edging the estuary's mudflats, these pastures are a spectacular sight in summer, spangled with wildflowers. Tiny meadow pipits, with their high-pitch piping call, nest in the fields, and you might spot lizards basking on the raised banks. Hebridean sheep also graze here sometimes, helping to manage the grassland and prevent it returning to thick scrub.

On the far side of the meadows, the walk rejoins the main track back to the start. This wild swim-walk can be rounded off perfectly with a pot of tea and a scone at the Discovery Centre café or by bagging the window seat at the Crown and Anchor in Kilnsea for the best sunset views over Spurn and the Humber Estuary.

DIRECTIONS

1 From the car park follow the grassy footpath, signed Spurn, that runs parallel with the road towards the point. Go through a gate. At the meeting point for Spurn Safaris you are officially on the peninsula. No dogs are allowed beyond here.

2 The track descends to a sandy beach and you need to walk across the sand for around half a mile. At the groynes a track rises onto a firmer, sometimes sandy, track.

3 On the seaward side there are several stretches of beach between the groynes for a swim in the sea. On the opposite side is the chalk bank which the return route takes in.

4 Return to the tarmac track and continue for just over a mile, with the lighthouse visible ahead. Just before you reach the lighthouse, bear left to the WWI signal station, and an information board about the military history of Spurn.

5 Return to the main track and continue to an enclave of houses (on the left) and the jetty (on the right). To appreciate Spurn's unique location you can descend to the beach on the jetty side and walk right round the point.

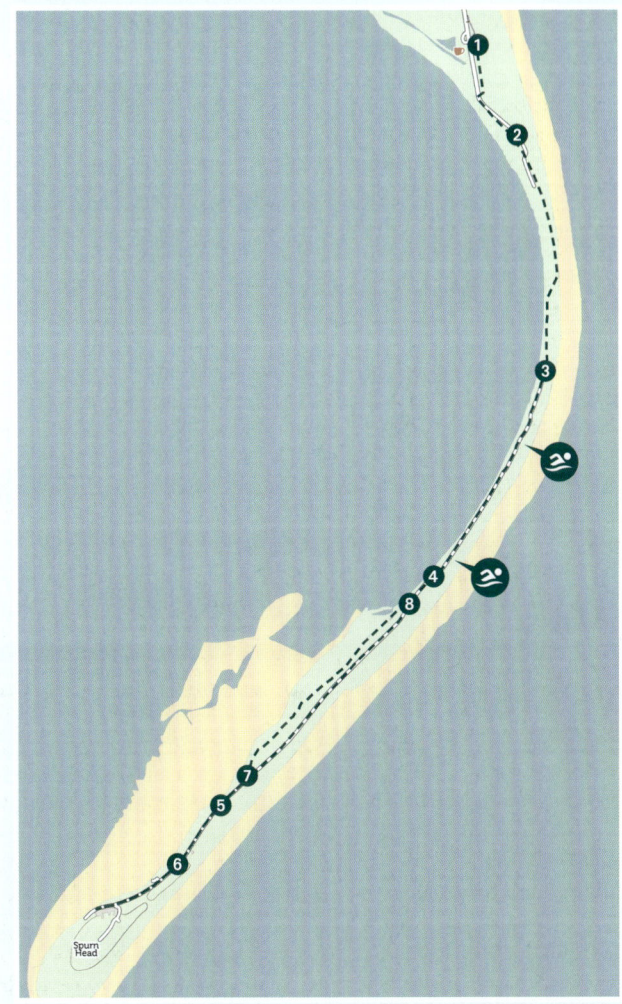

6 Alternatively, you can climb the steps ahead onto a raised mound and wander around the ruins of WWI shelters. After exploring the tip, rejoin the track for the return leg of the walk.

7 Look out for a wooden gate on the left, leading to the chalk bank meadows, a highlight in summer. Follow the footpath through the meadow to a bird hide and a gate on the right.

8 Turn left onto the main track and retrace your steps back to the car park.

Walk 25

LUDDENDEN DEAN AND MIDGELY MOOR

Explore one of Calderdale's most alluring vales before ascending to a pair of heather-fringed reservoirs with commanding views over the Luddenden Valley.

INFORMATION

Varied terrain including woodland footpaths, bridleways, country tracks and lanes. Some steps and stone squeeze stiles.

DISTANCE: 5 miles
TIME: 3 hours
MAP: OS Explorer OL21 South Pennines (Burnley, Hebden Bridge, Keighley and Todmorden
START & END POINT: Jerusalem Farm Education Centre car park, Luddenden Dean (SE 036 278, 53.7468, -1.9447)
PUBLIC TRANSPORT: Bus Service 574 (Halifax, Sowerby Bridge, Midgley) to Booth (one mile from the start)
SWIMMING: Pools and falls on Luddenden Brook, small waterfall pools on Warley Moor, reservoir at Midgley Moor (No Swimming signs)
PLACES OF INTEREST: Castle Carr, Luddenden Dean
REFRESHMENTS: Bob's Tearoom and Gardens (HX2 6XB, 01422 884354) is en route, serving homemade cakes, teas and coffees on Saturdays and Sundays. Cat I'th Well Pub in Wainstalls (HX2 7TR, 01422 618684) is just off the route. Its beer garden has superb valley views. Hebden Bridge is also nearby, with a range of cafés and restaurants.
NEARBY SWIM SPOTS: Gaddings Dam, Todmorden
EASIER ACCESS: Luddenden Brook is a short walk from the car park

The secluded valley of Luddenden Dean is one of the prettiest in Calderdale, and a pleasure to explore. Tucked away between Halifax and bohemian Hebden Bridge, this peaceful, verdant backwater is characterised by rolling pastures and pockets of ancient woodland, cut through by the babbling Luddenden Brook. Luddenden means Ludd Valley, or Valley of the Loud Stream, a reference to the tumbling peat-stained stream that was once harnessed to power corn mills here (and, later worsted-producing ones).

The leafy vale is bound on either side by the dimpled landscapes of Warley and Midgley Moors. This circular walk explores the Dean along woodland trails and footpaths threading through the valley bottom, before ascending tracks and country lanes to the moorland tops and a pair of sparkling reservoirs as well as magnificent South Pennine views.

Starting out at the nature reserve and campsite of Jerusalem Farm, the walk leads through a wooden gate onto a grassy track, bound by a mossy stone wall and a jumble of beech, sycamore and holly trees, to Luddenden Brook and Wade Bridge. Just before the bridge, fern-fringed steps drop down to a riverside meadow dotted with picnic tables - and tents if the campsite is open - where a small waterfall flows into a peaty pool ❶. You can take a dip before your hike or save it for your return. Keep an eye out for dippers, bobbing up and down on the rocks then plunging into the fast-flowing stream in search of small insects.

Across the bridge, several routes fan out into the woodland. Following the Calderdale Way ❷, the path rises up and away from the brook through mature oak woodland. These delightful woods

teem with life and birdsong. Tiny treecreepers and nuthatches search for insects to pluck from the bark of towering, twisted oaks while great spotted woodpeckers climb the trunks. They are not always easy to see but their loud drumming can quite clearly be heard. One of the first plants of the year to bloom here, in spring, is the splashy wood anemone, making the most of the light through the leafless woodland canopy. Drifts of bluebells follow, carpeting the woodland floor in a haze of deep violet-blue; their presence is a sign of a rare and special habitat.

Emerging into a glade, a wooden footbridge leads over a stream that trickles from a reed-choked mill pond. Instead of continuing through the woods, the path immediately rises up a wooded

bank towards a stone step stile onto a country lane. Passing a terrace of stone cottages, the route then picks up a footpath curving around the slope of the hillside ❸. In summer, this grassy bank is sprinkled with the crimson flower spikes of foxgloves, and hums with bumblebees, honeybees and moths. Ambling through this tranquil corner of Calderdale, it feels a million miles away from the urban bustle of Halifax, just a stone's throw away.

With height gained, the views are ever-more expansive, fields and moor punctuated by a few scattered farms and cottages. At a stone bridge, the route again encounters Luddenden Brook, cascading over a series of stone slabs. If the prospect of refreshments appeals, the Cat I'th Well pub is just around the corner ❹. Perched on the edge of moorland, the pub has an inviting beer terrace that overlooks the valley. Its name comes from a corruption of Catherine's Well rather than anything to do with a poor kitty stuck in a well; there is a spring here, in a stone trough set into the wall of the lane opposite the pub.

If you have resisted the lure of the beer garden, continue along the route, ascending steps to follow a grassy footpath high above the brook, then deviating up through a sloping field. A cobbled lane rises to the peaceful hamlet of Wainstalls; you can't miss the curiously named Tongue End, a street name which may relate to its location at the end of a 'tongue' of land ❹.

A cluster of traditional stone-built houses perch high on the hill here, surrounded by a mosaic of pastures, bounded by gritstone walls with splendid views over the Luddenden Valley towards Midgley Moor. Wainstalls was once home to Calvert's Mills, a worsted-spinning textile mill. The walk passes one of the 19th-century mill buildings, now converted into apartments. What a frenetic place it must have been in Victorian times, with the thunderous roar of machinery and stifling heat.

Leaving Wainstalls and skirting the edge of Warley Moor, the landscape feels increasingly wild. In summer banks of luscious bilberries and purple heather fringe the lanes, and the call of curlews and distinctive 'peewit' of the lapwings echo above. Look out, too, for hovering kestrels searching for mice and beetles in the moor grass. Just outside the village a series of falls tumble from Leadbeater Dam down the moorland slope to create mini plunge pools, almost at the roadside ❺. It can feel exposed up here if the wind is blowing but on a hot day you might be grateful for a cooling dip.

Descending along a bridleway towards the valley bottom, the sloping fields are brightened with foxgloves in summer. The shell of an abandoned railway carriage sits beside the footpath just before the ruins of New Hey Farm ❼. So seamlessly does it blend in with the landscape that it might almost be an Andy Goldsworthy art installation. Further along, beyond Upper Hey Wood, a country road winds round to an impressive castellated gatehouse ❿.

This was once the entrance to Castle Carr Mansion, a mock Tudor castle that once stood above Luddenden Dean. It was built for Captain Joseph Priestly Edwards in the 1860s, though he never saw it completed. Despite its Gothic grandeur, it was unloved, and plagued both by midges and by issues around rights of way. When it went to auction in 1962, bids only reached £9,250 so it was withdrawn and demolished. Today only the gatehouse remains, along with a small section of the mansion. Its water gardens, complete with a 40m-high fountain, open annually for charity.

After passing through the gateway arch, an enjoyable stretch of walking ensues along Catherine House Lane. Pleasant views stretch across the chequered fields of the valley, with the peaty brown brook flowing through its centre. The lane emerges at Bob's Tearoom ⓬, a good place to refuel before tackling the short (optional) excursion to the reservoirs of Midgley Moor, up a zig-zagging moorland track.

Positioned on the flanks of the moor, these two heather-fringed reservoirs offer up panoramic views ⓭. The furthest dam is particularly picturesque, fringed by trees with a crumbling stone barn in one corner. There are some timeworn signs discouraging swimming but this dark, peaty pond is a known local swim spot. After soaking up the superb views from these hilltop dams, the return route winds back to Bob's Tearoom and along the lane to the car park.

road edges open moorland to the right and, as the route flattens, look for a series of small falls and pools along Leadbeater Dam, a possible dipping spot.

6 After a few metres of road walking look out for a track on the left (signed Bridleway Only). Follow this past Upper Green Eden Farm, where the track becomes rougher.

7 At the road turn left. You can glimpse the lodge at Castle Carr from here.

8 Climb the stile on the left then follow the footpath beside a stone wall, passing the metal shell of an abandoned railway carriage, then the ruins of New Hey Farm. Pass the ruins and descend the field diagonally to a stone stile.

9 Climb the stile and follow a grassy path down towards a stone wall and into Upper Hey Wood. Cross a small stream and continue as the path becomes narrower, hemmed in by heather and bilberries, eventually reaching a stile onto the lane.

10 At the lane, turn right, passing a green bench on the right and a row of cottages further along on the left. Cross a stone bridge towards a castellated gatehouse. Swing left here, through the gateway arch and onto Catherine House Lane.

11 Follow this track for about a mile, with lovely views across the valley, to Bob's Tearoom on the left.

1 From the end of Jerusalem Farm car park, follow the footpath signed Wade Bridge/ Calderdale Way. Continue to a set of steps on your right leading to a meadow, some falls and pools. You could have a dip now, or wait until the end of the walk. Return to the steps and cross the bridge.

2 Follow the Calderdale Way path that rises uphill, not the path that runs alongside the brook. The correct path is edged with a small woven willow fence. Pass an overgrown millpond on your left and cross the small bridge then go through the gate. Look for hidden steps on the left that wind up to a track. Cross this track and continue up the next set of steps to a gap in the wall and stile onto a lane.

3 Turn left, passing a row of cottages on the left and Bank House on the right. Just after a driveway, signed Hock Cliff, look for a gap in

the wall on the left. Go through this onto a narrow grassy footpath that follows the slope of the hill. Go through two small gates next to Hock Cliff cottage and continue along the track to the road.

4 Turn left. The Cat I'th Well pub is a few metres further along if you want to stop for refreshments. Otherwise, look for a footpath sign and steps on the right just before the bridge, leading to a grassy footpath. As the path meets a mossy stone wall, look out for another set of steps on the right. Climb these, go through a gate and walk up the field with a stone wall to your left, to a bridleway beyond a gate. Turn left, past the cottages of Tongue End, into Wainstalls village along the tarmac and cobbled track.

5 At the end of the bridleway turn left onto a lane with sweeping views of Luddenden Valley. The

⓬ At a fork in the road, take the higher route and continue to a track on the right, signed Clough Lane. Follow this uphill to a stone wall. Another rougher track runs alongside the wall.

⓭ Turn left along this track and look for a derelict stone building on the right beyond the wall and, a little further along, a rustic metal gate. Go through this and follow the narrow track past a ruined pump house to the corner of the right-hand reservoir. Turn left to walk along the embankment to a bench. There are some 'no swimming' signs but the left-hand reservoir is a popular local swim spot, with access by the ruined building. Afterwards, retrace your steps to Bob's Tearoom.

⓮ Take the lower fork along the lane back to the car park on the left. If you want to return to Wade Bridge for a paddle and dip, take the footpath on the left, just before you get back to the car park.

Walk 26

WESSENDEN FALLS AND BLAKE CLOUGH

Explore the wild moorland of the South Pennines, bejewelled with sparkling reservoirs, then wander into hidden cloughs to find cascading waterfalls.

INFORMATION

Varied terrain including well-used tracks, narrow footpaths, some uneven ground and steep sections in the cloughs

DISTANCE: 5 miles
TIME: 2.5 hours
MAP: OS Explorer OL1 The Peak District Dark Peak Area
START & END POINT: Wessenden Head Road, lay-by parking (SE 077 075, 53.5648, -1.8848)
PUBLIC TRANSPORT: South Pennine Community Transport 357 (Holmfirth, Greenfield, Ashton-under-Lyme) and 352 (Holmfirth, Uppermill). Alight at bus stop on Greenfield Road/ Wessenden Road. Otherwise train station at Marsden then taxi.
SWIMMING: Wessenden Falls and Blake Clough
PLACES OF INTEREST: Marsden Moor
REFRESHMENTS: None en route but the towns of Marsden, Holmfirth, Meltham and Slaithwaite have an array of lovely cafés and bistros. Try the canal-side Handmade Bakery in Slaithwaite (HD7 5HA, 01484 842175), the perfect place to refuel after a moorland hike. Lu's Place in Meltham (HD9 4DS, 01484 850050) is a contemporary café in a beautiful setting.
NEARBY SWIM SPOTS: Sparth Reservoir, Marsden
EASIER ACCESS: Both waterfalls are remote. For a more accessible swim try Sparth Reservoir.

s a young man, the artist Ashley Jackson wrote in his sketchbook, *"To see the spirit of Yorkshire and its moors through your eyes is one thing, many people look but only a few will see and feel its very soul"*. Stand at the top of the expansive Wessenden Valley, at the beginning of this walk, and feeling that soul is now a little easier thanks to a metal frame spotlighting the view. One of six such frames installed across the county in 2014, the 'Framing the Landscape' art project was created by Jackson, now in his eighties, with the support of the National Trust.

The idea was to help visitors see the landscape as an ever-changing painting in an open-air gallery and Jackson's frame sets the perfect tone for this beautiful walk, which has views to savour at every turn, not to mention two magical waterfalls hidden in the valley's lush, fern-carpeted cloughs.

The Wessenden Valley forms part of the National Trust's Marsden Moor Estate in the South Pennines. This vast swathe of moorland intersects the conurbations of West Yorkshire and Manchester yet part of it also lies in the area of the Peak District National Park that's known as the Dark Peak – a reference to the layer of rugged millstone grit and shale which overlies its limestone bed. Geology is important here; the name Wessenden stems from Old English and means 'valley with rock suitable for whetstones', a nod to the fine-grained stone's use in tool-sharpening. The magnificent valley itself was sharpened, or rather carved out, by retreating glaciers and is still cut through by Wessenden Brook.

At Wessenden Head, the start of this walk, the path picks up the Pennine Way, a 268-mile national trail that runs along England's

rocky spine. The route then descends towards the shimmering water of Wessenden Head reservoir. The moors have been a water catchment area since the 19th century, when a number of reservoirs were created to provide water to power the mills further down the valley (and, later, to slake the thirst of Huddersfield's inhabitants).

A striking feature of the landscape, this bracelet of sparkling blue pools twinkles as you drop further into the valley. Unfortunately, we cannot advocate swimming in these outdoor pools, although many people do (no doubt you will see swimmers heading in their direction if it's a hot day). The dams are owned and operated by Yorkshire Water, which does not allow swimming in any of its reservoirs, and has installed officious signs warning of the dangers of doing so. Hopefully, in the not-too-distant future, groups such as Sheffield OUtdoor Plungers (SOUP) will succeed in their campaigns to allow access to sites like this reservoir at Wessenden Head.

For now, while these breeze-rippled lakes must be enjoyed from the shore, there are other delightful swim spots further along the trail. Diverting from the main path not long into the walk, a grassy track leads you to higher ground, and a fantastic view of Wessenden Head and Wessenden reservoirs fringed with tussocks of grass and, in summer, the pink spikes of foxgloves ❷. Listen out for buzzards keening as they circle overhead in search of food. These impressive birds of prey are not fussy eaters - everything from earthworms to rabbits or even carrion will satisfy their appetites- and this characteristic enables them to survive in a variety of habitats.

After rejoining the main track, the route rises, curving around the valley. In summer part of the route is hemmed in by ferns so you may find yourself wandering along, arms raised above the encroaching greenery. At Sike Clough a small waterfall tumbles down from the moors and a wooden footbridge crosses the stream ❹. Emerging from this deep ravine, expansive views stretch out ahead to Wessenden Reservoir and, beyond it, towards Wessenden Moor. Dropping down to the dam wall of Wessenden Reservoir and rejoining the Pennine Way, you will soon spot the tall, slender plume of Wessenden Falls tumbling over huge granite blocks.

Semi-obscured by a sea of rhododendrons, the pitted grey rock face here provides a habitat for gleaming mosses, well-rinsed from the spray ❼. Although the eye-catching rhododendrons look attractive, they are an invasive species and their thick foliage prevents native plants from thriving, not only across Marsden Moor, but in other parts of England too. The National Trust holds regular volunteer days to remove this flamboyant plant, introduced from the Mediterranean and Asia, and much-loved by the Victorians.

A faint path descends the fern-carpeted slopes to the falls, via a hop and a jump over rickety stepping stones and a scramble over rocks. It is a lovely place for a cooling dip in the peat-stained plunge pool, which is just large enough for a few strokes, before drying off and continuing along the track to the next cascade.

Following the outflow of Wessenden Reservoir as it wiggles along the valley bottom, the steep path descends to a footbridge where sand martins swoop above the sparkling stream ❽. The path upwards from here is arduous but the views are a good reason to pause every now and then to catch your breath. From the concrete block and mast at the crest, make sure to pick up the correct path; it hugs the fern-clad slopes of a gorge, with a cascading stream rushing down its rocky cleft. There's a remote feel to this spot and it offers a chance to savour the wild beauty of this landscape as you approach the head of the valley.

Multiple strings of white water cascade into copper-coloured pools that increase in size as you ascend. Some promise the potential of a dip, particularly as you near the main falls of Blake Clough ❿. Finding this secluded pool feels like such a treat as it is well-hidden and evades many who seek to find it. It is an enchanting spot with a dark, velvety plunge pool, perfect for bathing. As you float, grey wagtails may join you, flitting around the rim and hoping to catch a midge or two above the water.

After leaving the waterfall, the narrow, homeward path winds out of the clough, snaking round towards Wessenden dam to rejoin the Pennine Way and lead back to the start of the walk. If you are feeling inspired by this brooding Yorkshire moorland, you might like to visit Ashley Jackson's gallery in Holmfirth. He is one of the country's leading landscape watercolourists and his evocative paintings hang on some very prestigious walls, including those of former US president, Bill Clinton.

1 From lay-by parking on Wessenden Head Road cross the road and look for the NT Marsden Moor sign and the 'Framing the Landscape' picture frame. Go through the gate and follow the track (the Pennine Way) into the valley with Wessenden Head reservoir ahead.

2 After 500m, leave the main track and follow a grassy path on the right as it rises up the hill, offering a lovely vista of Wessenden Head reservoir and Wessenden reservoir ahead. Look for the ruins of some buildings on the right to check you are on the correct path.

3 The path descends to cross a wooden bridge then rejoins the main track as it winds around the hill.

4 After the entrance to a ravine on your right, look for a stony track that rises away from the main track. Follow this for a short way and then continue onto a higher path that runs parallel to the main path below. This higher path crosses a small metal platform over a gully before winding further into a deep clough. At the head of this gorge is a small waterfall and a footbridge. Cross the bridge and follow the path leading out of the clough then continue along the hillside path.

5 Keep an eye out below for a barn and a ruined stone building at the end of Wessenden Reservoir; these will help you identify the route down. The steep, descending path leads through a clearing in bracken

before meeting another path and a stone wall at the bottom.

6 Turn left towards Wessenden Reservoir, down some steps and rocky ground onto a gravel track that veers right, away from the reservoir.

7 After a few metres, look left across the valley to see Wessenden Falls, your first swim spot. Follow a grassy path to the falls, crossing stepping stones over a stream then clambering over boulders to reach the plunge pool. After your swim, return along the same path to the gravel track. Turn left.

8 At the Pennine Way fingerpost and an attractive 'Peak and Northern Footpaths Society' sign, turn left to descend a rocky path towards a stream meandering along the valley floor. Cross the bridge over the stream then climb up the steep, rocky path on the other side.

Don't forget to look behind you for far-reaching views of Blakeley Reservoir. At the crest of the hill is a mast, solar panel and concrete base. It is a good place to catch your breath.

9 From here, choose your route carefully. Follow the path to the left of the mast as you face it (with Wessenden reservoir ahead). This swings right, leading into another clough with a stream babbling below (on the left) with several pools.

10 Eventually you reach the waterfall of Blake Clough and your second swim. After your dip, cross stepping stones to continue along a path leading out of the clough and back to the dam wall of Wessenden Reservoir. Cross the dam wall to the track opposite.

11 Turn right for the return route, a gradual climb along the main track back to the start.

Walk 27

OXSPRING AND RIVER DON

An enjoyable walk tracing ancient packhorse routes and woodland paths beside the River Don, taking in the history and heritage of this peaceful valley.

INFORMATION

A fairly level walk along well-trodden footpaths, bridleways, woodland and riverside paths and tracks. There are two roads to cross. You may encounter livestock.

DISTANCE: 4 miles
TIME: 2 hours
MAP: OS Explorer 278 Sheffield and Barnsley
START & END POINT: Sports Field car park, Oxspring (SE 272 019, 53.5131, -1.5912)
PUBLIC TRANSPORT: Bus Services 20, 21, 21A (Barnsley, Penistone)
SWIMMING: River pools along the River Don
PLACES OF INTEREST: Packhorse Bridge, packhorse route
REFRESHMENTS: The Waggon and Horses, Oxspring (S36 8YQ, 01226 763259), is a historic 18th-century inn, serving hearty meat and potato pies, steaks, vegetable curries and sticky toffee puddings.
NEARBY SWIM SPOTS: River Don, Oughtibridge
EASIER ACCESS: The river at Bower Hill picnic area offers easy access from Oxspring

 huddle of traditional cottages and dry stone walls, Oxspring is around 12 miles north-west of Sheffield, in the foothills of the Pennines. A green oasis, away from the urban thrum, unsurprisingly its name comes from the large number of springs and wells in the vicinity. The River Don flows through the village, and on through the verdant dale beyond it, a watery lodestar for this swim-walk along the valley. The route occasionally drops down to the river, following woodland and riverside paths, ancient packhorse routes and parts of the 215-mile Trans Pennine Trail, a coast-to-coast route for walkers and cyclists, linking the Irish Sea to the North Sea.

From the car park, the walk starts with a gentle uphill climb through the village, passing the Waggon and Horses pub - once a farm and smithy, it was later used to house and feed labourers who came to work on the railway here. If you're visiting in the spring or summer you'll notice that many of the buildings are resplendent with dazzling hanging baskets. These are sponsored by local businesses, community groups and residents in a show of civic pride and are an eye-catching feature throughout the villages of South Yorkshire.

The lush, wooded valley of the River Don soon comes into view as the route joins an attractive flagged path down Willow Lane, part of an old packhorse route, to Willow Bridge ❷. The picture-perfect bridge was built to straddle the River Don, in around 1734, and is the subject of many photographs.

Just before the bridge, a trodden path leads to a secluded, sun-dappled pool a little further downstream, by the weir; the chance for an enticing dip in the dark, velvety water. The bridge itself, however, is a lovely spot to pause and admire the surroundings as

the river tumbles over rocks, overhanging sycamore and beech trees mirrored in the water.

There were at least three water mills in Oxspring in the 19th century - two corn mills and one cloth mill. If you stand on the bridge and look downstream, towards the left-hand riverbank, you can make out the line of the mill race, marked by a line of trees running parallel to the river. Large stones on the riverbank are the remains of the old sluice gate and weir, which raised the level of the water to fill the mill race. The race ran from here to a mill that once stood near the bridge on Bower Hill, which the walk later passes.

Beyond the packhorse bridge, the path continues along the cobbled route the packhorses would have taken on their way from Bradfield through Oxspring to Silkstone, and on to Wakefield and Leeds. Packhorses were first used by monks in around the 12th century and remained as a mode of transport until the 19th century in the steeper parts of Yorkshire. In the early days of the woollen industry in the north of England, packhorses were the only practical way to travel since they were suited to the hilly terrain. The horses could carry up to around 130kg, on packs fastened to a wooden saddle or pannier baskets. They travelled in groups of around 20 to 40 and, judging by the width of the bridge, you can imagine what a squeeze it would be getting all the ponies across.

The dog leg in the path, just beyond the bridge, was created to help the ponies manage the steep incline from the river but it's also beneficial for modern-day swim-walkers and Trans Pennine Trail-hikers. The following stretch of the walk runs along an ancient holloway (the run-up to ❸). Holloways were named as such because the constant footfall hollowed out these paths, causing them to sink below the surrounding land. Known locally as Holly Lane, the tunnel-like path here is flanked by dark, glossy holly bushes on either side. This dense shrub may have been planted to shelter travellers and their animals from the harsh winter weather.

Leaving the Trans Pennine Trail behind, the route then follows a field boundary with good views of Oxspring and narrow field strips, bounded by stone walls, on the opposite side of the valley. This was common land until the Enclosure Act of 1852, and remains unchanged to this day.

From Manor Lane the route passes the site of Oxspring Mill, which is thought to date back to medieval times ❺. The mill race that started at Willow Bridge filled the mill pond here, powering a water wheel. The water was then dispersed into the River Don. A short detour downhill from here leads to Bower Dell Riverside Picnic Area and nature reserve, a good place for a paddle or dip. With a shallow entry, the depth of the river depends on water levels. It is not very deep, although it flows slightly deeper downstream, allowing a short swim beneath a canopy of sycamore and beech.

Rejoining the main route, the footpath winds along a steeply-wooded slope above the river with more opportunities to drop down to the river's edge at a tranquil stretch of the river ❻. Beyond Cheese Bottom Farm, a footpath cuts across the field to Spring Wood, at the opposite corner of the field. Look out for buzzards soaring above you. Beyond a stile, the path rejoins the Don at a lovely twist of the river, where dappled light filters through the leaves and dances on the water's surface. There are

some deeper pools suitable for swimming here ❽ but access is tricky as the riverbank is bound by boulders so you need to check your exit points. Alternatively, you can continue to a stile and access the water from the meadow on the bend of the river, wading upstream to the deeper pools.

The imposing Rumtickle Viaduct, also known as Romticle or Romptickle, was built to carry the Sheffield to Manchester Railway ❽. Today this splendid structure and disused railway line is part of the Trans Pennine Trail. The Don runs more sedately here as it flows towards Cheesebottom weir, shrouded by swathes of Himalayan balsam in summer. A fish ladder has been installed by the weir to provide passage upstream for grayling, trout and salmon. Beyond a cluster of houses, including an Old Mill, you can see the remains of an old water wheel. The route then drops down to a line of smoothly-hewn stepping stones across the river ❾. A couple of these have toppled onto their sides, a reminder of how fast the water flows at certain times of the year.

The open-access land of Black Moor Common ❿ is one of the largest areas of western gorse and heath in the borough. Beech, oak and hawthorn jostle for space with an understory of lush, green ferns and brambles, while vibrant rowans flank the uphill path. Folklore has it that rowan, or mountain ash, trees protect against witchcraft and enchantment, something you may be glad of as you wind your way up through the woods.

Emerging from the trees, the homeward path is an easy stroll along well-walked tracks with views across the river valley as (in summer) sand martins flit above in search of flying insects. Dropping down through fields of corn, and under a railway bridge, the route soon arrives back at the start of the walk.

1 Turn left out of the car park and walk up Sheffield Road, past the Waggon and Horses pub, crossing Roughbirchworth Lane. Just after St Aidan's Church, cross the road and continue for a few metres to a footpath, signed Trans Pennine Trail, on the right.

2 Follow this footpath through an avenue of trees towards a packhorse bridge. At the end of the stone wall there is a gap in a wire fence on the right. A clearly trodden path leads to a weir and large pool, suitable for a swim. Retrace your steps to the path then cross the packhorse bridge. Follow the hairpin bend uphill along a cobbled path, keeping left as the route rises through the holloway of Holly Lane. At a Trans Pennine Trail waymarker, signed 'To ruins of Oxspring Lodge', turn right, crossing a step stile into a field.

3 Follow the field boundary around and slightly downhill to an open gateway on the left. Directly ahead are the ruins of Oxspring Manor, now overgrown. Go through the field gate then turn immediately right through another field gate. Follow the field boundary, with a stone wall to the left, to a stone step stile by a memorial bench. Go over this and continue straight on to a metal stile onto Manor Lane. At a stone outbuilding on the right, look for a stone stile leading into a paddock. Continue ahead to a woodland footpath leading onto a track.

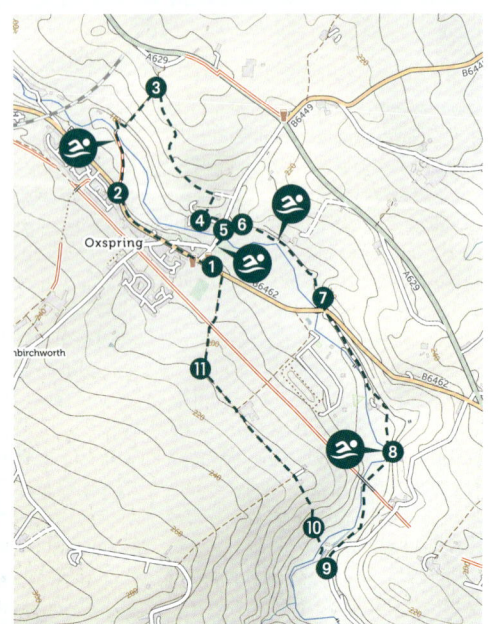

4 Turn left onto a track and continue to the road. Cross the road, carefully, towards an information board about Oxspring.

5 Turn right along the lane, crossing the bridge into Bower Dell Riverside Picnic Area, on the left. You can paddle and swim here. Afterwards, retrace your steps to the information board.

6 Look for a footpath on the right leading into woods. After a short distance a faint trail leads down to the riverside for more paddling and dipping. Return to the footpath and follow it as it moves away from the river, eventually arriving at the main road.

7 Cross the road then over a cattlegrid, following a tarmac track towards Cheese Bottom Farm. At the farm entrance, keep left on a narrow footpath running adjacent to the farmyard. Look for a gate and footpath on the right then cross the field, diagonally, to the far corner.

8 Cross the stile into woodland and pick up a riverside path. There is tricky access to the river for a swim. Continue along the woodland path and go over a stile on the right into a riverside meadow with the viaduct ahead. Pass beneath the viaduct and continue past a weir and fish ladder onto a path bounded by a

stone wall, passing the metal gates of the Old Mill. At a metal gate, go over a wooden stile on the left onto a tarmac lane.

9 Follow the footpath on the right down a narrow alley to the river. Cross over using the stepping stones, onto open-access land.

10 The onward path climbs slightly right through the woods, to a gate, before widening out to open countryside. At a fingerpost, continue straight ahead along a sandy track to a house. The footpath runs between the house and garden then keeps straight along a narrower, rougher path.

11 At a way marker, take the descending, right-hand, route along a track between arable fields to a railway arch. Pass beneath the arch to the main road and carry on back to the car park, on the left.

WYMING BROOK AND RIVELIN VALLEY

An energetic walk between the fringes of Sheffield and the Peak District, taking in the fairytale glen of Wyming Brook and Rivelin Valley's shimmering plunge pool.

INFORMATION

Steep, uneven paths through Fox Holes Plantation and Fox Hagg. Well-laid tracks in the Rivelin Valley, some road walking.

DISTANCE: 6 miles
TIME: 3 hours
MAP: OS Explorer 278 (Sheffield and Barnsley)
START & END POINT: Wyming Brook Nature Reserve car park (SK 269 858, 53.3688, -1.5967)
PUBLIC TRANSPORT: Bus Service 51 from Sheffield to Lodge Moor Terminus
SWIMMING: Small dipping pools along Wyming Brook, Rivelin Plunge Pool
PLACES OF INTEREST: Wyming Brook, Rivelin Valley Trail
REFRESHMENTS: The charming Apple Shack (S6 5SH, 07389 835957) serves homemade cakes, teas and apples on summer weekends. The Blue Moo Cafe at Wyming Brook Farm (S10 4QX, 07970 042995) is a take-away café in a converted horse box, open at weekends. The Three Merry Lads on Redmires Road (S10 4LJ, 0114 230 2824) serves home-cooked burgers, pizzas and pies, and real ales, overlooking the Rivelin Valley.
NEARBY SWIM SPOTS: The River Derwent at Bamford Mill, 10 miles west of Wyming Brook
EASIER ACCESS: Rails Road car park is about 300m from the Rivelin Plunge Pool

Two green oases lie to the west of Sheffield: the Rivelin Valley, a picturesque wooded glen where the city meets the Peak District National Park, and the Wyming Brook Nature Reserve, a bewitching cluster of tinkling streams, waterfalls, mossy crags and lofty pines. This exhilarating hike combines both of them, heading out into the countryside past dipping pools along the River Rivelin (the most celebrated of which being the Rivelin Plunge Pool, where a fan waterfall cascades into a cavernous, peaty pool) and returning via the fast-flowing waterfalls and river pools of Wyming Brook. Particularly beautiful in early summer, when the woods resonate with birdsong, the delicate woodland flora is at its best and the meadows are speckled with wild flowers, this is a walk to literally put a spring in your step .

The first part of the route can be tough-going, as the undulating woodland paths are uneven and rocky, so make sure you are wearing a sturdy pair of walking shoes. There are, however, plenty of opportunities to pause along the route, with well-sited benches offering superb views of the city and out towards the Peak District.

From Wyming Brook Nature Reserve, the route descends towards the brook itself before climbing through the attractive, deciduous woodland of Fox Holes Plantation ❷. Veteran beech trees, oaks, rowans, silver birches and downy birches cling to the steep slopes here. In springtime the delicate flushed flowers of pink purslane colonise the woodland floor while lime-green fronds of ferns unfurl beneath the slender birch trunks.

Beyond the trickling stream of Allen Sike, the path cuts through Fox Hagg Nature Reserve, where a patchwork of heather, bilberries, bracken and woodland cleave to the hillside. The land here

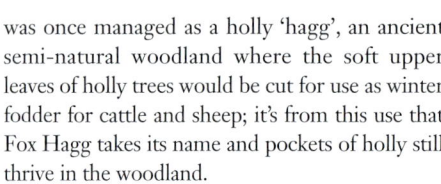

was once managed as a holly 'hagg', an ancient semi-natural woodland where the soft upper leaves of holly trees would be cut for use as winter fodder for cattle and sheep; it's from this use that Fox Hagg takes its name and pockets of holly still thrive in the woodland.

Keep an eye out along this stretch of footpath for a decorative metal signpost ❸. These lovely markers are the work of the Peak and Northern Footpaths Society, a registered charity that has been protecting footpaths for 120 years in the Peak District and other parts of Northern England. The society's signposts are its most enduring legacy; some of them are now over 100 years old.

After crossing vertiginous Lodge Lane, the route enters the western fringes of Blackbrook Wood. Having clambered up and down some arduous paths, you will feel heartened to see a pair of benches where you can pause to admire the wonderful valley views - towards the Rivelin Dams and the Peak District in one direction and Sheffield in the other ❹.

Continuing along the path, there are glimpses across the Rivelin Valley through the treetops. A little further along the cityscape of Sheffield rises above the canopy. Soon, the route drops down through Blackbrook Wood with Black Brook, no more than a trickle through the wooded gully, below to the right. After passing through an arch of holly, a path merges from the left. If walking this route in late spring or early summer, it's worth a short detour up this path to peer over the stone wall at the wildflower meadows; they are in full bloom from May to July. Further along the route, the charming Apple Shack is tucked between an orchard and a burgeoning allotment (just before ⑥). What started as a pop-up shelf selling cakes during the pandemic is now a popular place for walkers to refuel. Tea, coffee and a selection of delicious homemade cakes are served from tables in the garden during summer weekends. It's a delightful place to pause before descending to the Rivelin Valley.

The River Rivelin tumbles along the valley floor, where vestiges of old water mills and mill dams, some dating back to the 16th century, can be seen along the riverside trail. As well as powering the Rivelin Corn Mill, several other industries benefited from the river's fast-flowing waters. These included Sheffield's famous steel and cutlery plants, as well as paper and flour mills. As they became less dependent on water power, these industries moved to other parts of the city, allowing nature to return to the valley.

While the riverside path runs all the way to Sheffield, this route traces the river upstream, to dipping spots in dark, peaty pools shaded beneath the trees ⑦. The best is the Rivelin Plunge Pool, where a broad cascade tumbles into a large pool that shines like pewter ⑩. On sun-baked days, daredevils leap into the water here. It is deep enough to do so but always check the depth for yourself. The cool temperature of the water often means people don't hang around for too long so, if you find yourself in a huddle of other dippers, don't panic!

After a refreshing dip, the walk continues to a picturesque packhorse bridge. A short road climb

leads into Rivelin Rough, a conservation woodland that trills with birdsong ⑬. The woodland sits below the gritstone escarpment of Rivelin Rocks, a popular site among rock climbers, who know it as Rivelin Edge. The woodland trail can be obscured by bracken in high summer - you may have to beat a path through the ferns – but there are fine views across Rivelin reservoir as the path emerges onto Manchester Road.

The final ascent is through Wyming Brook, once part of Rivelin Chase, a hawking and hunting ground for the lords of Sheffield ⑭. Sweet-smelling pines and mossy crags cling to the sides of this idyllic glen and hillside streams rush down the rocky cleft, creating strings of white water that swirl into small pools. These are just about deep enough for a natural Jacuzzi-style dip to ease aching feet and limbs. Plump dippers frequent these fast-flowing waters, feasting on underwater insects.

At the end of the trail there is a pretty glade beside the water with stepping stones, dams and shallow paddling pools - a lovely place to unwind after an invigorating hike.

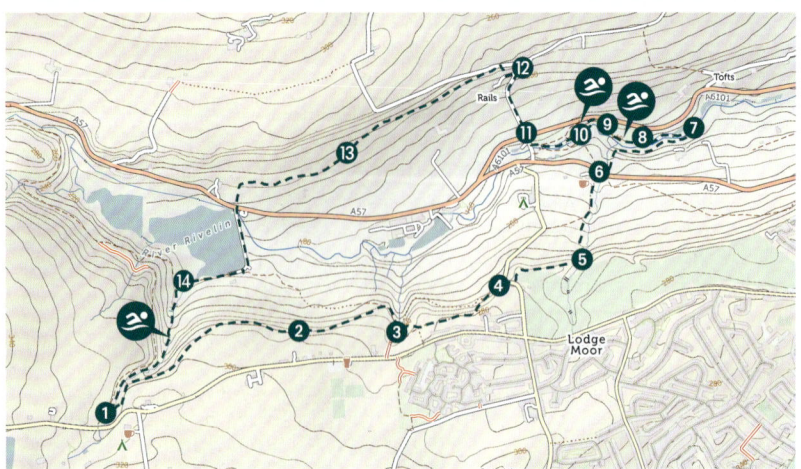

1 From the car park, follow the lower path beyond a wooden barrier and down some steps toward the stream of Wyming Brook. Cross the stepping stones, or continue beside the brook for a few metres to cross a wooden footbridge, then return to the stepping stones. Turn left up the first set of steps here, then almost immediately veer left onto an unmarked, rocky footpath into the woods, climbing above the brook.

2 Continue through the steep-sloped Fox Holes Plantation. The tree-top path rises with a stone wall to the right. After about 0.75 mile at a fork, keep straight. Don't bear right.

3 A decorative footpath sign indicates Redmires Road and Rivelin Dams before the path reaches a section of tarmac. Go down some steps on the left and cross a small stream. At a fork, take the right-hand footpath to climb up the valley side, continuing along the ridge. There is a small bench on the left with views through a clearing in the trees. Continue to the end of the track, and a junction with Lodge Lane.

4 Turn right onto Lodge Lane then cross the road. Walk uphill for a few metres to join a footpath on the left. Follow the narrow footpath beside a stone wall, with a golf course to your right. You will come to two benches where you can admire the surrounding views. The route continues high above the trees with a widening panorama of Sheffield.

5 Keep on this track until you reach a rocky path leading down through Black Brook Wood with Black Brook itself down to your right. Descend a wide set of rough stone steps then go through a tunnel of holly. As you approach the bottom of the woods, you will see the Apple Shack café, open during summer weekends.

6 The path soon veers right towards the road. Cross this road to join another woodland footpath opposite, leading towards the River Rivelin. The footpath curves right and weaves through trees with the river down below to the left.

7 Cross a footbridge over the river and continue left onto a path running between two low stone walls. The path then passes between the river on the left and a mill pond on the right.

8 The route climbs to a small tree-fringed meadow with a couple of benches. Choose your path carefully when leaving the meadow. Stick to the left-hand path closest to the river. Continue along this path, between the mill race and the river, to some stepping stones over the mill race. There are some shaded pools suitable for a dip here.

9 Follow the footpath sign up some steps, taking you above the river and onto a gravel track. Turn left then descend some stone steps a little further along, back onto the track.

10 Ahead is the Rivelin Plunge Pool for your next swim. There is plenty of space to change and a bench for your clothes. Afterwards continue to a stone packhorse bridge, then up the path towards Rails Road.

11 Cross the road, towards Rivelin Valley car park, and turn right, continuing up Rails Road to the main Rivelin Valley Road. Cross this road and continue up the lane on the opposite side.

12 After 500m turn left onto a track, towards a metal gate. Through the gate, turn right onto a narrow, overgrown path bordered by a stone wall. Climb the stone steps onto a tarmac lane. Then, turn immediately left onto a footpath with fields to the left and woodland to the right.

13 At a fork in the woodland path, take the right-hand, less obvious path (this may be overgrown in summer). Follow the footpath as it curves left towards Manchester Road. Cross the road carefully as there is a bend to the right-hand side of the road. Continue along the Rivelin Dam wall, passing a car park on your left. Follow the road round to the right, keeping a stone wall on your right. The reservoir is obscured by trees.

14 At the end of the straight section of road, go through a kissing gate and turn right. Then continue to a set of steps by a bench. The route now follows a path beside Wyming Brook where you will find myriad small pools before arriving back at the car park.

Robin Hood's Bay p165

Editor:
Rhiannon Batten
Cover illustration:
James Lewis
Design and layout:
Amy Bolt
Proofreading:
Tania Pascoe
Mapping powered by:

cycle.travel

Published by:
Wild Things Publishing Ltd
Bath, BA2 7WG,
United Kingdom
wildthingspublishing.com

WILD THINGS PUBLISHING

Acknowledgements

Firstly, thank you to Daniel Start for entrusting me with another wonderful project and to the team at Wild Things Publishing including my editor Rhiannon Batten and designer Amy Bolt for bringing this book to life. It has been an absolute joy to create. Thank you as always to my family for their ongoing support and encouragement. To my husband David, an enthusiastic companion on so many of these walks, always on the shoreline or river bank, holding the towel and pouring the tea! I couldn't have completed this book without you. To my three sons, Joe, Will and Ted - thank you for your cheerful camaraderie on more wild adventures and always posing for photos so willingly. To my parents, Margaret and Peter, for all your love and support - and for the outdoor childhood you gave me. To my friend and swim buddy, Camilla Simpson, for the fun and laughter on our swims together. To Paula Statham, friend, walking companion and fellow photographer. To the Friday 9am Swimmers at Pool Bridge Farm for welcoming me into your fold. To the fabulous wild swimming community, and in particular the buoying up from members of the Wild Swimming Walks Yorkshire Facebook group, especially those of you who joined me to 'test-swim' these walks. This book would not have been half as much fun to create without your company so a huge thank you to Paul Ashton, Lorraine Avery, Hannah Bowes, Sue Golton, Paul Gibson, Mandy Greatbatch, Mark Greatbatch, Joanne Grosvenor, Carole James, Rachel Keller, Helen Metcalfe, Jo Moseley, Sam Nichols, Rachael Reed, Karen Robinson, Anita and Ted Roy, Jen Scott, Sophie Sheppard, Heather Simpson, Mike Stansfield, Jean Taylor, Oliver Taylor and swimmers Brian Fletcher, Grace O'Malley and the Saltburn Mermates who I met along the way. To all of you, thank you and I hope to see you in the water again some time soon.

Facebook Group: Wild Swimming Walks Yorkshire
Instagram: @sarahbanksphoto

Photo credits

All photos copyright Sarah Banks except p24, top left, Helen Metcalfe. With thanks to David, Joe, Will and Ted Banks for additional help with photography.

Other books from **Wild Things Publishing:**

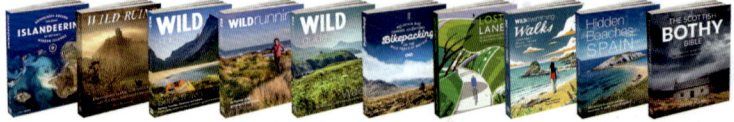